RICHARD HARDING DAVIS:

HIS DAY

RICHARD HARDING DAVIS, WAR CORRESPONDENT

FAIRFAX DOWNEY

RICHARD HARDING DAVIS

HIS DAY

CHARLES SCRIBNER'S SONS
NEW YORK · · · LONDON
1933

TO

MR. AND MRS. CHARLES DANA GIBSON

CONTENTS

ILLUSTRATIONS

RICHARD HARDING DAVIS:

HIS DAY

CHAPTER ONE

BIRTH NOTICE

I

"I AM Richard Harding Davis," he would announce in that superbly assured way of his. And for every one who listened unimpressed, there were a thousand to whom that name meant the breath of romance and the spirit of adventure, to whom it was a symbol of youth and success, a token of friendship or disinterested kindness, a gage of chivalry.

Print and personality were his passports throughout the world. Almost always doors swung wide and barriers vanished before one talisman or the other. Queen Victoria perused his *Princess Aline* and was not only amused but charmed. Boarding-school misses burned the midnight oil over many of his love stories, and cherished their coveted photographs of the author who could double for the dashing hero of his *Soldiers of Fortune* or his own elegant *Mr. Van Bibber*. College boys of the 'Nineties, said Booth Tarkington, speaking as one of them, were as familiar with his stalwart good looks as those of their own football captain, and, of all the great of the world, most desired to meet Richard Harding Davis. Charles Dana Gibson often drew him, and men reluctantly admitted that if any mere male could be worthy of the lovely, slender Gibson Girl it was this fine type of Gibson Man. He probably knew more waiters, generals, actors, and princes than any man who lived, wrote Finley Peter Dunne, and *Mister Dooley* circulated considerably himself.

Stirring events and Dick Davis seemed to have regular rendezvous. Millions saw skirmishes and sports, coronations and conventions, through his eyes. For reporting them, publishers paid him a thousand dollars a week, but that was only the lesser part of his reward from a life he loved.

It came to be said that no war was a success without the presence of this beau ideal of war correspondents, handsome, debonair, and splendidly equipped to chronicle it. His despatches from Cuba, featuring a colonel of the Rough Riders, helped to make a President of the United States. His magnificently vivid account of the entry of the German army into Brussels in 1914 crowned a career through which he wielded his pen like the sword of a Crusader.

"A perfect day for Mr. Davis," one caustic critic remarked, "would consist of a morning's danger, taken as a matter of course. In the afternoon a little chivalry, equally a matter of course to a well-bred man, then a dash from hardship to some great city, a bath, a perfect dinner nobly planned. Shrapnel, chivalry, *sauce mousseline,* and so to work next morning on an article which presupposed in others virtues his code compelled him almost to ignore in himself. Richard Cœur-de-Leon would not have disliked such a day, once he was used to shrapnel."

Enter, then, Richard the Lion-Harding, as they called him. D'Artagnan brandishing a pencil instead of a rapier. Enter Sir Galahad, not particularly in quest of the Holy Grail, but ready to carve the casques of the impure in heart. Enter Don Quixote, adamant against the outdating of knighthood, and Ponce de Leon, never disillusioned of his draught from the Fountain of Eternal Youth until nearly the end.

II

Richard Harding Davis was born with a silver pen in his mouth, the collaboration of a newspaperman and an author of fiction.

His father, Lemuel Clarke Davis, was an editorial writer on the staff of *The Philadelphia Inquirer*. By mid-April, 1864, he could view practically everything with alarm. Fort Pillow in the West had fallen to the Confederates and Bedford Forrest's gray riders had taken bloody vengeance on the taunting blacks in its garrison. All was quiet on the Potomac, stagnant with stalemate. Not for another three weeks would Grant drive for Richmond through the Wilderness and strew more dead among shattered trees than America would mourn again till Belleau Wood and the Argonne. Nor would the tramp of Sherman's legions marching to the sea echo the drumbeats of victory until those weary weeks had passed.

The city in which Clarke Davis wrote was a great base hospital. Fatal fever vied with convalescence to evacuate its rows on rows of beds. Dwindling currents of troops in blue streamed through from the North; recruiting was falling off despite an advance-bonus, the $250 bounty. The devoted women in hoop skirts and first-incarnation Eugenie hats who fed the soldiers at refreshment saloons sighed with prescience that many would return soon to occupy the crowded wards or never return at all. So it had been when the red tide of wounded flooded back after Gettysburg a year before. The city still shuddered to recall how near a wave of gray invasion had been to following.

Mr. Davis's paper reported the speech of Abraham Lincoln at the opening of Baltimore's Sanitary Fair on April 18 to raise money for hospital supplies, interlarding the quotation half resentfully with parentheses reading (Laughter). How could the man crack jokes at such a time? The President would speak at Philadelphia's fair that summer, and that metropolis, raising a million dollars, would begin to forgive him. Now it held him a grudge. He lately had superseded its native son,

General McClellan, in the chief command with that toper
from the West, U. S. Grant.

If all that were not enough for Mr. Davis to contemplate
with apprehension, there remained the local political machine,
which had called no truce for the duration of the war and came
as handy for scathing editorials as ever.

Clarke Davis, as an editorial writer, was perforce an anonymity. His wife, Rebecca Harding, was already a celebrity.
Before he married her, she had achieved the august *Atlantic
Monthly,* house organ of the sages of Concord, Boston, and
points Down East, with a short story and a serial which attracted considerable attention, praise, and condemnation. As
if she had not been bold enough in daring anything so un-
feminine and ungenteel as writing, she chose shockingly radical, frightfully unpleasant subjects. No lady should know anything about them. If she did, they ought to be secrets.

Her first story, *Life in the Iron-Mills,* published in *The Atlantic* of April, 1861, wreaked havoc with the sweet sentiment
and romanticism with which literature was sicklied o'er. Zola
or some raving Russian might have written it. It seemed incredible that a young American girl could have penned this
stark, disturbing tale of Welsh puddlers in the mills of Wheeling, creatures toiling on a line of furnaces "like a street in
Hell," slaves whose only escape was drunkenness. "If I had
the making of men," the author made one of her characters
declare, "these men who do the lowest part of the world's
work should be machines—nothing more—hands. It would
be kindness."

Premature was hardly the word for such startling remarks.
The time for labor reform was far from ripe in 1861, and the
name of Rebecca Harding Davis[1] would be forgotten like those

[1] Thomas Beer in *The Mauve Decade* and elsewhere resurrected the memory of this
highly remarkable woman. Anthologies include some of her short stories. Otherwise

of other apostles ahead of their day. There was trouble enough
now arising from another lady's story. The country was con-
vulsed over the freedom of *Uncle Tom* and his race, and it
was Harriet Beecher Stowe who would attain immortality,
for she had brought out her book at the crucial moment. The
question of another form of slavery must be tabled.

But the literati were struck by Miss Harding's contribution
to their favorite magazine. They were even moved to grant
that the fellowship of letters might be broad enough to include a woman, since she wrote like a man. A correspondence
began between Rebecca and Nathaniel Hawthorne. He could
appreciate the venturesome pioneer spirit, he who had been
defiant enough of puritanical canons to allow a heroine a scarlet letter and one awarded by a clergyman at that. Hawthorne
would have visited the promising girl author in Wheeling had
not inconsiderate Rebels torn up the railroad tracks.

So Miss Harding journeyed to Boston instead and sat awed
and alert at dinner with Emerson, Hawthorne, Holmes, Bronson Alcott, and other members of *The Atlantic* coterie. She
listened to them talk loftily and academically of the war, war
which she had witnessed in all its ugly actuality while West
Virginia was torn from the Old Dominion—political jobbery
and graft in both camps behind masks of patriotism—burning
homes and outraged women. She endured for a while Alcott's
windy panegyric on the waging of this conflict he called holy.
One of daughter Louisa's *Little Women* would have continued
to hearken respectfully and admiringly. Not Rebecca Harding.
Her eyes had looked too recently upon earthly cruelties and
hypocrisies to see in them the glory of the coming of the Lord.

her books gather library dust. She continued to write many years after her first flourishing in the 'Sixties but never again with such power. She seemed to have passed the
torch of her inspiration on to her son who, however, never wrote anything of such
grim strength as his mother's *Life in the Iron-Mills*. See Appendix.

She could not find it in her heart to cry allelujah. Instead she halted the orator in mid-career.

"War," she interrupted with unmaidenly frankness, "may be an armed angel on a mission but she has the personal habits of the slums."

Twinkling little Doctor Holmes laughed. *"Et in Arcadia, ego,"* he confessed. This girl had forewarned him of what he would see for himself when he travelled to the front to find his wounded son and furnish medical escort home for a future Justice of the Supreme Court.

Miss Harding prepared to quit her group of philosophers. They, she opined, were not guiding the world after all. They were in it but not of it and they would never see it as it was. She would not remain to sit in celibate discipleship at their feet and become one of the New England spinsters whom she would one day describe with devastating candor and welling pity as undedicate nuns. Rather, she made bold to scandalize the modern Athens with the dictum that women desire men, gathered her skirts and her portmanteaux and went home to be married.

III

Interest in writing had brought Rebecca Harding and Clarke Davis together. He, a native of Sandusky, Ohio, had settled in Philadelphia and begun his journalistic career. Reading a novel entitled *Margret Howth,* published anonymously in Boston in 1862, he was deeply impressed and took steps to learn the identity of the author. His surprise at discovering that a woman, a Miss Rebecca Blaine Harding, had written it was succeeded by a resolution to marry her, no less surprising. For in the book's pages was no trace of moonlight and roses. The story of a woman social worker, the sordid slums of its pages reeked and teemed with such sullen misery as no writer for many years would venture to depict. Only the pale lily of hope was permitted to bloom in its squalor. But Clarke Davis recognized honesty and fearless pioneering and character. He wrote her and followed his letter to her home and birthplace, Washington, Pennsylvania.

A snowball was their introduction. The visitor, ducking, caught sight of an attractive girl of sturdy physique. Her bright, sparkling eyes inspected a young man, not as tall as she but distinguished looking, with a clear, direct gaze and a flourishing period mustache. If her missile knocked off his stovepipe hat, she saw a fine, leonine head of hair which resembled Mark Twain's in grandeur.

Both came of good Anglo-American stock. Autobiographically, Rebecca Harding wrote, "It was your own grandfather who when he was ten years old had gone into a swamp, killed a huge beast that had threatened the settlement, and so won the proud title of Panther Jim. It was your own grandmother who had dined with Lafayette, and who hinted that Lady Washington had an ugly habit of idly scolding her husband and of boxing Nelly Custis's ears, which was hardly befitting a gentlewoman."[2]

War, as always, speeded courtship. Besides, Clarke Davis had found the lady all her book led him to believe and more; and Rebecca Harding knew her mind as few women do. Some of their early life was spent in Wheeling. Together they went through grim months of border warfare—the tragic splitting of families, elders holding loyal to the North, adventurous youngsters espousing the Lost Cause,—the devastation of homes and crops—ambushes and cattle raids—dwindling lard-

[2] Rebecca Harding Davis, *Bits of Gossip*. Cambridge, Mass., 1904.

ers, with coffee brewed from that forbidding vegetable, the parsnip, and potatoes for dinner welcomed as a treat. At length they crossed the mountains and established their household in Philadelphia.

Its traditional calm in grateful contrast, the one-time Quaker town received the young couple. While doing her part, Philadelphia remained outwardly as little perturbed as a metropolis could in war time. Ladies somewhat neglected their formal calls of a morning but the amenities were not altogether disregarded. Elderly gentlemen doing the family marketing early Wednesdays and Saturdays found that rite less leisurely and selection less copious, yet they catered no less faithfully. Turmoil in the city's activities was the fault of foreigners; Philadelphia does not consider bustle necessary to accomplishment.

The newspapers Clarke Davis scanned and the magazines for which his wife wrote reflected the life of the day in their advertisements. The couple could glance up from pages, peer out of the window and observe the reader appeal of the advertisements translated into a panorama of humanity. Those "straight ringlets or waving, massive curls" which escaped from beneath the bow-adorned poke bonnets of ladies sweeping through the streets were produced by handy hair curlers, as advertised. Unguent helped grow a share of those equally massive mustaches behind which many an officer and civilian strode. Flanking those adornments were often to be seen the popular sideboard whiskers, given newer name and vogue by Major-General Burnside[3] whose thanks for a combination pipe-and-pouch smoking apparatus were quoted in a testimonial. In that group of soldiers quaffing at a grog-shop, he who treated might be one of the "sixty voices from the Army of the Potomac (from

[3] When a shaving-soap advertiser made copy recently out of the General's whiskers, his descendants rose in wrath and threatened suit.

first lieutenant to drummer)" who testified in print to the value of B——'s pills in case of colds, chills, dysentery, typhoid, and other varied hardships of warfare.

Strains of music from yonder casement were to be recognized as one of the advertised patriotic duets for piano and violin. The latter instrument, played by a gentleman, was pressed against an enamelled collar, "moulded to fit the neck." That chatter betokened a ladies' whist party using cards decorated by French artists with love scenes and hence "combining pleasure with amusement." Veterans proudly wore badges pictured in the advertising cuts. Some rejoiced in the 75-cent pocket albums recommended warmly for their sixteen-picture capacity; no campaigner with a large family or a plurality of girls left behind him could be without one.

Headlines, which rose like a tower rather than spreading banner-like, chronicled the discouraging news from the front. Columns were required for the volubilities of Congress. Not a few type cases were emptied to do justice to flurries on the stock exchange, termed a panic by the modest standards of the day. With an eye to subscribers, marriages and deaths were grudgingly allotted some of the remaining space.

Birth notices could not crowd in. There was no public announcement that on Monday, April 18, 1864, a son was born to the Clarke Davises. Richard Harding Davis would be some years yet breaking into print.

IV

Mothers who bore children in those troublous times could not escape the foreboding that they were bringing up reinforcements for the next war. Least of all Rebecca Harding

Davis, for she was a realist and the mantle of the prophetess sometimes touched her. But that stamina which carried her and her husband through to peace was proof against the jangling post-war period and equal to bringing up a family among the ghosts and the chaos.

Dick Davis was born in a house at 1429 Girard Avenue, but the home of most of his early life was the three-story brick house on South Twenty-first Street, to which his parents soon moved. Philadelphia's family-tree streets: Chestnut, Walnut, Spruce, and Pine, were his neighborhood but not his birthright. That was a matter of no moment to him now. He was handy with his fists, he could swim like a fish, he could swing a baseball or cricket bat or boot a football with the best of the youngsters he knew, and those are the social credentials of boyhood. If any young blue-blood boasted his lineage, Dick would stagger him with a claim to descent from the Duke of Marlborough.

A younger brother, Charles Belmont, and a sister, Nora, arrived in the course of the next few years. Charley, dubbed Gus, was the ideal younger brother, ally, idolizer, and factotum, and he never altogether outgrew it. He cheerfully submitted to being strangled as the villain in the plays which Dick, the hero, had devised and directed.

The children adored their parents. Clarke Davis sailed with his boys, took them to the threatre, wrote stories for them. Although he lacked the height they could have wished for their paragon, they admired his courage the more when he sallied forth with a heavy cane for defense against Philadelphia gamblers, angered by his fearless editorial attacks on them. Mrs. Davis never secluded herself so long for her writing that she neglected mending and other maternal duties, to the amazement of those who branded her a feminist. Benign and unruffled, she held juvenile court for her brood with a just and tender understanding. "She had no delusions of grandeur and she spoke of God in a pleasant fashion that was respectful without patronage."

Severest trial to be borne was Dick's school reports which were periodic bad news. Teachers asked to comment on his progress in his studies were wont to reply evasively that he was good at sports. They might have foretold he would be a writer, so miserable was he at mathematics. Like the hero of his novel, *Captain Macklin,* he would rather take a field piece by assault than figure out its firing data. History he would look up when he had some use for it and he saw none now. Not maps but travel impressed him as the ideal system for learning geography. His spelling was never anything to boast of, but that mattered little to him, since he observed that people always gathered what he meant and corrected his errors before they became too public.

Fashionable Episcopal Academy accepted his attendance without scholastic satisfaction. Whatever good marks he obtained at least were come by honestly. He never cribbed and boys who did learned to conceal it from Dick Davis, not because he bore tales but because he could be and was just as morally indignant as any professor and more bitterly scornful. Popularity to be gained by school diplomats and politicians could go hang for all he cared. He was too outspoken, too insistent on leading, whether or no, to have many friends. Once (at Swarthmore) he was called with six other boys before the President to explain the disappearance of sugar bowls. The others denied any guilt, but Dick "merely smiled gravely," as he wrote his father, "and let the good-natured old duffer see how silly it was by retaining a placid silence and so crushing his base but thoughtless behavior and machinations."

School at most was only a tedious interlude between the

glorious summers at Point Pleasant, New Jersey, where the Davises kept a summer cottage. The boys had the Atlantic to swim in, the Manasquan River to sail on. Its tiny islands were theirs to search for buried treasure, to range as mighty hunters, to defend like true soldiers of fortune. They were surrounded with splendid settings for adventure stories. When Dick reached the age which compels the addition of that hitherto blithely disregarded character, a heroine, he sought farther afield, for what knight thinks to find his lady fair next door? There was a pretty little girl in a crimson bathing suit to be found down on the beach every day, but she was too young to engage the lordly notice of a fellow getting on in his teens. He might duck her once in a while as a polite attention to a friend of the family but usually he ignored her. Remembering his blindness later, he never was able to understand it. The girl was Ethel Barrymore.

Gayer Asbury Park drew the pilgrimages of Dick and his friend, Johnny Ruff. Dick had a way with the girls. He was given to talking to them about their souls and supplementing that excellent technique by serenading them with his guitar. What his voice lacked his good looks made up. The guitar supplied not only romance but transportation thereto and therefrom. Once Dick and Johnny wrung better than carfare out of a beach audience which gave ear to the troubadours and dug down into the pockets of its ample bathing suits for guerdon totalling two dollars.

These two comrades, having rendered the frivolities of life their due, held long and serious conversations. Dick confided that he was going to be a writer. He was, he avowed, no creature of circumstance; he had planned that career from the outset. What difference would what you were make in a thousand years? demanded Johnny, youthfully cynical. A big difference, decreed Dick with his customary authority and that settled the argument.

V

The bright glamor of literature and the stage filled the cottage at Point Pleasant and the house in Philadelphia. Mrs. Davis as an author of note, Mr. Davis as editor, dramatic critic of discrimination, and owner of playbills, portraits, and a library of rare books on the theatre, drew about themselves a brilliant and notable circle and held it by their own attractive personalities. Many a Saturday night at dinner, Thurston, the magician, enthralled their children with tricks. Frances Hodgson Burnett remained a Point Pleasant friend, though Clarke Davis took her out sailing and upset her, adorned in a specimen of her magnificent millinery. The boys held nothing against her, for she did not publish *Little Lord Fauntleroy* until 1886. They were grown then and beyond danger of the horrors of long curls, velvet, lace collars, and sashes which Mrs. Burnett, innocently abetted by the appealing illustrations of Reginald Birch, visited on protesting boyhood.

Louisa May Alcott came and wondered that Rebecca Harding Davis could still be a cheerful person after writing those gloomy tales of mills and slums. The talented tribe of the Drews and Barrymores was on intimate footing. Mrs. John Drew, Sr., one of the first woman managers, owned and ran the Arch Street Theatre. Her beautiful daughter, Georgie Drew, was a juvenile idol of Dick Davis's, as was her husband, handsome, witty Maurice Barrymore. Their children, Ethel, Lionel, and Jack, were friends of the Davis boys.

Most of the great actors and actresses of the day were as much at home in the Davis house as on the boards of that good theatre town, Philadelphia. Dramatis personæ lined the dinner table, their photographs papered the boys' room. Joseph Jefferson was often a guest. Lanky Edwin Booth stalked in and never failed to be regaled with his favorites, Madeira and waffles. Frizzled beef and smoked salmon, homemade biscuits and preserves, brandied peaches, scrapple, buckwheat cakes and maple syrup—all these delights of festive Philadelphian fare regaled royalties of the footlights at breakfast-luncheons, while Dick and his brother, relegated to the pantry until the ice cream, ate as heartily as the company.

Stately Henry Irving, actor on stage and off, graciously accepted the homage of young Dick. The radiance of Ellen Terry lighted the house. Dion Boucicault, his wit shining like his bald head, twitted the tragedians. Augustin Daly, slight, pale, and clad in sober black, frequented that informal Green Room, and with him some of the bright stars whose orbit he ruled like the force of gravity—Mrs. Gilbert, the incomparable Ada Rehan, and that promising young comedian, John Drew.

Once, entering a street car with his mother, Dick evoked some of the mightiest histrionics of the aging Edwin Forrest by stumbling over the thespian's gouty foot. "Whereat," wrote Charles Belmont Davis, "Forrest broke forth in a volcano of oaths and for blocks continued to hurl thunderous broadsides at Richard which included the Curse of Rome and every other famous tirade in the tragedian's repertory which in any way fitted the occasion."

These were the romantic figures which year after year made their entrances and exits at the hospitable Davis home. At the theatre, Dick from "down front" or the wings, where he was tolerated as the son of his father, saw them create a make-believe world so thrilling he could forget it was not real.

As these elder friends of his stepped out of life into a play, so could people one knew be transformed into characters for a book. You had only to wave that magic wand which is a pen. Drama was everywhere and anywhere for the eye open to see it and the hand skilled to write it down. Life was full of absorbing incidents and the world a storehouse of scenery. A writer could dramatize anything and anybody. Why, he could dramatize even himself.

CHAPTER TWO

SPORTS SECTION

I

Two pet snakes, collars on their approximate necks and leashes snapped to the collars, glided through the streets of Bethlehem, Pennsylvania, in the fall of 1881. The town and Lehigh University immediately took notice. Eyes travelled up the leashes to the jaunty young man at the other ends, blinked for a moment under the shock of the dazzling cricket colors on his blazer and skull cap. Tongues wagged with curiosity.

For once a sub-freshman, most negligible of beings, was a sensation. English, perhaps, by the accent? No, some Philadelphians talk that way. The name was Richard Harding Davis, with the middle stressed. Suspicions were correct. He was a nephew of the popular Professor Harding.

Earnest students in the engineering course, dressing the part in flannel shirts and dusty field boots, gaped at this exquisite. So did brawny youths from the steel mills, as they marked down a college dude on whom it would be a keen pleasure to swing in the next town-and-gown fracas. Demure maidens of the "Fem. Sem."—the Moravian Female Seminary—being promenaded, brightened as they gazed on the handsome young Adam with a brace of serpents and could not banish unruly thoughts of tempting apples.

Freshmen in the throes of being hazed were consoled by the sight of next year's most promising victim and balm in

Gilead. Fraternities listed him as a prospect. Although this sub-freshman seemed super-fresh, scouts reported him football material, track timber, glee-club tone, and editorial fibre for *The Burr* and *The Epitome*.

Davis had spent an unsatisfactory year at Swarthmore College. His present attendance at Ulrich's Preparatory School in Bethlehem was a relapse but a necessity, since intensive tutoring was called for if he were to rise to higher education. Ulrich's would ease him into Lehigh if anything could. Meanwhile, to all his intents and purposes he was a university man already.

Even in a larger seat of learning, the advent of Dick Davis would not have passed unnoticed. Due impress was made on little Lehigh, with its less than 300 students who overflowed from the dormitories into town boarding houses. Founded only in 1865, its campus still gave evidence of being hewn out of the wilderness, and Packer Hall wore the aspect of an outpost of collegiate civilization. But the Pierian Springs flowed freely and so did the beer. Eager youth attacked education with at least some of the zest with which visiting teams were tackled on the stern and rockbound gridiron. Traditions and Class ivy had been planted in fertile soil and both were sprouting.

Lehigh's most prominent sub-freshman breathed the air of freedom of college life. Away from home for the first time— Swarthmore, being so near Philadelphia, had not counted— he knew an invigorating independence. Studies took on a new interest, for they were the key to the gate of this inviting domain. In his uncle's spacious house, across the river from the university and the iron mills, was not even a restraining aunt, Professor H. Wilson Harding being unmarried. The pair of them kept bachelor-hall like old cronies. Although the pro-

fessor taught physics, he was no desiccated scientist, as testified
by the college catch he relished:

> Oh, do not pass without regarding
> The lectures of Professor Harding,
> So lucid, fresh and admir*able*
> And entertaining as a fable.

The light of the physics department was a large man but otherwise he resembled Napoleon III and had once been mistaken
for him while visiting Paris. Never since had he allowed his
goatee and mustache to become less imperial and more pro-
fessorial.

Along with his contemporaries who considered his house
something of a salon, Professor Harding was not proof against
the charm of his likable nephew. Iron company presidents,
congressmen, and attorneys became close friends of this amusing lad whose interest was flattering and whose enthusiasm for
life was so genuine and so naïve. "Bring yourself into contact
with new people," Dick's mother had written him, "and try
to act toward them as Christ would have you act." He obeyed
the first adjunct and his unsanctimonious effort to follow the
second failed less frequently than with the average of mankind.

Summer provided a trip to Boston and an interview with
Doctor Holmes who, Dick wrote home, "talked a great deal
about mother and a great many other things equally lovely."
With the coming of fall and his return to enter Lehigh, Mrs.
Davis asked her son to promise never to touch a drop of liquor
while he was in college. Guests in her home could have their
noggin of whisky before meals if they desired. She was not a
bigot on the drinking question.[1] But she was mindful of a

---

[1] Thomas Beer in *The Mauve Decade* tells this anecdote of Mrs. Davis. "In the early
'90's a lad got remarkably drunk one night, smashed furniture in a brothel and spent
some hours in jail. He found his mother's door technically locked in his face the next
morning, and went to refuge with Mrs. Davis, who considered his disorders and said

family black sheep—one gambols about alcoholically in many
a mother's memory—so she asked the pledge which Dick gave
and kept. It was not easy for him. Lehigh might have been
called a freshwater college but it drank its weight in beer.
Happily R. H. Davis, '86, could get as hilarious on ginger ale
as the next fellow on a series of steinfuls.

An epochal double event loomed above all else in that year.
Dick broke into print, the print of the outside world, with a description of the college cane rush which appeared in a local
paper. The $1.15 received for it was squandered on a pair of
brass candlesticks, one kept as a memento, the other sent to his
mother so that she could share in his joy. This triumph shortly
was followed by a mightier one when *Judge* accepted a contribution. The piece, entitled "The Hat and Its Inmate," was an
only mildly funny "short" about a brainless lady at a matinée
whose millinery masked the stage and whose conversation
drowned the dialogue. Its princely remuneration was a year's
subscription. But what was payment beside the glorious array
of type over the initials, D. D., in a real magazine?

These were thrills of a lifetime, intimations of immortality.
Arrays of print to be read and reread—conned till had by heart.
To be mentioned off-hand to unfortunates who had not discovered them. To be shrugged aside when those who had
noted remarked on them—to be dismissed with all the nonchalance at one's command with an "Oh. Did you see that?"

This proud author flung back his head, sniffed the intoxi-
cating fragrance of printer's ink and marched on to the Promised Land revealed by this shining signpost.

briskly, 'Go up and take a bath while I get you some breakfast, you silly child!' She
fed him and packed him off to young Richard in New York, with orders verbal that
a job was to be found for him at once."

II

Davis knew that he was about to fight a Waterloo on the playing-fields of Lehigh. Not an undergraduate but cast this conspicuous, new-fledged freshman in the rôle of Napoleon. "The fellows looked on me as an object of ridicule on account of the hat and cane, walk, and so on," he wrote his father. Natty suits of an English cut, double-breasted waistcoat, a tam-o'-shanter, and a crooked stick had alternated with the cricket blazer. How were the undergraduates of Lehigh to know that a mediæval gallant with all the Renaissance love of colorful costume was reincarnated in their midst? That this young chap with drama in his soul possessed the boy's and the actor's fondness for dressing up? That shyness and not a desire to show off was a chief characteristic? And what would they have cared if they had known?

A college student could not be "different" with impunity in the 'Eighties—not by some decades. Most of those who tried it decided it was not worth while when the Committee on Conformation waited on them.

"Silly, undignified, and brutal," was the Davis indictment of hazing. His third count was strongest. Hazing might have its uses in reducing the swelling of egos, but it was all too often a field day for the bully, a blanket massacre of the innocents. As such it offered Sir Richard a Cause. A choice between being a champion and a "good sport" never gave him any hesitation.

From the moment he matriculated he knew he was leading a life of the hunted. Should he rally his class and fight it out? he wondered. No, the lone hand always appealed to him most. This after all was his party.

Unescorted by a bodyguard, he went to a performance at

the Opera House one night. No sooner was he seated than an electric tension warned him there would be alarums and excursions without. Word spread through the college that a heavy hazing session was on the cards—that Davis's exit from the theatre would be better than anything in the show.

Johnny Ruff,[2] torn between loyalty to Dick and his duty as an upper classman not to interfere, was hovering outside, not having the price of admission. Another henchman, Mark Antony De Wolfe Howe,[3] was attempting to rouse a Roman mob of freshmen but not having the luck of his namesake. There was only one of his class in Davis's vicinity and that poor wretch clearly felt like a man who had unwittingly accepted a martyr's invitation for a stroll which had ended in an arena full of lions.

Impatiently the audience awaited the conclusion of the performance. Down dropped the curtain and Davis, closely followed by his unhappy classmate, walked out. A sophomore grabbed him by the arm. He jerked away and made them a little speech. They were not going to set him down as stubborn and hot-headed if he could help it. They must recognize that this was a matter of principle.

"If this means hazing, I'm not with you," he said. "There's not enough men here to haze me but there's enough to thrash me, and I'd rather be thrashed than hazed."

The sophs hooted with glee. Hazing? That was the last thing they'd think of. No, indeed, Davis, old fellow, you're mistaken.

The miserable freshman companion pulled at Davis's coat and begged him to duck out of the mess. Davis strode off with the pack in full cry at his heels. At the next corner he turned

2 John D. Ruff, mining engineer and Philadelphia newspaperman.
3 Editor and biographer.

on them. "I give you fair warning, keep off. I tell you I'll strike the first man, the first one, that touches me."

With that they jumped him. He got in one blow and went down in the gutter with four pummelling sophomores on top. When he struggled to his feet, he was bedraggled and muddy, with one eye blackening rapidly. "Now," he shouted, "you're not able to haze me and I can't thrash twelve of you, but I'll fight any one man you bring out."

The faithful Ruff was beside him now and other upperclassmen were calling out for fair play. The hazing was not going so well, no co-operation being received from the victim. The whole process depended on that. Otherwise it had the look of cowardly odds. A second and a third time—knights always blew three blasts on the challenging trumpet—Davis demanded, "Will one of your men fight fair?" The hazers hesitated. Then there was a rescue rush of police and supporting mill hands and the sophomore class was saved from an awkward situation. It was all over but beefsteak for the embattled eye and beer for the rejoicing freshmen.

A triumph was given the victor next day at the meeting of the Athletic Association. When the freshmen nominated for committeeman a class member agreed on in caucus, a leading sophomore jumped up. He was pleased to place in nomination the name of Mr. Davis, and his classmates enthusiastically seconded him. Nominees were forced to stand up. Up rose Dick, one eye decked with the black badge of courage. "Davis! Davis! Vote for D!" yelled the sophomores. Davis insisted on withdrawing his name in spite of cries of "No!" Johnny Ruff, the staunch, hugged him all the way back to the Harding house, where Uncle Wilson approved heartily.

"You see," ran Dick's letter to his dad, "I am now the hero of the hour, every one in town knows it, and every one congratulates me, and, 'Well done, me boy,' as Morrow, '83, said, seems to be the idea. One gets taken care of in this world if you do what's the right thing if it is only a street fight."

His father's answer was prompt and hearty. "Dear Old Boy," the little editor wrote his son, "I'm glad the affair ended so well. I don't want you to fight, but if you have to fight a cuss like that do it with all your might, and don't insist that either party shall too strictly observe the Markis o' Queensberry rules. Hit first and hardest so that thine adversary shall beware of you."

III

Davis was not a revolt, he was revolution. Down with the cane rush. Its fairly severe casualties weren't worth the fun in it. Lehigh could take it from him, too, that there was over-much "ponying" going on; too many fellows who, like one junior, could sign their exam. papers "& CO." No student needed first aid more than Davis, but he would not stoop to it. Neither would he attend the Allentown Fair, an annual collegiate saturnalia.

Slinging ink at the devil, Davis published an article in the college paper denouncing by name a student who was exerting an evil influence on younger men. The student was expelled.

Down with fraternities with their secrecy and limitations on independent action. Vainly they offered bids to the reformer with the courage of his convictions. And what should the zealot do but add injury to insult by starting clubs to suit his own ideas! He formed the Arcadia Club, gay with conviviality and rollicking choruses, composed by the founder, in praise of "pipes, books, beer, and gingeralia." What cared he who made the Greek letters of Lehigh, if he could but write its songs?

His fellowship of the "Mustard and Cheese," which was the seed of the college dramatic club, he organized along the lines of Harvard's Hasty Pudding. Davis's stimulating personality and leadership were its mainspring. Once a week the small membership met for spreads costing thirty cents a man, delivered profound sentiments on life and literature amid a haze of tobacco smoke[4] or acted the amusing burlesques and melodramas which the president provided for any occasion.

Long into those unforgettable nights the Davis guitar twanged merrily. The Davis voice, a second tenor,—Brother Charley arrived next year with that greater rarity, a first tenor, —was lifted in song: Offenbach, Sullivan, or something moderately original. He loved it so, he sang with such verve that even the real singers condoned his somewhat hoarse and throaty tones. Sometimes the Arcadians condescended to go serenading and fair ones appeared at their windows duly delighted. Had they realized that the singers were more entranced with their own close harmony than romance, beauty would have tossed its bang and switched its bustle in pretty pique.[5]

Songs and hops, friends and long talks, tennis, track, and football—a man could ask no more for bright college years. But the piper had to be paid with mathematics and the like. Davis took fervent part in the trial, hanging and burning in effigy of King Calculus after exams were over each spring, but inevitably the old tyrant would rise from his ashes to plague him next fall. Chemistry he flunked just as regularly. Professor Harding for his conscience's sake seems to have managed to keep his nephew out of his physics class; he had

[4] From pipes and cigars, of course. Cigarettes were then regarded as a mere juvenile smoke.

[5] The abandonment of the hoop by this time and the reefing of voluminous skirts aft in bustles was welcomed by the ladies. Perhaps that was why some of them coyly crowned that rear elevation with sprigs of orange blossoms and other posies.

enough lobbying to do with colleagues of the faculty. One subject after another went by the board, leaving as a residuum the "Davis Special Course." Its backbone was determined to be English literature and guitar playing.

But there was one ray of light in the educational gloom. The lad could write, could write simply, clearly, and entertainingly. His vocabulary never comprised much more than 900 words; yet he could do wonders with that noble 900. His pen was the mainstay of *The Lehigh Burr* and *The Epitome* of which he was chairman when only a sophomore. He wrote verse (happily, judging from samples, soon abandoned) but devoted himself more to forceful articles and to fiction, popular with his college readers. His character, *Conway Maur,* was the forerunner of *Van Bibber.* Flushed with triumph, for he had contributed to *Life* and *The New York Evening Post,* he collected his undergraduate efforts in a privately printed volume entitled *Adventures of My Freshman* and sold it at twenty-five cents a copy.

For a first book it seemed to be doing rather well. After a discouraging interval, booksellers reported it sold out. The excited author besought his mother to finance a second printing. Her refusal hurt his feelings. Some years later he understood when he found the bulk of the first edition cached away in the family attic.

But Davis would win fame with his pen. "Bish" Howe, a fellow editor, was sure of it. Even then he truly appraised the spirit of confidence and enthusiasm which turned everything Dick undertook into an adventure—the brave and humorous playing of the game of life, the true heart, the wholesome body and soul of his friend and classmate. Those were qualities to win a most-likely-to-succeed vote in spite of eccentricities.

However, future achievements out in the wide world were

vague and unimportant speculations now. The pristine football fortunes of Lehigh were demanding immediate doing or dying.

IV

The day of Lehigh's first football game, un-story-like, dawned dull and rainy—December 8, 1883. Captain Jake Robeson, of the sophomore team representing the university, nevertheless donned his white jacket. Wet weather or not, it was only right he should. There had been nothing as fetching as that garment in all Lehigh's athletic wardrobe when elections were held and it had won Robeson the captaincy.

Now similar jackets at seventy-five cents the copy were donned by Halfback Davis, Halfback Howe, and the rest of the team. Each pressed on the back of a well-thatched head a white skull cap, mindful of the rule that he must not wave it distractingly at an opponent about to make a fair catch. Each scanned admiringly his brown-and-white-striped jersey, his Rugby shorts, his shoes free of projecting nails and iron cleats, according to regulations. Some rubbed a little dirt on their virgin uniforms to gain a veteran appearance, but none resorted to forbidden greasy substances to elude tacklers.

Without a final fight talk from coach and trainers, for there were no such aids, the eleven trotted forth. It was greeted by a cheering crowd which had not struggled for the coveted pasteboards and complained of being allotted seats behind the goal lines, since there was no grandstand. Nearly 300 partisans lined the ropes along the sidelines: loyal undergraduates, excited maidens in fashionable dolmans or revealing jerseys, unsuspecting professors not yet confronted by the dilemma of flunking a football player. There were cheers for Jake Robeson in his original model, for "Bish" Howe, light but fast, for

THE LEHIGH FOOTBALL TEAM IN DAVIS'S TIME

R. H. Davis is the second from the right, standing; C. B. Davis, the second from the left, standing.

RICHARD HARDING DAVIS, 1884, EDITOR OF *THE LEHIGH BURR*

Associates, (on the left) W. W. Mills, (centre) Charles Clapp.

unhazed Dick Davis, the human declaration of independence.

The visiting team of sophomores of the University of Pennsylvania were eyeing the gridiron apprehensively. Its rocks, tin cans, broken bottles, and muddy quicksands convinced them that only formidable foemen would practise on such home grounds. While the rules forbade throttling, butting, tripping, or slugging with closed fists, they said nothing about rough tactics by the field. It might be better to give up the ball than be downed on that terrific terrain.

The whistle blew, the ball sailed through the air, a runner was collared. Teams lined up and the snapper-back flipped the pigskin to the quarter. Such mighty forward passes as would soon disappear in the evolution of the game and not be restored for years soared through the air. Bucking the line was condemned and there was practically no interference. When a man ran the ball, his teammates trotted along after him out of courtesy and interest to see how much ground he would gain.

Robeson and Howe were Lehigh's tower of strength. Poor Davis, winner of hurdle races and high jumps, was not a good mud horse. "The captain," he confessed, "did not know much but at least he had sufficient judgment to pass the ball to the other half, and I never got it by any chance unless he fumbled it and some one else did not fall on it first. And as our side never got the ball except on those benificent chances required by the fourth-down rule, I had plenty of time to study the game and count the stripes on my jersey and try to keep up with the other side's score. It was not difficult to keep tally of our own." He modestly failed to declare that he was a bulwark of the defense.[6]

[6] Frank Dole, coaching Pennsylvania two years later, remembered Davis as one of Lehigh's best offense men, steady, fast on his feet, a crackerjack dodger, and hard as nails in bucking the line.

At last even the indefatigable Howe, when Robeson signalled to him to carry the ball by the customary nod in his direction, called out: "Don't pass that ball to me, Jake, I'm stuck in the mud and can't get out!"

Two forty-five-minute halves, with ten minutes rest between, passed into history, engraving a score of 16 to 10 in favor of Pennsylvania. Yet Lehigh had fought hard. None could doubt it after gazing at the sterling cast in the mud of the field imprinted by the features and knitted woollen cap of Posey of the U. of P. when several Lehigh men stood on his head.

Stalking back to its quarters, the team, grimy and battered, was halted by Davis. Thus, fresh from combat, they must have their tintypes taken, he insisted, and they were duly snapped.

The Davis sense of drama could not resist a little grandstanding at times. Once he was slightly hurt in a scrimmage and it was in the guise of a dying gladiator that he was supported off the field by a comrade. But he never equalled the bravado of another Lehigh football stalwart, the doughty Rafferty, who, suffering a compound fracture of his collar bone, retired behind the ropes and broke training enough to light a cigar. Thereupon he knocked off its ashes on the bone sticking through his jersey.

There were plenty of hard knocks and little glory in those early years of Lehigh football. Its rival Lafayette won their first game 56 to 0. The contest was remembered as a series of personal encounters with spectators and Easton cops "who had an instinctive prejudice to Lehigh men which they expressed by kicking them on the head whenever one of them went under the ropes for the ball."[7] Rutgers conquered Lehigh by 61 to 0. The old college spirit could hardly have been in there

[7] From *A History of Lehigh University* by Catherine Drinker Bowen. Bethlehem, Pa., 1924.

fighting with the Varsity, for the undergraduate body scorned its record and grudged it fifty-two dollars from the athletic association treasury for new uniforms.

Lehigh football would rise from the slough.[8] A second game with Lafayette showed at least a gleam of better things. It was lost, but the string of zeros was ended by a score of 34 to 4. Those four points were the result of a run and a touchdown (as then scored) by R. H. Davis who was thereupon enshrined in athletic annals. He often declared that he took keener satisfaction in making that first touchdown for Lehigh than in all the verses and short stories he ever wrote.

Before the football season of '85 was under way, it became evident that one star halfback would be missing from the Lehigh line-up. Although he had broken through Lafayette, the faculty had stiffened and would hold. Davis would never gain enough scholastic ground to reach Banner Day next spring and graduate amid the joyous clamor of traditional hand-organs.

His failures puzzled him slightly. He told one professor who flunked him that he did not understand because he had used the same notes as Howe. He neglected to add that he had made none of his own.

The inevitable happened. Solemn professors assembled in august conclave to pronounce a decree of expulsion upon Davis, '86, for failure in scholarship. Dean Elwood Worcester, later chaplain of the university, relates in his *Life's Adventures* how Davis, "well aware of his own power," faced the faculty and declared:

"You don't think I am worthy to remain in this school. But in a few years you will find that I have gone farther than you will ever go."

[8] Davis went back to college to help coach the victorious team of '93.

It was a hurt, defiant youngster who was speaking and his words sounded like nothing but braggadocio. And yet by 1890——

So Dick Davis bade farewell to his second alma mater and transferred to Johns Hopkins, there to study political economy and labor problems. Those subjects, he believed, would stand him in good stead in newspaper work. So they might have, but they were not to be mastered by an incurable romantic. This one did not seriously try. His economics professor rated him as willful, untractable and conceited. When that teacher ventured to criticize the literary style of one of the hasty Davis essays, he faced a spoiled-boy exhibition—an angry youth who demanded if he realized that he was the son of Rebecca Harding Davis, the writer, and Clarke Davis, the Philadelphia editor.

Neither of his parents would have thanked him for such advertisement. Mrs. Davis was striving to guide her son out of his cock-sure immaturities. She would praise him for his dramatic eye, his quick perception of character, for his keen sympathy with all kinds of people, his humor. Wise woman! she knew that with each compliment not altogether deserved she gave him an ideal to live up to. Writing, she warned him, was not inspiration but practice. Let him remember that he had not yet conquered his art; that he was only a journeyman, not a master workman.

Until spring he studied social sciences by attending numerous dinners and dances with the ever-charming Baltimore girls. There was football to play, too, and magazines not entirely hostile to contributions. A year at Hopkins seemed enough. It was time to put aside education and step across the threshold of the journalistic career which was beckoning him by paternal example. He was leaving his third college without any sheepskin evidence of having been among those present, yet it was a rare city editor who, in taking on a new cub, would ask for a look at his diploma. On the contrary, if a fellow had one it might be as well to keep it dark.

You will look vainly through the books of Richard Harding Davis for heroes who went to Swarthmore, Lehigh, or Johns Hopkins. Almost all who were college men went heroically to Yale, Harvard, or Princeton. *66066*

He once confided in a young Harvard friend—this was before the day when his remark would have been a collegiate *faux pas*—that it was the regret of his life that he had not been able to go to Princeton and play football there. Perhaps it was best he did not. Big Three gridiron gods, who might have fulfilled some more original destiny, have been side-tracked all too frequently into the bond business.

CHAPTER THREE

GENTLEMAN OF THE PRESS

I

FOLLOWING in his father's footsteps, Richard Harding Davis took the rough road which is littered with copy paper, pungent of printer's ink and strident with the whirring of presses. A newspaper job was virtually a birthright of Clarke Davis's son. Graciously *The Philadelphia Record* granted the request of its distinguished colleague of *The Inquirer* that his eldest be given an opportunity to break in.

Davis faced his first city editor with the assurance of an initiate in the writing craft. He smiled his boyishly eager smile and reported for work. From behind the barricade of his desk, James S. Chambers, Jr., responded with a baleful glare which was a masterpiece even for a city editor.

That hard-bitten newspaperman incredulously surveyed the combination fashion-plate and reporter hired over his head by the powers upstairs. He almost gaped at a spectacle so unique in a newspaper city room of 1886. The young man wore a suit of nobby English cut and actually carried a cane, an ornament of such massive proportion that it was forthwith christened the Davis railroad tie. Not for many years would the like be swung by reporters and then the guilty ones would be New Yorkers. Chambers was ready to suspect his applicant of owning a dress suit, a college education, and a willingness to drink afternoon tea—anything but entrance requirements for the Fourth Estate. Most obnoxious of all was the pair of kid gloves which completed the Davis ensemble. One of those effete gauntlets might as well have been flung at the editorial feet in knightly challenge to mortal combat.

Davis stood unfeazed by the scathing inspection of this editor whose steely eyes, stubby brown beard, and brusque manner gave him a striking resemblance to General Grant in one of his more ruthless moments. It was Chambers who opened hostilities with a scornful offer of chance work, but Davis, accepting, won the first skirmish with the blithe remark that such an arrangement would leave him more time free for his outside writing. The war was on.

There would be no fancy extra-curriculum effort by any cub on Jim Chambers' staff. He soon surprised his new and elegant addition by shifting him to full time—eighteen assignments or so a day at $7 a week, such assignments as are the woeful lot of novices. Davis was condemned to the gloomy toil of the undertaker "run" with its short "obits." of worthy but unimportant citizens. If any one of prominence died, his eulogy fell to experienced reporters. For veterans were the thrilling three-alarm fires; for Davis the puny blazes that never amounted to anything—nobody burned up, nobody rescued, minor property damage. His not to cover the murders but the meetings of women's clubs. His not to reason why but to charge out and interview nonentities who sent word to the editor they had a "great story" for the paper. His to listen patiently to hopelessly confused people who were under the impression that advertising was news.

Cub reporter versus city editor is a struggle where the odds are heavy on the latter. Yet while Chambers[1] could and did quell a rebellion of *The Record's* copy boys when they brand-

[1] Other tales of the redoubtable Chambers remain in the folk-lore of Philadelphia newspaperdom. Once when he served as correspondent at a convention and found that he "owed himself money," he inserted in his expense account an item of $30 "For upholding the dignity of the *Record*." It was questioned by his immediate superior but allowed by his chief as cheap at the price.

ed him "Boy Killer" in a round robin, Davis staggered ahead under the weight of his accumulating assignments, unconquered, unexhausted, and not ungloved. He plodded miles through the city in quest of trite items. Clad in a long yellow ulster with light-green stripes, he attended his quota of fires. In spite of his English clothes and a copy of *The London Athenæum* protruding from a pocket, he reported Irish labor meetings and escaped intact to the amazement of his antagonist of the city desk.

It was the dullness of the cub's routine and the disheartening destiny of his literary flights that made Davis fatally careless. Of course he overwrote at the slightest excuse after the manner of repressed tyros. An undeveloped news sense telling him neither what to put in nor what to leave out, his pencil scribbled feverishly over page after page. In the glow of accomplishment he laid his story on the sacrificial altar of the copy desk. There the carnage commenced, as words, sentences, and paragraphs were cold-bloodedly "killed."

"The copy editor's cigar was tilted near his left eye-brow,"[2] Davis described the sadly familiar scene. "His blue pencil like a guillotine ready to fall upon the guilty word or paragraph was suspended in mid air, and constantly, like a hawk preparing to strike, the blue pencil swooped and circled." Strike it did. There was prey a-plenty in copy where "which" was spelled "witch" and where padding was as prevalent as in a mattress.

Davis from a distance would watch his edited story forwarded at last to the composing room. Eagerly he would rustle through one of the first papers off the press, finally to find

[2] From *The Red Cross Girl*. In this tale Davis made a dream come true. The fell designs of the copy reader on the hero's story were balked, although it was a combination editorial, essay, and spring poem. It was so good it had to be run intact or killed, and it was run.

his yarn buried inside, cut down from half a column to a stick and a half and barely recognizable. Such is the fortune of cub reporters. Theirs is a dispiriting apprenticeship to a spirited profession. A severe school, but for directness, simplicity, and conciseness in writing there is none better, and the Davis style always bore its mark.

Yet to Davis's temperament it was especially galling. As he hurried through the streets on some piffling assignment, it was his habit to picture himself in the midst of an exciting situation; some big story breaking which he would cover to the Queen's or even to the Chambers taste and beat the town. It only happened in imagination and story-books. Actualities were dry and discouraging. That he was having elementals pounded into him, that he was cultivating a nose for news— these were compensations beyond his present appreciation.

He wondered why he was wasting his time writing three-line squibs for this sheet, he who had published in real magazines and had a book out. Why must silly girls keep asking you on your day off if reporting wasn't a fascinating career? The only interest Davis saw in it was the sports department and they would give him no chance there. Always the eagle eye of Jim Chambers was on him and a new chore was ready. The quality of mercy in a city editor is not strained; it is diluted or entirely evaporated.

Tense from a thousand going-to-press deadlines, burdened with a million details, Chambers still could not forget the gloves on his stylish subordinate who dressed like a journalist, not a newspaperman. Davis contended he only wore them when it was cold, but his boss took oath he clung to them in a temperature of eighty and even wrote in the things. Stubborn young Mr. Davis was resolved to fight it out along those lines with General Grant's double if it took all fall.

That was all it took. In three months Chambers had all he could stand of gloves and incompetence. If the fellow had gone out and got drunk once in a while, that would have been different; an astonishing amount of insobriety was condoned in newspaper offices, if the drinker produced in between flings. This cub just did not seem to have the makings. One night the city editor marked his victim dawdling beside the sports desk with an important (to Chambers) assignment unwritten in his pocket.

"Take off your gloves and your coat and get to work," his boss directed gruffly.

Reluctantly relinquishing his perusal of scores, Davis sat down and wrote his story—with his gloves on. Chambers read it like a man biting into a sour apple. In a voice which, wafted without, was one of the louder noises of Chestnut Street, he summoned the culprit to judgment.

"You can take a long vacation at once," was the verdict.

Said Davis: "Well, I guess I am fired. Is that it?"

"That," interpreted the editor, "is the English of it."

It was a heavy blow. Still one had to stand up under it like a man. Davis's reply was infuriatingly sporting.

"Well, old chap," he remarked, "I suppose I'll have to take my medicine."

Whereupon he offered the city editor his gloved hand.

II

The Davis persistence sent him out in search of another job and he applied to Albert H. Hoeckley, city editor of *The Philadelphia Press*. Admitting that he just had been discharged from *The Record,* Davis explained:

"Jim Chambers gave me nineteen assignments at $7 a week, and"—adding a line that belongs among Alexander Woollcott's classic examples of understatement—"I don't think he liked my gloves."

Hoeckley hired him and did not regret it. Soon he was rating his new hand as a good reporter and a modest one, rapidly developing into a star man.

For the shock of being fired made Davis shed gloves, ulster, and cane and get down to work. Years later he confessed to Chambers that his forced exit had chastened him into a readiness to take assignments as they came and put his heart into them all. It was a priceless lesson, a Godsend. Taking trouble with the trivial tasks he had ignored, he found and imparted the human touch, the tiny, trenchant, compelling details which make an item a story. He was learning now that "reporters become star reporters because they observe things other people miss and because they don't let it appear they have observed them."[3]

Uncomplaining he betook himself to the zoo, that distant bourne whither city editors at their wits' end send reporters hanging around the office. He registered bison births and news of gnus. Better luck attending, he reported that intensely dramatic event, a big hotel fire. He interviewed Modjeska and the not-unreceptive Sarah Bernhardt whose genius for publicity won her the nickname of Sarah Barnum. Financiers and captains of industry talked for him, patronizingly or cordially, cagily or incautiously. He discovered that "some people like to place themselves in the hands of a reporter because they hope he will print their names in block letters, a few others— only reporters know how few—would as soon place themselves in the hands of a dentist."[4]

Society theatricals, jolly to cover and good copy from the prominent subscribers' angle, were in the Davis orbit. In line

[3] From *The Red Cross Girl*. Published in *The Saturday Evening Post*, March 2, 1912.
[4] From *The Red Cross Girl*. Published also in a book of short stories.

of duty, he visited behind the scenes at burlesque shows, and no young man was safer in those somewhat precarious surroundings.

Like the hero of Stephen French Whitman's *Predestined,* he "contemplated degradation, he intruded on anguish, in awe he looked down on the mysterious masks of suicides and murdered men." Degradation, because a reporter cannot shut his eyes to life. Intrusion, because "I've got to do it," is the American newspaperman's motto and he is not permitted to exercise the blessed forbearance of English pressmen. Suicides and murders, because those violent finalities are always news.

The Press was a lively paper and Davis was up to its tempo. At last he knew the joy of making the front page, the satisfaction of handling competently a story on which a first-string man had fallen down. He tasted that heady brew, the power of the press, whose instrument he was. J. O. G. Duffy, then and for many years afterward a veteran editor, classed him as somewhat deficient as a fact digger but a first-rate feature man, with a flair for brightening his descriptions with interest and humor. Other reporters, conceding him to be a good craftsman, put him down as no hail fellow well met. Uppish, they decided, as they contemplated his aristocratic and exclusive air, his clothes, his familiarity with more literature than was any use to a newspaperman. And yet there was something to upset their judgment in his warm-hearted way, in his generosity to his friends, in his enthusiasm when all hands sat around the city room awaiting assignments or talking over stories in the morning paper. When the staff assembled for a shad breakfast, it was Davis who made the party go by unlimbering his guitar and rendering "When Kerrigan Struck High C."

In the Sunday *Press* lay a field of glorious endeavor for Davis. It abounded in feature articles illustrated by neat line-cuts. Bill Nye[5] was regularly syndicated in that edition—two long, unleaded columns or more of wise and witty stuff, which might be envied by any modern "colyumist." Space, tight on weekdays, loosened up Sundays, and Davis revelled in the chance to let himself go.

Armed with a letter of introduction from Talcott Williams,[6] his managing editor, he sallied forth to Camden to interview Walt Whitman.[7] It had its amusing aspects, this meeting of ·the sage and the unsophisticated young reporter. . . . Davis earnestly striving to plumb the complexities of the Good Gray Poet in one afternoon. . . . Whitman, gun-shy of reporters, dodging questions on politics. . . . Davis mindful that his mother considered Walt a seer and a spokesman for the gods but condemned him for vulgarity and indecency and "always writing poems to every part of his own anatomy." . . . Whitman more interested in studying his interviewer than answering his queries. . . . Davis flattered and impressed but fastidiously deploring the fact that the oracle's finger nails were dirty.

"So you say he is the son of Rebecca Harding Davis?"[8] Whitman asked his disciple, Horace Traubel, afterward. "I thought him an Irish boy: I liked him—he was so candid, so interesting. Such tall, wholesome-looking fellows are rare among American youngsters."

His interview written and printed, Davis made bold to forward it to Robert Louis Stevenson. His recompense was a cordial letter containing advice, precious to him and to any newspaperman.

---

[5] In an article syndicated in *The Press,* Nye delivered his ideas on "How Some Writers Write." Whittier, Nye declared, dips his pen in bluing; Ella Wheeler Wilcox makes her typewriter sound like a zylophone trying to convince a lawn mower of the error of its ways; Oliver Optic is threatened with pen paralysis; Edgar Saltus writes with his nerves on plain paper.

[6] See ACKNOWLEDGMENTS at the end of this volume.

[7] Christopher Morley based a one-act play, *Walt,* on this episode.

[8] From Horace Traubel's *With Walt Whitman in Camden.* New York, 1908.

"If you are to escape unhurt out of your present business," wrote R. L. S., "you must be very careful, and you must find in your heart much constancy. The swiftly done work of the journalist and the cheap finish and ready-made methods to which it leads, you must try to counteract in private by writing with the most considerate slowness and on the most ambitious models. And when I say 'writing'—O, believe me, it is rewriting that I have chiefly in mind. If you will do this I hope to hear of you some day."

III

Davis meant that Stevenson should hear of him some day. He was keeping busily at his magazine writing. There was, for instance, that pirate story he had sent to *St. Nicholas*. Only a few years before Stevenson had won fame himself with a book about pirates.

A letter from *St. Nicholas* arrived one morning when Davis and his fellow-reporter, F. Jennings Crute, were having breakfast together. It might be just an offer of a subscription at reduced rates. No, there was a letter inside and a check, a check for fifty dollars—the sum his mother had received for *Life in the Iron-Mills*.

Dazed at a payment which seemed no less than magnificent, Davis gasped helplessly: "It's for fifty, Jenny."

Crute stared back in wild-eyed incredulity. "Half a hundred dollars, and on your day off, too," he murmured.

The wealthy author, having gazed his full in awe at the check, brought himself to cash it and spent the rest of the day paying debts for clothes, buying more, and writing the glad tidings to his family at the seashore.

Mrs. Davis was delighted. But no son of hers was to be allowed to rest on the laurels of his first fiction acceptance. "Have you done anything on Gallagher?" she demanded.

Gallagher was a copy boy on *The Press,* and Davis had made him the hero of a short story. A gem of character, a real individual was Gallagher. For other juvenile couriers on the paper's retinue, lazy or oversmart, the traditional summons of "Boy" or "Here, you" was enough when "takes" on a late story were to be rushed to the composing room and galley proofs sped back to the city desk. Not for Gallagher. He had won the accolade of a name. Dick Davis, always fond of children, was devoted to this ten-year-old youngster who "wore perpetually on his face a happy and knowing smile, as if you and the world were not impressing him as seriously as you thought you were, and his eyes, which were very black and very bright, snapped intelligently at you like those of a little black-and-tan terrier."[9] He "possessed the power of amusing *The Press's* young men to a degree seldom attained by the ordinary mortal. His clog-dancing on the city editor's desk, when that gentleman was upstairs fighting for two more columns of space, was always a source of innocent joy to us," wrote Davis. It was he who gave the lad dimes to jig on that august spot.

Best of all, Gallagher was possessed by a detective complex. It was beyond Davis's power to resist weaving a story of newspaper life around the lad and his earnest sleuthing, a tale of a murderer who wore gloves, by the way, but for good reason. Of a raided prize fight and a valiant race by a copy boy to catch the last edition—a simple, genuine, moving yarn which gives you a catch in the throat at the end. Gallagher, of course, was the original of the copy boy and his patron, the sports editor, was Davis. The prize fight, they say, was the century bat-

[9] Davis: *Gallegher, a Newspaper Story.*

tle between Mike Mallon of Pittsburgh and Jack Dempsey the Nonpareil of New York.

The story was, as Mrs. Davis told her son, by far the best work he had done. He ought to send it to Editor Richard Watson Gilder in spite of the fact that it contained the word "brandy," for *The Century* had now attained the broad tolerance necessary to permit such mention in its text. But Dick, not so greatly daring as to storm such magnificent portals, preferred to try *Gallegher* on lesser magazines, rewriting it after each rejection. In due course, Mr. Gilder would see it and so would a great many other people, though not by grace of Gilder.

Well, Davis had done something on Gallagher, though nothing seemed to come of it. He forgot it and joked with the story's inspiration, telling the boy that they two would be managing editor and city editor of *The Press* in five years. In less than that Gallagher, as a title (slightly misspelled), and his biographer-patron as an author, would be associated in far greater fame.

IV

Davis, inventor of a fiction plot on little Gallagher's endeavors as a man-hunter, found himself taking the same rôle in a dangerous business in real life.

Philadelphia was suffering from a plague of yeggs. One successful burglary after another had been pulled off, and the police, the newspapers sarcastically remarked, were baffled. Perhaps, came the bluecoat retort, the papers could do something about it themselves besides knocking.

The Press accepted the challenge, its well-dressed Mr. Davis volunteering for the assignment. Into the wardrobe went all

R. H. D. FROM A PHOTOGRAPH TAKEN IN BETHLEHEM, PA.

R. HARDING DAVIS AT THE AGE OF NINE

R. H. D., REPORTER   IN BURGLAR DISGUISE

R. H. D. AND OTHER GENTLEMEN OF THE PRESS AT THE
JOHNSTOWN FLOOD IN 1889

Davis stands in the front row to the left of the barrel.

the splendid raiment. The unshaven tough guy who emerged in shabby suit, dirty flannel shirt, and cap cocked on the side of his head was perfectly disguised. He slouched into the reputed hang-out of the thieves, keeping to himself until his able mimicry had picked up the argot and manners of the hardboiled. He had a real talent for acting, had Davis; Daly, the great manager, once offered him a place in his company.

For days Davis lived in the dives, scraping an acquaintance with the gang who had committed the burglaries and winning their confidence. The slightest suspicion that he was a reporter would have meant a swift and unpleasant death, but no such slander entered the heads of the crooks who welcomed him as a recruit of unusual promise. This young fellow's bright ideas when he helped them to plan their next job aroused their professional admiration. What might have been Philadelphia's most brilliant burglary never came off. The police, tipped off by an insider, were waiting at the scene, arrested the gang and obtained convictions and jail sentences on evidence furnished. *The Press,* by a coincidence not at all strange, had the whole story.

The walls of Davis's room took on the look of a museum of crime under their new decorations of souvenir pistols and blackjacks. But more than mementos, a newspaper "beat" and a reputation for daring were results from the exploit. When later readers of stories by Richard Harding Davis followed the adventure of *Van Bibber* and his burglar[10] and of *The Disreputable Mr. Raegan,* they noted strong evidence that the author's knowledge of burglary and disreputability was based on research into source material.

Davis's energy was boundless. Besides his newspaper work,

---

[10] In this story Davis has *Van Bibber* let the burglar go. It is a fair presumption that helping to send the Philadelphia gang to prison came hard to him.

he plunged into editing a weekly theatrical sheet called *The Stage*. Morton MacMichael III was editor-in-chief and Barclay H. Warburton and Edward Fales Coward were associates with Davis. Between them they were editorial staff, advertising, subscription and mailing departments, Paris and London correspondents. The publication folded up before long after consuming the several stocks in trade: Davis's time and the others' money.

Work, work you loved, was an absorbing affair, but a little relaxation now and then was relished by the most earnest young men. One so personable as Davis had ample opportunity. Doors opened hospitably to a chap who could "sing for his supper." Did it matter so much if, when a calculating hostess issued her invitation, she sweetly added, "—and be sure to bring your guitar"? You brought your appetite, too, and a fair return was no robbery. At one imposing party, Arthur Hall, a young railroader and fellow-troubadour, having supped, was fetching his banjo. In the hallway he met Davis, distraught, clutching his guitar.

"Say, can you tune a guitar?" he begged the banjoist. "Mine's got all off key and I can't do anything about it. My sister always tunes it for me before I leave home."

Hall could tune a guitar, so all was well and shortly the enthusiastic, if uncultivated Davis voice was lifted in a favorite of the day suiting the singer mightily:

> "Last night a copper ran me in.
>   Judge Duffy let me go,
> Says, 'He's a swell. I know him well.
>   He's Donahue, the beau.'"

A night off now and then was not enough. Even a dynamo like Davis needed a rest occasionally. He took it reluctantly, realizing he ran the risk of missing a big story.

Exactly that happened. Davis was off duty when one of the biggest stories in American journalistic history broke with the suddenness of the disaster itself—The Johnstown Flood.

V

A dam stopped the mouth of the south fork of Stony Creek, a tributary of the Conemaugh River, at a point 75 miles east by south of Pittsburgh. Built in 1852 to provide a storage reservoir for a canal, it was retained to form a fishing preserve for a sportsmen's club. Warnings of the weakness of the earthen wall went unheeded. It had held for years. But under the pressure of waters swollen by unprecedented rains, the barrier burst on the afternoon of May 31, 1889. Behind a foaming crest 20 feet high, a roaring, grinding avalanche of water, 70 feet deep and 700 acres in area, rushed down the valley. A few gallant horsemen raced it, shouting alarms until they reached the high ground or sank beneath the waves that caught them. Down swept the torrent to inundate Johnstown and seven villages in its path. A railroad bridge held under the mass of wreckage heaped high against it and there miserable victims spared from drowning perished on a huge pyre as the débris crackled into flames. Nearly 3000 lives and $12,000,000 in property were destroyed.

The first brief Associated Press flash[11] sent out that evening was enough to bring correspondents converging on Johnstown from every large newspaper within striking distance. Davis dashed to the office as soon as he heard the news. He was too late. *The Press* already had despatched Crute and other good men who were obeying literally the unwritten newspaper commandment: Get what you're sent for if you have to go through

[11] The General Manager of the AP was a passenger on a train marooned on the mountain side by the flood.

fire and water.[12] Davis watched their copy, written on barrel heads by candlelight, tick back over the wires. Jealously he scanned their columns on columns of front-page stuff, accounts of the catastrophe gleaned from dazed survivors, of drunken ghouls plundering the corpses of the drowned; tales of heroism and horror. He was missing all this because of a mere rest. At last his paper yielded to his poignant disappointment and sent him on.

The story of the flood and its havoc had been ably handled by his predecessors, but Davis won the honor of a by-line on a despatch based on the human interest details he had learned not to overlook. Searching through the backwash of the calamity, he found a railroad passenger car picked up like a match by the flood, carried half a mile from the depot tracks and buried beneath the floors and the roofs of demolished houses. On the side of the car was still legible a sign: "Any person injuring this car will be dealt with according to the law." Here lay a catcher's mask flung off as quickly as for a foul fly. There rested a mahogany bar, complete with nickel rail, high and dry. The only firm stretch of the road he was treading caught Davis's attention. It was composed of thousands of cigars spilt out of a ruined factory.

And yonder inside the door of the still-standing stone jail hung a bunch of keys. Davis grasped them, unlocked the rusty, complaining doors of the cell block. In one slumped the body of some poor wretch, drowned like a rat. Who was the man? It was the job of a good reporter to find out, chaos or not, and Davis hustled for facts until he discovered the tragic irony that crowned the story. The prisoner had been locked up for twenty-four hours to recover from a Decoration

---

[12] From *The Making of a Journalist*, by that great reporter, Julian Ralph. New York, 1903.

Day spree and there in his cell the sudden deluge had trapped and overwhelmed him.

Later Davis, substituting for the men first in the field, did thorough work in covering the relief efforts and played a part in bringing the plight of the devastated region[13] to the notice of the country, which raised a $4,000,000 fund for aid and reconstruction.

VI

The sports page of *The Record* had snared Dick Davis that night Chambers caught him on the hip. Now the same page of *The Press* had him in its toils. He could think and talk nothing but cricket, for all Philadelphia was engrossed in it.

That cricket stronghold of the United States was hanging on the selection of a picked team from local clubs to represent it against the amateur teams of Ireland, Scotland, and England. Elsewhere hurried Americans displayed a certain apathy to a game where a four-inning match might stretch through one or two days. But Philadelphian furor, increased by the recent visits of British teams, had spread to include everything English from canes to coaches and gaitered grooms; from col-

---

[13] The tragic drama of the Johnstown Flood made an impression on the nation which did not fade for years. Fairs and expositions featured sideshows; stages set with a miniature Johnstown, swept into a mechanical collapse by an onrushing torrent, while a monologuist shouted the reputed words of the warning horseman, "My God! The dam has burst!" These shows supplanted the Civil War cycloramas and in turn gave way to early motion pictures such as *The Great Train Robbery*. The country also was deluged with a flood of verse by earnest though unskilled poets. One, a medical student, thus described the ride of the Johnstown Revere:

> He announced the danger of the coming abyss,
> Warning people not to take it amiss.

Two other couplets of his must be quoted for the gems they are.

> Pianos found exit through the opening walls,
> Forced by the flood from embellished halls.

> During the first two weeks of distress,
> People stood around apparently purposeless.

ored jerseys and caps for girls to alarmingly tight Bond Street trousers to cramp masculine legs. As boys and undergraduates and graduates of the University of Pennsylvania and Haverford, the young men of the Quaker City were constant cricketers. They spent their summers no farther away than the suburbs instead of flitting to resorts and they played cricket from spring through fall.

Every newspaper featured the choice of the Gentlemen of Philadelphia, a team of star players which included Davis's friend, MacMichael, George Sterling Patterson, R. S. Newhall, D. P. Stoever, William G. Morgan, Jr., E. W. Clark, Jr., Francis E. Brewster, R. D. Brown, Henry J. Brown, Joseph W. Sharp, Newbold Etting, and A. G. Thompson. And every newspaperman coveted a chance to accompany the team as a correspondent. Davis, cricketer from his youth and sports enthusiast always, burned for this prize assignment which meant longed-for travel abroad.

But Davis's claim to go ranked below that of a member of the regular sports staff of *The Press* who got the assignment. Nevertheless when the boat sailed in June, Davis was on board as a representative of *The Philadelphia Telegraph,* a temporary transfer in which one seems to see the fine editorial hand of his father. With the team he landed at Queenstown and listened with awe to the speech of welcome in Latin which preceded matches with Trinity College and the Gentlemen of Ireland. Along with the Gentlemen of Philadelphia, he ducked hastily when their special train, carrying also an Irish agitator under arrest, was fired on by a riotous crowd of sympathizers. He cabled reports that his team was holding its own against the Gentlemen of Scotland, and in England enjoyed to the utmost the hospitality of country houses extended to the American cricketers and correspondents.

Like Patterson, who at luncheon in a Kentish village found himself seated between a former Governor General of Bombay and the local barber, he marvelled at the democracy of cricket on its native soil. Many a dinner was enlivened by Davis's talent as a raconteur or by "Dixie" sung to the accompaniment of his trusty guitar.

Yet it was not altogether a happy trip. Davis had a quick temper and he often lost it when teased. Considerable kidding being inevitable in a crowd of college men, he was forced to take his share and his failure to take it well hurt his popularity. Because he was abnormally sensitive, he sometimes saw himself as a reporter who did not "belong" being snobbishly treated by a bunch of young aristocrats, and once a sally of rough fun brought tears to his eyes.

What was he to do about this sensitiveness he never had been able to overcome? Hardening an impulsive and ingenuous nature like his was impossible. Life was bound to hurt him. The only answer, the only defense seemed to be—fight the devil with fire. If you met some one who was likely to snub you, give him as good as he sent. Out-snub the snobs. There was a danger in that. It might rate you as considerable of a snob yourself. But if you were born to carry your heart on your sleeve, you must shield it from bruises somehow.

Davis loved England. It was full of stories he must write some day. Travel had fascinated him since an earlier trip to Santiago, Cuba, where scenes of stirring adventure had shaped themselves in his imagination and the characters of a novel to be called *Soldiers of Fortune* were waiting to be born to people them. He was sorry when it was time to sail home.

But the port of New York docking his ship opened up a glorious vista. Here was the literary capital of the nation, the gateway to enterprise. Here the Mecca toward which every

good newspaperman faced prayerfully. If zealous scribes made
the pilgrimage from San Francisco via Chicago and way stations, the journey sometimes requiring weary years, was Philadelphia, then, so far from New York? In that great city were
many magnificent newspaper shrines as yet unmerged by Munsey, the Merciless, the Uncompassionate, and every now and
then one of them had a job loose.

As a reporter in Philadelphia, Davis had been successful. In
time he might climb the ladder to editorships like his father
before him. And yet at Lehigh and elsewhere he had been
pretty free with prophecies of how far he would go in a few
years. His native city, said one of her wisest inhabitants,[14]
lacked discriminating enthusiasm for her own children and
the work of their hands. While New York, if you caught her
fickle fancy, could not do enough for you and sang your praises
loud enough to be heard everywhere.

"To put a good newspaperman on a Philadelphia paper is
like inviting a good musician to prove his skill on the jew's-
harp."[15] Thus some supercilious New Yorker once expressed
the attitude of his town. Base calumny, of course, but still it
was true that the greater opportunity lay to the north. For a
while after his return from abroad, Davis continued on *The
Press*. Then in December, 1889, he resigned and took a train
for New York.

[14] From Agnes Repplier's *Philadelphia, the Place and the People.* New York, 1898.
[15] From *The Book Buyer*, New York. A sketch of Davis published in the days of
his early fame.

CHAPTER FOUR

PARK ROW

I

Davis stood poised in City Hall Park. Behind him rose the trim marble front and frugal sandstone rear of the Colonial City Hall. To his left the Elevated engines, playing at being a real railroad on stilts, emitted steam, whistles, and soot. Beyond, a steel span soared gracefully over the East River—that bridge which, as he was to discover, connects Brooklyn with New York but not necessarily New York with Brooklyn. Street cars rolled by at the leisurely jog trot of their motive power.

Around him the park trees were beginning to outnumber surrounding telegraph poles, thousands of which had been hewn down by the Bureau of Incumbrances, with billions of feet of the city's arbor of wires buried underground. The current dynasty of bums stared up from their benches lazily, contemptuously or enviously at the handsome, square-shouldered young man in tweeds, Ascot tie, and derby hat, while moribund aspirations twitched at the look in his brown eyes. Those eyes scanning the magical panorama of Park Row's newspaper offices saw none of their shabbiness, only the infinite allurement of the "Alley of Ambitions."

Davis had written his mother from the Philadelphia station that he was only going to make a little reputation and to learn enough of the business to enable him to live at home in "The Centre of the Universe" with her. Now that he was in New York, perhaps he realized already that he would never leave it for long. The city would cast its spell on him once he found a job in one of those buildings across the way.

Which should he try? *The World's* office was no more imposing than the rest, but the framework of its new quarters hard by were towering tallest in the city toward the skies to be crowned by a golden dome, token of Pulitzer brilliance and sensationalism. There stood *The Tribune* of sturdy tradition. *The Morning Advertiser, The Evening Telegram,* and *The Recorder* all were better housed than *The Sun* at Frankfort Street and the Row, but to that tumble-down structure of muddy, discolored brick the gaze of the young man in the park turned most often. Relinquished by the braves of Tammany for their new Fourteenth Street wigwam, it had been purified by the presence of the illustrious Charles A. Dana's paper and its offspring, *The Evening Sun,* now two years risen. There was likely to be more opportunity on the new edition, a berth there meant day work, and Davis knew its managing editor, Arthur Brisbane. His decision made, he crossed Park Row and like Childe Harold to the dark tower came.

Entering through the business office, accessible as business must be, Davis reached a spiral iron stairway and wound his way upward through a gloomy shaft. About him the walls echoed and trembled to the rumbling vibration of the presses tended by grimy figures in the shadowy pit below. He climbed past the second and third floors, domain of the talented staff of *The Morning Sun* and their sense of superiority. A typewriter, the only one in the building,[1] clicked behind the door of the third-floor sanctum of Mr. Dana and his son Paul; clicked hesitantly since the secretary who operated the con-

[1] Installation of typewriters in newspaper offices was a slow process. Because of non-visible writing and other cumbersome mechanical features of the earlier machines, longhand writers outsped them and laughed them to scorn. Finally improvements and obvious advantages of speed and legibility forced their adoption. By that time there

traption must needs raise the roll to see what he had written. Sound and fury increasing with his ascent, Davis stepped onto the tobacco-stained, paper-strewn fourth floor to witness *The Evening Sun* in the throes of creation.

The dark and dismal loft was a madhouse conglomeration of all departments except the press and delivery rooms which were in the basement. Pandemonium, as reporters so frequently wrote, reigned. Machines clanked and men shouted. Stereotypers flung themselves on the locked type forms from the make-up men and produced matrices with the wet blanket reek of their trade. Molten lead in bubbling cauldrons added its fumes where half-naked, sweat-streaming founders cast a plate from each matrix and despatched it to the presses in the nether regions. Reporters strolled or hurried in, sat down at little tables, hats on heads—for whence is headgear less likely to be taken by mistake?—and scribbled out their copy. Some besides their own notes consulted the faintly pencilled carbon "flimsies" from the O'Rourke service for city news or the United Press. Clouds of tobacco smoke[2] from corncob pipes attested the fevers of literary composition. Occasionally a rewrite man struggled with murmurings from the single coffeegrinder telephone on the wall. Copy boys with winged or leaden feet, according to the strength of lungs of their summoner, carried stories and proofs on their appointed rounds. A sheet from the previous edition, bearing the august blue pencillings of Dana himself, demanded the instant action of the

were enough decrepit, second-hand typewriters to meet all journalistic demands; only in recent years have treasurers loosened up and purchased new machines. Nevertheless, reporters, using the two-forefingers, hunt-and-find method and composing direct from their notes, developed considerable rapidity. Linotypes (ingenious machines making leaden casts of type and saving long delving into printers' cases) were introduced on *The Tribune* by the progressive Whitelaw Reid in 1886. These, too, were slow coming into general use.

[2] That inspiration to the muse and soother of tenseness was banned from *The Sun* by Frank A. Munsey when he bought that paper. His wraith still prohibits except in a club room ruled off the reservation.

city desk. A little apart, editorial writers mused on whither we were drifting with a rare concentration which even the apparition of cockroaches from their table drawers failed to disturb.

Davis was led through the racket of the familiar, ever-thrilling daily drama to the desk of Brisbane. There was a quick sympathy between these two, that strange attraction of characters in many ways opposite. Brisbane, the somewhat austere intellectual and executive of multitudinous affairs, greeted the candid young unsophisticate whose early mentor and lifelong friend he became. Was there an opening on *The Evening Sun?* Davis asked. He had stopped in to see on his way to *The World*. A reporter of his proven ability, believed the man to whom he was now applying, would doubtless get a job there.[3] Any intelligent editor would have engaged him, in the opinion of Arthur Brisbane, who, coming emphatically under that head, suited the action to the conviction.

So Davis went to work for *The Evening Sun* and in his second week became a man of mark, a reporter who not only collected news but made it. He was crossing from Jersey City on a ferryboat when a notorious confidence man known as "Sheeny Mike" reconnoitred his frank and open countenance, his ruddy complexion and his English clothes. Here seemed to be a newly arrived Johnny Bull, ripe for the swindling. "Sheeny Mike" approached and opened negotiations for the sale of a "valuable" painting. His intended victim listened, as much outraged at the "con. man's" trade of preying on the innocent as at his taking Richard Harding Davis for a sucker.

---

[3] The late Charles Belmont Davis in his *Adventures and Letters of Richard Harding Davis* states that his brother had visited a number of newspaper offices without success and was sitting, tired and discouraged, in City Hall Park; that he was about to return to Philadelphia when Brisbane happened along and gave him *The Evening Sun* job. This story, more complimentary to the benevolence of fate than to the reputation of R. H. D., is directly denied by Brisbane.

Davis let him talk until they had landed and walked to lower Broadway. Then, looking around for a policeman and seeing none, he collared the rascal himself and shouted for the police at the top of his lungs. What had been a hurrying, busy crowd massed rapidly into an excited mob of several thousand. Police appeared and the party adjourned to the Tombs Court where "Sheeny Mike" was convicted and sent to the Island, while his nemesis returned to the office to write the story.

The capture of the "green-goods" merchant made a good yarn. William M. Laffan himself, the general manager of *The Evening Sun,* took note and suggested the headline. What if the veteran from Philadelphia was annoyed by seeing himself described as "Our Green Reporter"? He was off to an auspicious start.

II

Davis landed in an ideal berth at an ideal period. He was of the vanguard of college men coming into the newspaper picture, alert young fellows of the immense energy and decent appearance demanded by Dana and *The Sun* executives under him. The sloppy, food-spotted clothes and chronic whisky breaths of Bohemian journalism were on the decline along with other old traditions.

The Evening Sun started him at thirty dollars a week; cubs began at half that. At the end of his fourteen months on the staff he was getting fifty dollars, which would be doubled or trebled for a star man today. That salary was anything but easy money. He slaved for it and like other good newspapermen earned it several times over. More complete and more readable news boosts circulation which in turn raises advertising revenues, but reporters must largely content themselves with a reward in intangibles.

The bonus given Davis and other able toilers on Dana's papers was not cash. Yet they prized it none the less—that privilege of theirs of writing as the spirit moved, of presenting news and feature with a freedom that would later flower into "colyums." Drama and color could embellish the compilations of facts which stood starkly alone in the older type of journalism, although the essential facts must be pursued with relentless thoroughness. An *Evening Sun* reporter could turn news into literature if he were capable of it. Dana in Olympian seclusion in his office was known to approve. Brisbane encouraged. The copy desk under good-natured Charles P. Cooper seldom grew bilious at the sight of originality. There was often a festive, Sunday magazine air about *The Evening Sun,* as when it followed up a noted execution with an effusion on the death penalty in all ages, profusely illustrated by line cuts. Sometimes the very advertisements, catching the contagion, disdained the conventional. Proclaimed one enterprising firm of merchants, "We are restless. Our stock of overcoats must move."

The watchword of Dana's papers: "If you see it in *The Sun,* it's so," was no empty slogan. But the staffs strove "to make an interesting story in spite of the fact, and not on account of the fact, that it is a true one," as Davis neatly put it.[4] Algernon Blackwood, a young Britisher who shortly joined and suffered as a cub but recovered to make a name as a writer of supernatural stories and fantasies, complained that the good, the beautiful, the lovely were very rarely news to *The Evening Sun.* He might have been answered that eternal verities should not be considered as news. But while Blackwood found himself in a cynical school and believed that any New York reporter was lucky to escape with a single rag of illusion to his back, it was not so with Dick Davis. His buoyancy shed cynicism as readily as his vitality responded to electrical impulses

[4] Davis, *The Editor's Story.*

from the supercharged battery who was his city editor—William G. McCloy.

McCloy, who succeeded Brisbane as managing editor, was at this time the youngest city editor in New York. He was a boss after Davis's own heart. A small, thin man with the slightest and frailest of bodies, nervous hands, gimlet eyes, and high-pitched voice, he "lived on wires," in the words of Blackwood's excellent description;[5] he had "a general air of lightning speed and such popping, spouting energy that I felt he might any moment flash into flame or burst with a crackling report into a thousand pieces. . . . Buried among these mechanical perfections, however, I caught, odd to relate, an incongruous touch of kindness, even of tenderness. There were gentle lines in that electric face. He had a smile I liked." The just and sympathetic (when he had time) McCloy, molding a reporter as a good city editor can, sent Davis out to cover stories and learn the town.

The "L," swiftest conveyance of those pre-subway days, transported Davis for a ten-cent fare. He rode in coaches, each with a name in the best Pullman tradition. While the soft-coal soot of its engines took toll of his own immaculacy and etched ladies' faces with their veil designs, its speed conserved the perishable goods he gathered—news. He could reach his office in time to write his own story. If he had to stay on the scene, he despatched installments by Johnny Reaper, the wizened East Side copy boy who was Gallagher's successor, or other couriers. Stories possessed an eye-witness value which a later era of telephone and rewrite man sacrificed for speed's sake.

Beyond and between "L" lines were vast stretches of blocks to be covered only by slow horse cars, an occasional new-fangled cable car, costly carriages or leg work. Leg work it must

[5] From *Episodes Before Thirty*. London, 1923.

be for a reporter whose assignment could not be marked "Rush" and eased into an expense account, alias a swindle sheet. Davis trudged, fascinated, through the city and learned it with a thoroughness no other method could afford.

In a few months he was writing a comic guide to New York for his paper, an amusing piece illustrated with stock cuts from the printer's case. There was insight under its humor. Each letter of introduction carried by a visitor to Gotham, remarked this quick initiate, is good for one dinner if presented uptown and one lunch if downtown. Thereafter tourists might dine at Beefsteak John's if they brought napkins and did not eat pie with a fork. "Delmonico's is another place where you can get a good square meal, well cooked and fitly served, for about seventeen dollars. [This was incautious; the author would soon be guilty frequently of the extravagance on which he now vented his sarcasm.] The Metropolitan Museum is three-quarters of an hour from any known spot. [So it is still.] The Hoffman House Bar is located near the Hoffman House, so called because it is run by a man named Stokes. Its chief objects of interest are Billy Edwards and Bougereau's painting of the Seven Northerland Sisters." But it struck Davis that it was cheaper to drive some place else, pay the cab and get a drink there. Coney, he found, was an island entirely surrounded by water filled with bathers, old shoes, and decayed bananas.

The Metropolitan Opera House was patronized by the "400" and Ward McAllister. People who did not care to receive at home rented apartments of two rooms each on the second or third tier of the Metropolitan and asked their friends to drop in and chat with them. Of course it was true that the singers and musicians made too much noise, but arrangements were being completed for Wagner in pantomime next year. Another object of interest, according to the Davis guide, was the

Knickerbocker Club where very young and very beautiful gentlemen in high-standing collars were as conspicuous in the windows as if the place were a laundry. One of those window dressings was to be appropriated by Davis and called *Cortlandt Van Bibber,* but he was not much interested at the moment, for this was society stuff. And as he and his fellow craftsmen agreed, there were two kinds of reporters on a newspaper: reporters and society reporters, the latter being classified as the lowest form of journalistic life.

The explorer learned to know the Bowery, tawdry, tough, and perilous for countrymen or any stranger, and the Bowery learned to know him. There would be no more burglar disguises, but he could and did make friends with characters like his *Disreputable Mr. Raegan,* mighty swimmer of the waterfronts. Davis, known as a newspaperman, was as safe as any precinct detective in that vivid segment of the Orient around Pell, Mott, and Doyers streets where the "heathen Chinee" was still sufficiently peculiar to wage tong warfare with hatchet, knife, and erratic revolver. Roaming west into the Tenderloin, he invaded in line of duty the Haymarket, for eighteen years New York's most notorious house of assignation. It fell to him to write that dive's obituary when reform sentiment forced the withdrawal of its liquor license and its consequent closing. A colorful piece he made of it. Indeed he wrote so graphically of brothels, gamblers, and the purple sins of the city that he was genuinely worried when Brisbane twitted him that a certain story of his would lead any one to suppose that his evenings were spent in the boudoirs of the horizontales of Thirty-fourth Street. With the indignation of innocence he rushed off a letter home avowing that it was unfair to assume that a man must have an intimate acquaintanceship with whatever he writes of intimately.

The best general assignment men on *The Evening Sun* did considerable police reporting. Sitting majestically by the judge, Davis often unearthed gems of stories in those dusty and malodorous mines, the Jefferson Market Court and the Tombs Police Court. The coveted post at Police Headquarte s itself was the inalienable right of his colleague, Jacob Riis, that paragon of police reporters. But Davis worked on many a crime story and knew cops from Inspector Byrnes, into whose terrible, non-sleeping, yet calculating eye he gazed unawed, down to the unfortunate patrolmen banished to the goats (predecessor of the sticks) of Harlem. Firemen all over Manhattan augmented his list of friends. Reporters, policemen, and firemen all are doomed to working on Christmas and the Fourth of July and between them are other points of sympathy and communal effort, to be disturbed only by dishonesty or inefficiency. Davis bestowed the accolade of praise in print on his friends of the precincts and firehouses when deserved. They showed their gratitude by giving him the news he sought and, better, inside tips. He had a way of finding a story where there seemed to be none, as in the case of a tramp burned to death in his sleep in a cheap-lodging-house fire at 6.30 one morning. Worth only a stick of type, if Davis had not turned up the dead man's charred alarm clock. It was set to ring at 7. When you can measure the margin of life and death and contemplate the inscrutable workings of Fate—then you have something to write.

III

The pages of newspapers are, of course, current history and they serve the humbler purpose of comprising fragmentary diaries of the reporters whose stories make them. Davis's journalistic day book for 1890 showed that he was engaged in helping to record a ghastly affair, the first execution by electricity.

In New York State, agitation for a more humane method of inflicting the death penalty than hanging had resulted in the invention of the electric chair by Doctor A. D. Rockwell, assisted by Doctor Carlos F. Macdonald and Edison. Immediately the "hot seat" moved on to the front pages of the papers and stayed there for weeks. First, the law establishing electrocution was attacked by the Westinghouse Electric and Manufacturing Company, because its products were driven by alternating current, the type used in the chair, and the firm feared ruin for its business through a sinister and deadly association in the public mind. But the constitutionality of the law was upheld both against that assault and the eloquent objections of W. Bourke Cockran, counsel for William Kemmler, the first man sentenced to die in the chair.

Kemmler had committed a particularly brutal murder. After running away with another man's wife, he had quarrelled with her and hacked her to pieces with a hatchet in the presence of her small daughter. Three trials were required before the verdict of death in the electric chair, the efficiency of which had been demonstrated on animals, was made final.

Davis was among the newspapermen waiting outside the walls of Auburn Prison when, the last reprieve having expired, the execution of Kemmler took place on August 6. In the confusion and through neglect of the absent inventor's instructions, the performance was bungled. The correspondents shuddered at the details they wrote, and *The Evening Sun* headlined the story in heavy black type: "WRITHED." A thrill of horror ran through the world to subside only when subsequent successful use of the electric chair established it as a comparatively merciful method of capital punishment.

A few months later another sensation of the year pre-empted the front page—the Annie Goodwin murder.

"If a man falls dead, believe it's a suicide until you've proved it is not," Davis made one of his characters say in *The Editor's Story*. "If you find a suicide, believe it is a murder until you are convinced to the contrary. Otherwise you'll be beaten." It was with such reportorial scepticism that he regarded a short reference in his paper to a missing girl. At least she would not be found in the Haymarket now. He went to McCloy with his suspicions. "Boss, I can cover that," he suggested. "You're the man. Go ahead," ordered the city editor.

It developed into the type of crime and sex story which the civilized deplore but which everybody reads. A keen detective on an "L" train overheard a conversation regarding the disappearance of Annie after getting "in trouble." Gradually the gory details unfolded. Annie Goodwin, "shown by her picture to have been of rare beauty," was a worker in a cigarette factory. Taken by the lover who had betrayed her to a den in Harlem, she died under an illegal operation by a seventy-year-old doctor. Late that night the aged abortionist bundled the corpse into a carriage beside him and drove to a lonely cemetery where the body was later exhumed to send him to prison for fourteen years. Davis's description of the drive was high melodrama. "The something that sat beside him wrapped in a quilt on the front seat, as he drove through the silent street in the glimmering gray of that early dawn, past policemen on their beats, past a thousand sleepers secure in their beds, between rows of lamps that blinked knowingly at him and his odd companion—that something was a corpse, the body of the murdered Annie Goodwin."

IV

More cheerful pages of the Davis journal in type showed football games, for at last he had proven to a sports desk that he was a sports reporter *par excellence,* and the big games were the prerogative of star men, whatever their usual run might be. The one-time Lehigh halfback lived for the crisp, fall days when New York flung off its still half-cultivated air of being too tremendously busy and sophisticated for such things and went frankly collegiate. When the roses of Harvard, the violets of Yale, and the chrysanthemums of Princeton bloomed on many a fair and indubitable bosom. When the old "grads." and the men who wished, as at no other time, that they had gone to college mingled with the detraining, joyous throngs from the campuses. When the coaches-and-six, wealth in topper and topcoat at the ribbons, and beauty, fashion, and finance enthroned beside and behind, rolled grandly from the Holland House out Fifth Avenue to the Polo Grounds, with mighty tally-ho flourishes every few blocks. Davis, sharing the sidelines at the field with other reporters, personages, coaches, and substitutes, followed the flying wedges and mass plays of the shock-haired warriors on the gridiron with the air of a connoisseur. The stands were a stormy sea of color as enthusiasts waved pennants unabashed and clamorously cheered a touchdown. Swiftly Davis scribbled the details and handed his copy to telegraphers close by to be wired to his paper.

That night he roamed through the noisy revelry of celebration or consolation, as the college boys (or those passing as such) stormed the hotels, restaurants, and theatres. Twenty-deep they and their supporters lined the famous bars. They surged snake-dancing through the streets, and doormen scattered before revivals of the flying wedges of the afternoon.

The long, low, smoky hall of Koster and Bial's on Twenty-third Street rang to their songs. They jammed into Harrigan and Hart's and all the musical shows, raising the roof with their hearty rahs and sis-boom-bahs of approval or ringing down the curtain with catcalls of condemnation. Supper at the Silver Grill, cane rushes into dance halls, and parades up and down Broadway continued until dawn or the nightsticks of the "Finest," crushing high, bell-shaped hats or denting silver flasks, restored the quiet and budding dignity which New York had forfeited by its twenty-four-hour metamorphosis into Princeton or Cambridge or New Haven.

It was at the Yale-Princeton game at Eastern Park, Brooklyn, on Thanksgiving Day, 1890, that Davis risked his job. At the edge of the gridiron he was confronted by no less than his managing editor. Mr. Brisbane had a sidelines ticket but he was accompanied by a friend who was behind the fence without one. Let Reporter Davis turn over his pass to the friend and retire to the stands. Davis refused point-blank and with undiplomatic emphasis. He was reporting this game, it was best done from the sidelines, there was his post, and there he was staying, he informed his chief. Otherwise, he remarked, McCloy would take his head off. Rather than the fury of his city editor, he would chance the wrath, once removed, of his managing editor. Brisbane and guest relegated themselves to the stands.

When Brisbane told the story at the office that night, a subordinate asked him if Davis was to be fired. "No," said the editor. "Raise his salary."

V

Freed after a strenuous day, 8.30 to 6.30, from the demands of *The Evening Sun,* Davis returned to his room at 108 Wa-

verly Place in still-unexploited Greenwich Village. The evenings were for plugging away at fiction or jolly parties with
Charley Davis up from Philadelphia to visit. Feasts at a Sixth
Avenue fifty-cent table d'hôte, *vin compris*. Gay adjournment
to Broadway and the comic operas of Francis Wilson and De
Wolf Hopper, friends to be relied on for passes. Pretty girls,
champagne, and cigars in the dressing-room of the jovial Hopper. Afterwards, invariable custom of the brothers, a delicious
breakfast at Martin's on University Place.[6] Then a little sleep,
if time was left for it, and back to work with the resiliency of
youth.

Unfailingly Davis put his whole self into his reporting.
Gradually he evolved that newspaperman's philosophy which
he set down in *The King's Jackal, The Derelict, The Reporter
Who Made Himself King,* and other stories of which reporters
are the heroes. Nowhere better than in the third named.
"The Old Time Journalist," he wrote in that sprightly narrative, "will tell you that the best reporter is the one who works
his way up. He holds that the only way to start is as a printer's
devil or as an office boy, to learn in time to set type, to graduate from a compositor to a stenographer, and as a stenographer to take down speeches at public meetings, and so finally
to grow into a real reporter, with a fire badge on his left sus-
pender, and a speaking acquaintance with all the greatest men
in the city, not even excepting police captains.

"That is the old-time journalist's idea of it. That is the way
he was trained, and that is why at the age of sixty he is still
a reporter. If you train up a youth in this way, he will go into
reporting with too full a knowledge of the newspaper business,
with no illusions concerning it, and with no ignorant enthu-
siasms, but with a keen and justifiable impression that he is not

---

[6] The present Lafayette, still renowned for a fine French cuisine.

paid enough for what he does. And he will only do what he is paid to do."

The pay was not paramount. That fact became increasingly clear to Davis, although he loved the pleasures and comforts money would buy. He realized that he was being compensated also by experience, that precious commodity which ekes out the meagre stipend of the hospital interne and the law clerk. As he went on to assert in his wise and honest creed: "Now, you can't pay a good reporter for what he does, because he does not work for pay. He works for his paper. He gives his time, his health, his brains, his sleeping hours, and sometimes his life to get news for it. He thinks the sun rises only that men may have light by which to read it. But if he has been in a newspaper office from his youth up, he finds out before he becomes a reporter that this is not so, and loses his real value. He should come right out of the university where he has been doing 'campus notes' for the college weekly, and be pitchforked out into the city work without knowing whether the Battery is at Harlem or Hunter's Point, and with the idea that he is a Moulder of Public Opinion and that the Power of the Press is greater than the Power of Money, and that the few lines he writes are of more value in the Editor's eyes than is the column of advertising on the last page, which they are not. After three years—it is sometimes longer, sometimes not so long—he finds out that he has given his nerves and his youth and his enthusiasm in exchange for a general fund of miscellaneous knowledge, the opportunity of personal encounter with all the greatest and most remarkable men and events that have risen in those three years, and a great fund of resource and patience. He will find that he has crowded the experiences of the lifetime of the ordinary young business man, doctor, or lawyer, or man-about-town into three short years, that he has learned to think and to act quickly, to be patient and unmoved when every one else has lost his head, actually or figuratively speaking, to write as fast as another man can talk, and to be able to talk with authority on matters of which other men do not venture even to think until they have read what he has written with a copy boy at his elbow on the night previous."

There was bound to be dissent on Park Row with a man who lived by such a philosophy and did not hide his light under a bushel; dissent, honest or envious or partaking of personalities. It was not so much the Davis sartorial splendors that irritated confrères now, although the cane had reappeared and was joined by a hatbox for trips to Philadelphia. David Graham Phillips had been known to array himself in white flannels to report a Pennsylvania coal strike, and there were other elegant gentlemen of the press. It was, as Chester S. Lord, managing editor of *The Morning Sun,* so well stated it, the Davis enthusiasm and naïveté, his rigidity of code and self-dramatization which clashed with the cynicism and surface sophistication of many newspapermen and caused them to dislike him.

Davis was the first in the office to rush over and congratulate a man who had written a good story; and his precious guitar sometimes reposed in a pawn shop because a fellow reporter needed the eight-dollar loan its chancery brought. Yet the lone hand appealed to him more than easier co-operation on a story with reporters of other papers. He was not much given to joining the boys in the back room of Perry's Drug Store for yarning and absorbing the jolts of its whisky blend. And he was suspected of being favored as a protégé of Brisbane's. Some of Park Row began to put him down as no reporter but a fiction writer, a dilettante.

Brisbane differed. He rated Davis as an excellent reporter,

as well as a good writer, all his life. McCloy, another in position to know, concurred, calling Davis both a good news and a good feature man, punctilious, on time, never shirking and never considering any task too small for him. The city editor never forgot a certain tiny, unimportant assignment Davis covered for him.

Some one had to carry a small sum from *The Evening Sun's* charity fund to a distressed family on Thirty-fourth Street. Davis was handy in the office and McCloy unhesitatingly gave him the errand, with orders to come back and write a stick and a half about it.

Several hours elapsed before Davis reappeared, looking weary and subdued.

"Been off on a vacation?" came the ironic query from behind the city desk.

Davis told of the destitution and misery he had seen when he delivered the money. He had walked back to Park Row, he said, and that had taken the time.

"Boss," he pleaded, "don't send me out on anything more like that. I pulled out every cent in my pocket and gave it to 'em."

VI

The charge that Richard Harding Davis was a fiction writer was doubted even by the accused. He had written fiction, certainly, but he could get little of it published. Well, he was making good as a reporter. A catch in a newspaper career, however, was its scant liberty. *The Evening Sun* relinquished Sundays to its staff, but if they desired more time off they must fill the gap with print. One day was too short for Davis to make a satisfactory weekend visit to Philadelphia to spend with his mother. What could he do for the Saturday paper that would release him after work Friday? An entertaining opus for the back page to take the place of regular news reporting would do the trick.

A travel piece on New York to Philadelphia from a car window served once. It would not work twice. Davis would do any amount of extra work to have an extra day to spend with his adored family. If only he could hit on an idea with stamina for a series!

The resourceful Mr. Brisbane came forward with it.

It was a good idea. It was good for a thousand and one Philadelphian nights. It was good for a great deal more.

CHAPTER FIVE

VAN BIBBER'S TOWN

I

THE idea Brisbane presented to Davis was embodied, most elegantly embodied, in the fictitious person of *Mr. Cortlandt Van Bibber,* clubman, man-about-town, and knight errant of New York of the 'Nineties.

That young gentleman's name presumed proud and unbroken descent from the old Dutch aristocracy of New Amsterdam. Few knew that there was a bar sinister in his escutcheon. The truth is that he was out of a French newspaper by a minor author, one Manchecourt. Brisbane read the inspiration-story in the original and translated it for the benefit of his reporter. It dealt with a young French nobleman who came home the worse for wear, and, when he awoke the following morning, asked his valet what orders he had given the night before to learn what his condition had been when he went to bed.

Then and there Davis adopted and christened *Van Bibber.*[1] At first *Van Bibber* was bibulous, following the bad example set him by his rake of a French ancestor. But as Saturday after Saturday he held the fort for his literary father, absent in Philadelphia, the grateful Davis grew fond of him, sobered him up and made him a real hero. *Noblesse oblige. Van Bibber* deserved it on more counts than one, for he shortly became a

---

[1] A certain Doctor Van Bibber, of Baltimore, whose shingle may have been memorized by a certain Johns Hopkins student, was kept busy explaining to enthusiastic young women patients, that he was not the original of Davis's character.

personage. No real young New Yorker was as well known and as popular.

Van Bibber strolled out of the Knickerbocker Club, where Davis had watched his counterparts ensconced in the windows, and sauntered onto the back page of *The Evening Sun* to capture the fancy of the town. Readers flocked after him in imagination, as, resplendent in evening clothes, Inverness, and top hat, he betook himself to the opera. They followed him into the glamorous backstage realms of the theatre. Delicious shivers ran down Puritanical spines at the thought of invading, even by proxy, those wickedly Bohemian, almost inaccessible purlieus. The more daring theatregoers, matinée-idol girls, and stage-door Johnnies, envied *Van Bibber* his intimacy with the fascinating folk of the footlights. He was free of a land of mystery of which they achieved only glimpses. As a line in William Crane's play, *Henrietta,* put it, a Johnny need only show a friend pictures of chorus girls on the walls of his room to be thought a devil of a fellow. Gay young bloods won their reputation merely by sending bouquets of hot-house flowers to dressing-rooms; and as for the chaps who took ladies of the chorus out to supper, a bird and a bottle, with sometimes a toast drunk from a little slipper,—they were high-flyers indeed. Nor were the actors reluctant to have *Van Bibber* personally conduct tours through this enchanted world of theirs. He neither branded it naughty nor destroyed its allurement. Many of them hard-working, moral people, they lived, almost pariahs, in cheap boarding-houses, sustained by the spell of their profession when mundane sustenance was scant. The other world was beginning to know them as Davis did and was inviting them out as social curiosities.

Sun subscribers dined and supped in state with *Van Bibber* at Delmonico's and lunched at Martin's. They courted *Miss*

Cuyler, Miss Catherwaight, and other blue-blooded damoiselles with him, and jealous maidens sighed with relief when he remained the bachelor beau. They would have echoed Davis's dismay when Brisbane once jokingly threatened a marriage in the Saturday paper between *Van Bibber* and *Maggie,* the tough character of a series by a police reporter. The very thought of such a mesalliance! Yet when the author of *Van Bibber's* literary being permitted him to condescend now and then to consort with hoi polloi—prize fighters, hotel servants, burglars, and such—devotees smiled patronizingly. It only made their hero more human, and besides *hoi polloi* never forgot their place and took advantage of young *Mr. Cortlandt.*

The *Van Bibber* stories were lifting Davis out of the ruck of reportorial anonymity and swiftly making a reputation for him. There is no surer method of establishing and nourishing fame in the field of periodicals than carrying a likable and amusing character through a series of regular appearances. Authors and artists already had discovered that: comic-strip producers and "colyumists" later would cash in on it heavily. Granted the fertile imagination that makes such a character long-lived, the only difficulty is the launching.

And for that all-important feat Davis could have been vouchsafed no more apposite era in American history. New York City under the eyes of the country had twirled the separator busily and evolved the cream of Society. The calculating gaze of Ward McAllister, social entrepreneur extraordinary, had estimated the capacity of the ballroom of his patron, Mrs. William Astor, fatefully cut the invitation list to fit, and lo! the magic figure 400 appeared. It clicked into the headlines, as the newspapers chronicled the guests ennobled to dance in the mansion at Fifth Avenue and Thirty-fourth Street.

Lowly society editors perked up. Now copy that *was* copy

was coming their way. Make space, they could cry like heralds, for a newly created American nobility, based not on letters patent but on power plutocratic. For the ever-fascinating division of the sheep and the goats. For pomp and pageantry. For thinly disguised Lord Ronalds and Lady Clare Vere de Veres in the plain, democratic U. S. A. For ceremony and for crests imported from abroad with their impecunious owners to gild the calling cards of American heiresses.

Into this day of dudes, debutantes, and dowagers in diamond dog-collars marched young Mr. Davis's young *Mr. Van Bibber,* cream of the cream, scion of wealth and leisure, cotillion leader, and luminary of "The 400." Those potent numerals had focussed the nation's attention on Society with an intensity to be lost forever in its latter, many-ringed circus days. Now social functions and intrigues were burning topics at boarding-house tables. Fashionable weddings drew throngs of sidewalk spectators, breathless with interest. A few years later the proletariat would rumble like a French Revolution mob at the alleged extravagance of the Bradley Martin fancy-dress ball[2] at the Waldorf-Astoria. But now it was entranced by news from Newport, Washington Square, Murray Hill, and Fifth Avenue.

Even the hinterlands could not foreswear its lure. Jealous sister cities, small towns, and farms shared a craving for New York society gossip. By the same token, they took to that howling swell, *Van Bibber,* and adopted him as a symbol. He had a host of rustic readers, especially after he was enclosed in book covers, although his adventures never took him to anything nearer a farm than a Long Island country estate. Of course his social equals in real life welcomed him—sometimes with open arms, sometimes with raised eyebrows, yet they welcomed.

[2] Its cost was quoted as $9000. In the lush winters of 1915–16 and 1928–29, a New York débutante's coming-out party cost $10,000, or her father was a piker.

So much was *Van Bibber* doing for Davis. More subtly but as surely he was doing a great deal to him. Davis, using his character at first as a lay figure, placed him in certain situations and caused him to act in them as his author's imagination and his observation as an outsider dictated. *Van Bibber* was limited by the experience of his creator. Why shouldn't Davis share more of the entertaining exploits of his imaginary clubman?

Popularity was beginning to open doors for him. Though he lacked both money and social position as a birthright, then as ever there were hostesses pleased to receive a literary lion, particularly one so good looking and attractive. His contacts as a reporter proved helpful. One comely society maiden, seeking the aid of the press for the working girls' clubs which were her hobby, received Mr. Davis of *The Evening Sun*. She poured her plans into ears so sympathetically attentive that she never suspected that girls' clubs are not a favorite Park Row assignment. Here was a nice boy who was evidently "a gentleman, though a journalist." She invited the artful fellow home to tea and a friendship began which was to be of great social value to him at home and abroad.

Some ill-natured persons sneered that *Van Bibber* was an office boy's idea of a gentleman, but they were largely ignored. The ladies, the true arbiters, were gracious when Davis and *Van Bibber* stepped out together. This clever new writer was fresh and unspoiled and enthusiastically romantic about society.

So Davis, looking into the mirror of his imagination, saw himself as *Van Bibber*. It was a conscious reflection, the result of a pose but an honest one. Davis, declares one of his best friends, derived his original ideas of aristocracy from the stage, picturing a gentleman as a fellow in a figured dressing gown breakfasting late in his chambers from a tray, with letters from

ladies neatly stacked beside the toast. He went to the opera
because it was the thing to do—a reason frequently shared by
the highest-born. When he acquired a valet, he never grew
quite used to him—a failing duplicated by other self-reliant
Americans. What if the Davis shield lacked the quarterings
of ancient lineage? It was borne by a knight *sans peur et sans
reproche.*

Robert Bridges aimed a gentle satire[3] at his friend, Davis,
appropriating his characters for his illuminating dialogue:

Miss Cuyler: Oh, is Mr. Davis in town? I thought he was
abroad.

Van Bibber: He was: just arrived yesterday on the *Paris.* No
end of new toys—lovely coaching coat that touches his heels—
beautiful collars with a sheer to them like a racing yacht—a
new shade in gloves, and all that sort of thing. . . . But frankly now, Miss Cuyler, I'm not the sort of a cad he put in those
stories, am I? I don't pose as such a dreadfully superior person, do I, and patronize people who are less lucky than I am?

Miss Cuyler (sincerely): No, no, you are never that. The
only thing I don't like about you is your accent, and that's im-
proving. Where *did* you pick it up?

Van Bibber (hastily): In England. Thought it was the real
thing, and have just found out that it is cockney. . . .

Miss Cuyler: We New York girls are not half the prigs Mr.
Davis takes us to be. One might think from his stories that
we are a combination of gorgeous frocks and intense sentiments—a sort of virtuous *Camille,* if you can imagine that type.

As Bridges added in a postscript, Davis's stories showed he
saw a good deal and had an eye for dramatic effect; that color
was one of his best literary weapons. Color and vigor were

---

[3] Mr. Bridges, editor emeritus of *Scribner's Magazine,* collected the sketch quoted
with others for his book, *Overheard in Arcady.* New York, 1894.

indeed predominant features of the *Van Bibber* tales. While some of them are episodes, plotless, and few approach the artistry of O. Henry and H. C. Bunner, they match the work of those short-story writers with their rich flavor of New York of that day.

For Davis roved through the town and the *Van Bibber* saga is the record of his rovings. *Van Bibber* lunches at Martin's and acts as an extemporaneous best man at a wedding in the Little Church Around the Corner. His incomparably trained "man," *Walters,* holds one of those terraced tables at Delmonico's which command a view of St. Gaudens's Diana atop the Madison Square Garden tower and orders dinner for his master and guests. When they fail to arrive, *Walters* yields to temptation and feasts on the delicious repast after the *Van Bibber*-Davis taste: Little Neck clams first, with Chablis, and pea-soup and caviare on toast, before the oyster crabs, with Johannisberger Cabinet; then an entrée of calves' brains and rice, then no roast but a bird, cold asparagus, with French dressing, Camembert cheese, and Turkish coffee. A girl at a football game asks *Van Bibber,* her escort, why umpires wear whistles on chains around their necks, like *lorgnons,* and he gravely informs her that it is to keep from swallowing them in excitement. The bachelor apartment in the Berkeley Flats, Fifth Avenue, where *Van Bibber* (in *Her First Appearance*) called to restore a small daughter to her father, was reproduced on the stage when Robert C. Hilliard dramatized the story as *The Littlest Girl.* A list of the properties for its setting breathes the spirit of the 'Nineties: Upholstered leather chairs, screen, cigar stand, rubber plants, decanter, stand of armor, statue of Venus, deer heads, Ottoman, silk pillows, stuffed birds, and crossed rapiers.

Everybody was talking about the timely *Mr. Van Bibber.* Yet

THE HORSE SHOW, MADISON SQUARE GARDEN, BY C. D. GIBSON

The figure on the left is practically a portrait of Davis.

TWO DRAWINGS BY OLIVER HERFORD WHICH ILLUSTRATED "THE
HOUSEHOLD OF RICHARD HARDING DAVIS" BY ROBERT BRIDGES
—*OVERHEARD IN ARCADY*

A GIBSON ILLUSTRATION FOR
VAN BIBBER AND OTHERS

From Scribner's Magazine, 1890.

"WHY, IT'S GALLEGHER," SAID THE NIGHT EDITOR

An illustration for *Gallegher* by C. D. Gibson.

this emblem of the Quality was forced to give way as the prime
benefactor of his sponsor to a ragged juvenile character who
antedated him, to *Gallegher, Press* copy boy and amateur detective. *Van Bibber* had taken readers backstage. *Gallegher*
would lead them into equally strange and magical confines—a
newspaper office.

II

Gallegher, a Newspaper Story, had made the rounds of half
a dozen lesser magazines since it was written in Philadelphia.
It had travelled for its health, the author having revised it
painstakingly after each rejection. Finally Davis with the courage of despair moved to the assault of the Big Four: the *Century, Harper's, Harper's Weekly,* and *Scribner's.* Only daring
novices ventured to submit to that awesome quality group of
the 'Nineties. On their dignified pages sparkled the names of
eminent literati and they were illuminated by the work of the
hands of Edwin Austin Abbey, Winslow Homer, Frederic
Remington, R. F. Zogbaum, A. B. Frost, and W. A. Rogers.

Richard Watson Gilder, of the *Century,* seated in the highest seat of the editorial mighty, cast his piercing black eyes on
the Davis contribution. He recoiled from *Gallegher's* slang—
he recently had been criticized for printing some of the same—
and he perused the manuscript hastily. He rejected it in that
gentle caressing way of his which, in the words of Bill Nye,
made disappointed scribblers come from thousands of miles
around to thank him for his kindness and stay to dinner. That
decision, he magnanimously admitted later, was a regrettable
mistake.

Scribner's Magazine, having lent an ear to the helpful Mr.
Brisbane, offered hospitality to *Gallegher* at last. The story

was published in its August, 1890, issue, with illustrations by a rising young artist, Charles Dana Gibson. Subscribers read the tale of the gallant little copy boy and were stirred to an enthusiasm which no subscription list could contain. Word of mouth, louder than rolling drums and pealing trumpets, spread the gospel of *Gallegher* at home and abroad.

Richard Harding Davis, popular through *Van Bibber,* was suddenly famous, famous by virtue of a single short story in a magazine.[4]

It could not happen today—this swift flash of fame from such a simple and inconspicuous candle. But in the smaller, less preoccupied and hurried, more open-eyed world of 1890, it was a wonderful possibility and a not infrequent fact. The light of a man and his deeds gleamed bright and became a beacon. All with little or none of the artificial glare which publicity later would generate to dazzle—and to fade.

Everywhere people were asking who Richard Harding Davis was and toasting a name they would never forget in his lifetime. For *Gallegher* was no isolated freak of achievement nor *Van Bibber* a coincidence. Magazines competed for his stories now, *Harper's* having printed *A Walk Up the Avenue* in the same month with *Gallegher*. "Herewith Davis mounted into celebrity as gracefully as he might have swung his fine body in its handsome dress to the cushion of a waiting cab. He rode, a figure of pleasant sophistication and fresh good humor, among passengers who lacked those qualities precisely, and boys laboring with manuscripts looked up and saw a star."[5]

All over the United States such young fellows, reporters

---

[4] Various factors contributed toward the success of *Gallegher:* the simple appeal of the story itself; growing interest in more highly esteemed newspaperdom; the increasing national consciousness of American literature and declaration of independence from English models by American writers, noted by Mark Sullivan in *Our Times*. Basically, to use a slang phrase at which Mr. Gilder would have shuddered, Davis had the stuff and he got a break.

[5] From Thomas Beer's *Stephen Crane.*

drudging on dull assignments, and lads earning their bread and butter on uncongenial jobs and scribbling half the night to win deliverance, heard the tale of a dream come true. Hope sharpened stubby pencils and quickened ambition raced them over miles of foolscap. Eager voices begged every detail of the career which had led so soon to the glittering goal, and Dick Davis glanced back to see an army of youth striving to tread in his footsteps.

It need not be so long a struggle after all. Recognition had come to Davis and he was only twenty-six. Youth and success were coupled and human hearts were captivated by the combination as they have been throughout history.

"Youth called to youth," Booth Tarkington wrote of him. "All ages read him, but the young men and young women have turned to him ever since his precocious fame made him their idol. They got many things from him, but above all they lived with a happier bravery because of him. Reading the man beneath the print, they found their prophet and gladly perceived that a prophet is not always cowled and bearded, but may be a gallant young gentleman. This one called merrily to them in his manly voice and they followed him. He bade them see that pain is negligible, that fear is a joke, and that the world is poignantly interesting, joyously lovable."

The college campuses took Richard Harding Davis to their hearts. Once more the screeds of the Greeks and the Romans and the Elizabethans were neglected for stories signed by two names which seemed suddenly to reveal to startled undergraduates, confessed one of them,[6] the astonishing fact that the thing called literature might conceivably have something to do with them. Rudyard Kipling and Richard Harding Davis were those

[6] H. W. Boynton in *The New York Evening Post*, April 15, 1916. John Dana of *The Sun* said that all the lads were trying to imitate Davis. Many of them became reporters because he had begun as one.

two names, and harassed faculties observed them far too often on the title-pages of extra-curriculum reading. Not theses but writing Mr. Davis for his autograph engrossed the disciples of higher education. High school students chose him as the subject of their orations. Headmistresses of boarding schools worried over increased gas bills traced to midnight study of works by a New York newspaperman. "A battle raged among the virgins of a family school for girls in the Hudson Valley over a signed photograph of the new god stolen by one young female from a brother."[7] Even the heroes of the gridiron, the diamond, and the shell must step down from their pedestals and yield them to this writer chap as stalwart as they and once a football star himself; both classmates and fair admirers demanded it. As for statesmen from the President down, for millionaires and such, and even matinée idols—they would be well advised not to appear in the same vicinity with the author of *Gallegher* and the *Van Bibber* stories, if they did not care to go unnoticed by the crowd.

Curiosity burned more brightly as each Davis opus appeared in print, demanding biographical details. He filled in data for one of the "mental photographs" in vogue, data lightly given but revealing:

"What I admire most in women—Clean gloves." (The fastidious fellow half meant it.)

"What I admire most in men—To sit opposite a mirror at dinner and not look in it." (And he couldn't resist it to save his life.)

"What I enjoy most—Being photographed and detesting the results." (But he didn't really; the results were usually handsome like the sitter.)

Laurels sat so gracefully on the Davis brow and the brow

---

[7] Beer: an article on Davis in *Liberty*, October 11, 1924.

A TENDER HEART.

He : I HAVE THREE THOUSAND A YEAR. YOU COULD CERTAINLY LIVE ON THAT.
She : YES : BUT I SHOULD HATE TO SEE *YOU* STARVE.

Copyright Life Publishing Co.

From the cover of *Life*, May 22, 1890. A drawing by C. D. Gibson
for which Davis posed.

became the laurels so admirably. If glimpses or the pictures which deluded publishers broadcast had revealed a near-sighted, odd-looking scribe, the story might have been different, with worshippers limited to the not so gratifying contemplation of a brain. But here appeared a splendidly clad Greek god who looked as romantic as his stories read. Illustrators of his tales could use him for a model and did, notably young Dana Gibson whose charming pen-and-ink drawings were taking the town by storm. Gibson gazed on his contemporary chronicler of social life and noted the absence of a Gibsonian antipathy, the mustache of the period, and marked the presence of features that would make a mere man fairly fit to be on the same page with a ravishing Gibson Girl.[8] His friend Dick Davis often sat for him, and many of those delightful double-page drawings in the centre of *Life,* which everybody turned to first, showed him rendering homage to beauty in drawing-room or on the beach, happily reinforced by one or a dozen Gibson cupids.

When the excited whisper ran from table to table at Delmonico's or from box to seat at a theatre that the original of one of the Gibson Men, the sports editor of *Gallegher,* and *Van Bibber's alter ego* was present, how necks craned, eyes popped, and conversation hummed. Nor could the young fellow of twenty-six help but take an utterly human and rap-

---

[8] Mark Sullivan in *Our Times, I:* notes the almost universal vogue which the drawings of Gibson, called the American Du Maurier, reached in the later 'Nineties, establishing a type for the American girl, formerly vague and nondescript. Mr. Sullivan quotes the observation of *The New York World* that American men acknowledged the Gibson Girl as their queen and the girls themselves held her as their own portrait and strove to live up to the likeness. "Thus did nature follow in the footsteps of art, and thus did the Gibson Girl become legion, and the world took her to its heart as the type of American womanhood. . . . Gibson also created a type of man, the square-shouldered, firm-jawed, clean-shaven, well-groomed, wholesome youth for which he and his friend, Richard Harding Davis, were the models, and the American young man, less self-consciously than the American girl, set himself to follow the type. It was Gibson's pen which sent mustaches out of fashion and made the tailors pad the shoulders of well-cut coats."

turous satisfaction in the stir he made. There were plenty of
invitations now. Those free Saturdays and Sundays *Van Bibber* had won him might have been spent most entertainingly
in New York and its fashionable suburbs. But belles of Father
Knickerbocker's town must find another beau than the most-
talked-of author for their weekends. Those were invariably
reserved despite fame and its trappings. Davis followed his
daily letters home to Philadelphia, where he held his mother's
hand and told her and his father what a marvellous affair life
was turning out to be.

III

Clarke Davis, prominent editor of *The Public Ledger,* used
to complain quizzically during those weekends that he had
been known for years as the husband of Rebecca Harding
Davis and now was identified only as the father of Richard
Harding Davis. His family, mutually admiring and mutually
devoted, laughed. At their home, which they called "The Centre of the Universe"—to them it plainly was—still gathered
many of the old theatrical crowd and such lights of the new
as shy and charming Maude Adams. The Davises had shifted
their summer base to Marion, Massachusetts, and that resort
had widened their circle of Philadelphia guests to include
President Grover Cleveland and the beautiful bride he had
married in the White House; the editorial Gilders; that stout
yachtsman, Commodore Benedict, and his witty daughter,
Helen. Also came young men making their mark in the pro-
fessions: John Russell, the publisher, Roland S. Morris, lawyer,
and Kenneth Frazier, artist. There was always a merry company at the Saturday morning pre-matinée breakfasts and at
the post-edition suppers in the Twenty-first Street home, pre-

sided over by Clarke Davis, back from putting *The Ledger* to bed. Mrs. Davis would leave her writing desk, Dick, Charley, and Nora would gather the guests at the board, and Nottingham, the old Negro butler, would bear in his tray-loads of scrambled eggs and sausage, cold meats, fruit, beer or whisky and sodas.

What jolly evenings they were! Mrs. Davis would tell the anecdote of the messenger boy called by her husband, busy at his office nights, to take her home from a party—how the small escort reaching a dark corner hid behind her ample skirts and confessed, "I'm alus sorta skeered of this place." Clarke Davis would extract from a girl, still aghast at the display of legs by the chorus of young Joe Jefferson's show, *The Circus,* the blushing admission that she never had seen any legs before but her own. Dick would narrate some amusing adventure of his in New York, such as his and Brisbane's rivalry for the favor of a wealthy widow—of how they went a-wooing on horseback and Brisbane came off first but he came off quickest.

Philadelphia in her restrained manner took note of her emigrated son. Down at *The Press* office one day Gallagher was shown a popular book with his name on the cover, a book by his former reporter-patron, and objected heatedly that it was spelled "Gallegher." Along Walnut Street in the after-church promenade walked a lovely young teacher of an élite finishing school for girls, and pupils who had snobbishly cut her the previous Sunday bowed effusively now that she was accompanied by Richard Harding Davis. That warm-hearted celebrity, having heard the story of past rudeness from his sister, a friend of the schoolmistress, had made a point of calling at the church door and offering escort. It was this same teacher who picked up a book in the Davis library one day and was alarmed by a shower of one-dollar bills fluttering out of its pages. Mrs. Davis explained that her prospering son had been taken with the quaint conceit of using the book as a bank, placing one dollar on page one, two on page two, and so on to see what he could save.

Monday and back on the job at *The Evening Sun*. They realized there that there would be a reportorial vacancy soon. Davis would be a reporter all his life and proud of it, but the shackles which chained him to the daily grind of run-of-the-mill newspaper work must soon be loosed. That vision of every toiler in his craft, the rosy dawn of reputation which brings offers of editorships, special correspondence, and the glorious freedom of the free-lance, was reality for him now.

IV

Emancipation appeared in the electric and eccentric person of S. S. McClure, who was galvanizing the staid magazine world as Joseph Pulitzer was journalism. His card snapped down on Davis's desk and his offer snapped out:

"I have sent my London representative to Berlin and my New York man to London. Will you take charge of my New York end?"

"Bring your New York representative back and send me to London, and I'll consider it," Davis shot back. "As long as I am in New York I will not leave *The Evening Sun*.

"Edmund Gosse is my London representative," McClure shifted. "You can have the same work here. Come out and take lunch."

"Thank you, I can't; I'll see you on Tuesday."

"All right, I'll come for you. Think of what I say," the publisher persisted. "I'll make your fortune. Bradford Merill told me to get you. You won't have anything to do but ask people to write novels and edit them. I'll send you abroad later if you don't like New York. Can you write any children's stories for me?"

"No. See you Tuesday."

Pleased with his nonchalance and hoping to enjoy further bidding, Davis on Tuesday refused the post at $75 a week. He feared it might shelve him, and writing short stories independently for *McClure's* seemed safer and more profitable. He was sure of it when he received $300 for *The Reporter Who Made Himself King*. Also another and better opportunity was forthcoming, again by benefit of Brisbane who recommended his reporter to his friend, J. Henry Harper. That gentleman took more Davis stories and finally took their author, seating him in the managing editor's chair of venerable and estimable *Harper's Weekly*.

Farewell to the city desks of Park Row. Franklin Square now and another circular iron stairway, the famous ascent to Harper's worn shiny by footprints likewise discernible in Mr. Longfellow's sands of time. There were traditions to be maintained on *Harper's Weekly* and Davis rose to their call. He published stories by Kipling, Henry James, and by Gertrude Atherton who confessed she was having trouble selling to more hidebound editors. His articles dealt with news, science, personalities, politics. Growing national interest in athletics was appreciated by a regular column on amateur sports. He continued to fill pages with those grand and generous drawings which had achieved distinction and subscribers for the *Weekly* from Civil War days through the time of Tweed when the deadly pen of Thomas Nast transfixed the Tammany Tiger—those drawings whose fascination photographs never have equalled. Society and club scenes (courtesy of

Van Bibber), the theatre and all the life of the town from Fifth Avenue to the Bowery. Pictures of life on the farm and in foreign lands. Graceful Gibsons, the dashing cavalrymen and Indians of Remington and Zogbaum, Rogers cartoons, the comic darkies of Frost, and the panoramas of Thoré de Thulstrup.

The hard-pressed reporter never had known such leisure and leeway as the editor's muse possessed. Davis writing for his own and other magazines was increasing his reputation and bank account. One night he came home to his rooms at 10 East Twenty-eighth Street, now shared with Charley Davis, to find a royalty statement and check for his first collection of short stories, *Stories for Boys*. The check for nine hundred and odd dollars[9] set the brothers whooping and dancing around the hall table, and off they rushed to celebrate the occasion with a dinner. Delmonico's was decidedly indicated.

It was always an event when Richard Harding Davis dined at Delmonico's even when it became an almost daily occurrence. It was a rite for any civilized person to partake of its unmatched cuisine. There, declared a devoted patron, one dined; elsewhere one merely fed and sustained one's wild nature. Under Delmonico tutelage Davis learned to order a dinner and developed a taste in wines creditable to a Continental connoisseur. He never, as the saying went, "dined too well," but maintained the rule of sobriety he had laid down for *Van Bibber* after his first fling. The song and poetry of the grape expressed his regard for it, and he ordered champagne not with the flashiness of the parvenu but with the air of a gentleman of the old school commanding the best vintage for his friends.

9 Indicating an excellent sale for a collection of short stories.

Copyright Life Publishing Co.

GIBSON GIRL AND GIBSON-DAVIS MAN

Delmonico's,[10] gradually having moved uptown since its foundation on Beaver Street in 1836, was in its heyday in the early 'Nineties at Fifth Avenue and Twenty-sixth Street overlooking Madison Square. The quiet elegance of its atmosphere, its crimson hangings and polished mirrors, its veteran waiters in trim jackets and spotless aprons, all distinguished it and pitched the tone of its clientèle. When Davis lunched there he watched the Avenue's parade of broughams, hansoms, and lumbering stages (entered from a rear door shut by a leather thong running to the driver's seat) from a table which any one else seldom ventured to usurp. It was the same when he made his evening entrance, arrayed in double-breasted dinner coat, boyishly delighted to be causing a stir, bowing to all his friends and stared at from all sides both because of his fame and his good looks.

Davis and Delmonico's are inseparably linked. They both have become period pieces. A novel (published, 1932), laying part of its scene in their day, thus characterizes its heroine:[11] "Once dining at Delmonico's, she had met Richard Harding Davis and fallen in love with him immediately."

Legends, too, grew up around the celebrated restaurant and its celebrated patron. His friend, Franklin Clarkin,[12] once told him one of them to amuse him, a tale current in Park Row—how Davis, finding a stranger at his favorite table, was supposed to have remarked: "I beg your pardon. My name is Richard Harding Davis and you are in my chair." "Do not

---

[10] Delmonico's final move to the northeast corner of Fifth Avenue and Forty-fourth Street took place in 1897. There it flourished for years, but crude oil is said to have lured members of the Delmonico dynasty away from salad oil to indulge in disastrous speculations; and Prohibition was the death warrant of the famous restaurant, the site of which is now occupied by an office building. However, the name and tradition are preserved in an apartment hotel at Park Avenue and Fifty-ninth Street; in its kitchen one of the old Delmonico chefs still rules.

[11] *The House of Vanished Splendors,* by William McNally.

[12] Newspaperman on staff of *New York Times.* War correspondent.

mind," replied the usurper. "My name is Jove. Many swear by me. If you are one, sit down."

The anecdote left Davis gravely thoughtful. "How can they think such things of me?" he wondered. "It isn't even a well-arranged story."

Yet there was little real conceit about Davis. Bravado sometimes covered diffidence and dramatics always were irresistible, but he stood his sudden celebrity remarkably well. How could he help enjoying being equally the rage with Carmencita, the Spanish dancer,[13] who was packing them in nightly at Koster & Bial's music hall? Red-and-yellow frills and flounces covered Carmencita's shoulders and legs as modestly as the conventional corset compressed her middle. But through her graceful fandangos seeped sufficient of that seductiveness, which is an old Spanish custom, to bring the gentlemen rallying around. The ladies, breaking through a taboo on "refined vaudeville" for their sex, came to see what the gentlemen were up to. One can still seem to hear a husband of the 'Nineties expatiating on the art and appeal of Carmencita, while his wife counters with the art and appeal of Richard Harding Davis.

None responded more heartily than Davis to the toast, "The ladies—God bless 'em," or more willingly agreed to a post-prandial shall-we-join-them. They were a grateful spectacle to his eyes—tiny slippers, voluminous skirts flowing from hour-glass waists over plural petticoats, mutton-leg sleeves, and soft hair knotted to crown proudly held heads. By day the Oriental charm of a veil raised to disclose cupid's-bow lips enthralled him. By evening he gazed enchanted at slim and stately forms in the silken ballgowns which Gibson drew with

13 An article by Julian Ralph in *The Sun* began her vogue. Similarly, an appreciation by Davis of Ada Lewis as a tough girl from the Bowery in a Harrigan and Hart show launched that actress's popularity.

such fashionble éclat that some declared *Life* ran a Butterick pattern section. He admired slender arms in long, white, immaculate gloves, and rounded shoulders rising above a decolletage no bathing suit would venture. Yet one of Davis's characters, an actress, did expose herself to sunburn on a beach, suffering retribution by accumulating a tan which prevented her appearing in an evening dress for a month.

Girls liked to glide a waltz or hop a polka or schottische with such an excellent dancer as Dick Davis. They acclaimed the carnation in his lapel, his double-breasted waistcoats, twice-around ties, and patent-leather boots. His high silk hat and splendidly filled frock coat distracted their attention from the ring at the Horse Show in Madison Square Garden. Parlors full of femininity languished when he strummed his guitar and sang "Thy Face," "Fourteen Tarriers on a Rock," "Casey's Flat," or his own setting of "Danny Deever." He was always in love with one or more society girls or actresses and not a few were secretly or openly enamoured of him. His courting, they still remember, made a girl feel like a queen. Yet before the queen could unbend and step down from her throne, young Mr. Davis was back at his eternal writing or off to Philadelphia to see his mother. More than once some fair charmer was bitterly chagrined at scratching a cavalier and finding no Casanova.

V

The editor's easy chair, as it is euphemistically called, is normally confining. Davis, restless soul, had foreseen as much and had arranged with the Harpers that he would divide his time between editing and travelling for material to write. For his first trip he picked the only point of the compass he had neglected so far and set out in January, 1892, for the series of

articles which appeared in *Harper's Weekly* and later as a book
under the title, *The West From a Car Window.*

The vast distances of Texas staggered the city chap, an-
chored to his car seat by the weight of silver dollars given him
in change for his greenbacks. At Laredo he overcame his in-
hibitions and coinage and detrained. Troop G, 3d Cavalry,
was about to pursue Mexican revolutionists. Davis longed to
be a war correspondent and here was a chance to start in the
primary grade. Attaching himself by War Department permission, he swung into the saddle.

It was only one of those periodic chases supplied by bandits
who obligingly crossed the Border to exercise the U. S. Cavalry, but it was strenuous field service. Few could have expected that tenderfoot editor, much less *Mr. Van Bibber* of
New York, could ride the 30 to 50 miles a day he did and
stand up under sun and dust and thirst with hard-bitten troopers. One day he was in the saddle for 33 hours to cover 110
miles. He helped capture and disarm supposed bandits. It was
useful experience for the future, this brief campaigning with
a fragment of the vanishing Old Army of the Indian wars era
—those gallantly picturesque troopers in battered campaign
hats, bandanas at throats, short blue jackets, and yellow-striped
breeches in spurred boots, galloping over the plains with ready
carbines and rattling sabres. Remington drew them magnificently to illustrate the *Weekly* articles. And into Davis's soldierly heart entered something of that love of the Service to
which most men must be born or reared. You can glimpse it
in his *Ranson's Folly* and in *Captain Macklin's* broken cry
after he had been dismissed from West Point for running the
sentries to dance with a girl at a hop: "I shall never see U. S.
on my saddle-cloth, nor salute my country's flag as it comes
fluttering down at sunset."

On to the oil fields of Oklahoma he journeyed and up to
Denver and on the boom mining camp of Crede, Colorado,
where he delighted in the Bret Harte atmosphere. He marked
the loutish, apologetic air of the man who shot Jesse James
in the back. He saw a drunk slap Bat Masterson in the face
and live, saved by his condition. He knew the thrill of meeting
Westerners who knew him by reputation, and he found two
young Harvard men whose sole possessions were a tiny cabin,
silver-mine shares, five dollars in cash, two banjos, hope, and a
large picture of Richard Harding Davis.

VI

"I think any man who can afford a hall bedroom and a gas
stove in New York City is better off than he would be as the
owner of 160 acres on the prairie or in one of those small so-
called cities."

Thus Davis, setting down his travel impressions with an ag-
gressive honesty hardly diplomatic for the editor of a national magazine. "The West," ran his final verdict as his
train sped eastward, "is a very wonderful, large, unfinished,
and out-of-doors portion of our country and a most delightful
place to visit." Let Westerners reply if they would that New
York City is a very sinful, large, unfinished, indoors portion of
our country, good enough to visit but God save them from
having to live there. They could chime in with the city editor
of Davis's *The Red Cross Girl* and grumble: "There's nothing
to New York except cement, iron girders, noise, and zinc gar-
bage cans"; you never sight the sun nor the moon in that burg
of street canyons unless you stand in the middle of one and
bend backward, and no flowers bloom except on women's hats.

For all that, Davis had pledged his allegiance. He sought no more far horizons but the view across the New Jersey flats where the skyscrapers marshalled by the Equitable Building and the twin spires of the Cathedral rose majestically through the smoke. He had encountered enough statuesque Indians and dashing cowboys; his eyes longed for the vision of Diana of the Tower and bronze Farragut to greet him daily as he strolled through Madison Square to Delmonico's, there to be tendered a *carte du jour* which made no mention of bacon and alkali water. He was eager to hear the blast of the horn of the Country Club coach tooting above the roar of the Avenue, noisier with the dawn of the Auto Age. To promenade that thoroughfare past the fortress-like walls of the Croton Reservoir at Forty-second Street,[14] To watch discreet matrons sipping cocktails out of teacups in the confectionery shops of Madison Avenue. To foregather with their spouses in the bars of the Holland House or the old Fifth Avenue Hotel where Tom Platt issued orders from the Amen Corner. To push through the Election Night jam in the Hoffman House.

He might have despatched the homesick message which *Meakim,* the grafting Tammany police commissioner of *The Exiles,* sent from his foreign refuge: "Just take a drink for me at Ed Lally's—I don't know nothing better than Fourteenth Street of a summer evening with all the people crowding into Pastor's on one side of the Hall and the Third Avenue L cars rattling by on the other."

For New York is many things to one who knows her as Davis did. Iron girders were hidden by tall towers. Cosmopolitan crowds trod her cement sidewalks, and the rattle of traffic on the cobblestones of Broadway was the symphony of one of the great streets of the world. What if the moon hid behind housetops? The gas footlights shone bright at Weber

[14] The site of the present New York Public Library.

and Field's, Harrigan and Hart's, and Koster and Bial's. It was slander to say flowers were only millinery. The keen gaze of Bunner could see "a pitcher of mignonette in the tenement's highest casement."

So Davis came out of the West and all the wide border and returned joyously to a beloved New York, *Van Bibber's* town and his.

CHAPTER SIX

THE LUCK OF R. H. D.

I

New York having proved its magnetism relaxed it. Alluring illustrations in English and French magazines on Davis's desk beckoned, and advertisements reminded him that a first-class passage to Europe cost only fifty dollars. He was freer than ever, for he had resigned the editorship of the *Weekly,* assured that the Harper presses would be hospitable to his free-lance work.

American interest in Europe was blazing up and growing American fortunes were its fuel and motive power. Sons graduating from college were reviving the Grand Tour. Mothers and daughters were launching argosies in search of titles, gowns, and culture. Fathers were furnishing the sinews of travel and being dragged along, like Gibson's *Mr. Pipp.* The birth of that European major industry, the American tourist trade, was announced by happy hootings of steamship whistles. Davis listened to those new national slogans, All Aboard and *Bon Voyage,* and sailed for the England he had liked so well on the cricket trip, bound to establish a closer relationship with "our English cousins."[1]

No American ever chose a more difficult method of claiming that distant kinship, never readily acknowledged across the Atlantic. Davis dared settle down at Oxford with the view of entering into the undergraduate life of Balliol College. And

[1] Chosen by Davis as the title for his book made up from articles which appeared serially in *Harper's Magazine.*

this was in a day when Cecil Rhodes was still unprepared to arrange *coups d'états,* let alone scholarships.

A young Englishman, H. J. Whigham,[2] who met Davis there and saw the attempt accomplished, expressed astonished comment:

"Any one at all conversant with the customs of universities, especially with the idiosyncrasies of Oxford, knows that for a person who is not an undergraduate to share the life of undergraduates on equal terms, to take part in their adventures, to be admitted to their confidence is more difficult than it is for the camel to pass through the eye of a needle or for the rich man to enter heaven. It was characteristic of Davis that although he was a few years older than the average university 'man' and came from a strange country and, moreover, had no official reason for being in Oxford at all, he was accepted as one of themselves by the Balliol undergraduates."

Just how Davis managed it is something of a mystery. His genuine enthusiasm for things English and the success his pen had won played a part. "The typical Oxonian is a combination of audacity and shyness," he wrote and, having exactly described his own disposition, he was bound to find kindred spirits. Soon he was rooming congenially with an "English cousin" and adopting an alma mater in all respects but studying. It struck him as an ideal collegiate existence.

It was a far cry from Lehigh. There were traditions but such fine, venerable ones. The former rebel was moved to no revolt when he was fined for passing the gates after nine o'clock or smoking after ten. He delighted in arraying himself in evening clothes and dining with the dons at a high table lit with candles, while gowned students sat below and rattled pewter mugs engraven with the college arms. Decorously he

[2] Editor of *Town & Country.*

carried his napkin and paraded to Commons for port, nuts, and raisins; then followed the dons to another room for cigars and brandy and soda. An Oxford don, he decided, mixes some high living with his high thinking.

Once he took coffee with the Master of Balliol.

"Oh, yes, you're from India," said the "dear old man."

"No, from America," the guest corrected.

"Oh, yes, it's the other one," the Master admitted. "The other one" turned out to be an Indian princess in a cashmere cloak and diamonds who looked so proud and lovely and beautiful to young Mr. Davis that he wanted to take her out to one of the seats in the quadrangle and let her weep on his shoulder.

The lively American was the ringleader in an expedition which cut the chain a crusty landowner had the effrontery to stretch across Shakespeare's Avon. His friends, knowing how he liked to dress up, inveigled him into wearing old clothes at a rowing victory dinner of celebration with the excuse that a succeeding bonfire would ruin raiment. The flustered Davis arrived to find everybody attired in his best. The last laugh was his when the bonfire lived up to predictions.

The opening of the season drew him to London, a sentimental journey. There in the glamor of empire reigned Queen Victoria, sensible of the obligations of royalty to a pageantry-loving people and to all story-tellers. There abounded belted earls and duchesses, some of them presiding over literary salons. There glittered gorgeous uniforms and all manner of colorful costumes for regattas or guilds, for hunting or costermonging, donned by tradition and for occasion and drawing none of the jibes Davis had suffered for his clothes at home. He loved it all for its color and correctness, its orderliness and its heritages. So fervently did he wish he might play a part in it that later, when he was made a Chevalier of the Legion of Honor, he naïvely had his calling cards engraved: "Chevalier Davis." Kind friends quickly confiscated them.

His anxiety that the English should like him and other American cousins led him to scold American girls for racing through hotel corridors and warned them they would be talked about if they persisted at dances in "twosing" with young men in corners, on stairways, and behind statues in gardens where Mr. Davis, unwittingly intruding, was most embarrassed. "A young girl," ruled this stickler for propriety, "must remain in evidence, she must be where her parents can reach her, and where whoever is looking after her can whisper to her to hold herself straight, or that she is dancing her hair down. If she wants to talk to a man alone, as she sometimes does, and her mother approves of the man, she can see him at her own home over a cup of tea any afternoon after five." As for English girls, he disapproved Primrose Dames visiting bachelor apartments to canvass votes in elections. Nor could he be accused of failing to practise what he preached. One night he escorted home two hard British blondes, who had been on a party with Nat Goodwin, and maintained an attitude of chivalrous reserve.

He roamed London as he had roamed New York, looking for adventures, playing parts. Disguised as a boatman, he poled down the Thames with an eye out for floating corpses. In a ragged suit and a growth of beard to resemble somebody out of Dickens, he scoured Whitechapel for Jack the Ripper. Each masquerade was a joy and very real to him. His imagination captured what might have happened and down it went vividly in a story.

The Derby entertained him until a mob flung itself howling on a welsher trying to flee his betting losses and almost killed

him before bobbies made the rescue; Davis always mentioned
the incident when English people asked him about American
lynchings. Most of all he enjoyed helping a friend win a stirring campaign for a seat in Parliament. He would never forget the candidate's homecoming from the triumphant vote
counting—his admission through a door of the stately mansion
only used for great events—the assembly of the tenants in their
best clothes and the servants in livery and powdered hair—
the Lady of the House, a red silk cloak flung over her shoulder,
awaiting her victorious son—the candidate kissing her hand and
making his last speech of the campaign. Watching the English loyalty, pride of race, and time-hallowed tradition of it all,
the gaze of the American outsider blurred with emotion and he
was proud of his descent.

II

Home and off to the opening of the World's Fair at Chicago, where police considered the Davis coat one of the more
extraordinary sights and a crowd of several thousand people
cheered him as the Prince of Wales. Back to New York for a
while, then off for a Mediterranean cruise. The now inveterate globetrotter knew none of his fellow passengers but
most of them had brought *Gallegher* and *The West from a
Car Window* for their steamer reading. He was kept busy au-
tographing and giving favorite quotations for flattering young
women in yachting caps, reefers, football sweaters, and billow-
ing skirts.

When he woke one morning, "Gibraltar was a black sil-
houette against the sky, but toward the south there was a line
of mountains with a red sky behind them, dim and mysterious
and old, and that was Africa. Then Spain turned up all ame-
thyst and green and the Mediterranean as blue as they tell you
it is."

Davis wrote his travel books[3] as if he were a Marco Polo, completely assured that none of his public ever had visited the climes he was discovering. Readers, even seasoned travellers, caught his fresh enthusiasm. He made people visualize what he saw by comparisons with familiar objects at home: the Great Pyramid would reach to such-and-such a story of the Equitable Building. Somehow he could impart a bit of common knowledge with a charming naïveté which made it seem almost news.[4]

He landed eagerly on Gibraltar. That impregnable rock would never be attacked, he decided, since only Americans were clever enough to invent a way of taking it and they were far too clever to attempt the impossible. How he loved the scarlet uniforms of the officers of the British garrison (he tried on spare ones in wardrobes)—the toast to the Queen at mess— all the old regimental traditions—"Learoyd" and "Mulvaney" in the ranks at guard mount—dinner with the Governor not accepted until that official had hesitatingly, much to Davis's amusement, agreed to attend a luncheon in honor of Washington's birthday.

Morocco. Tangier's foul prison, worse than a precinct station in New York. Davis, climbing a roof to photograph it, found himself the object of hue and cry. He was on top of a

---

[3] *Cf.* C. B. Davis: "If Richard took it for granted that the reader was totally unacquainted with the peoples of these cities and their ways it was because he believed that that was the best way to write a descriptive article, always had believed it, and believed it so long as he wrote. . . . And when he suggested to an editor that he would like to write an article on Broadway, or the Panama Canal, or the ruins of Rome, and the editor disapproved, Richard's argument was: 'It hasn't been done until *I* do it.' And it was not because he believed for a moment that he could do it better or as well as it had been done. It was simply because he knew that the old story was always a good story, that is, if it was seen with new eyes from a new standpoint."

[4] Davis, said a critic, could inform readers that Washington was the first President of the United States and interest them. It might be added that his travel books would have benefitted vastly from the gay and intimate touch characterizing his letters to his family. Yet travel was then seldom written in that vein, and Davis studiously avoided the egotistical—in print.

harem. Exit with haste and embarrassment. Malta—wraiths of knights and Saracens out of Sir Walter Scott. Cairo, with its Biblical flavor and its Citadel looking like the Croton reservoir superimposed on Madison Square Garden. *Gallegher* was on sale in Cairo. Davis named one of his hired donkeys for it and called another "Van Bibber," but the donkey boys called it "Von Bebey," so he doubted if it would help the sale of that book. A call on the Khedive. Joining Stanford White to climb the pyramids. The impertinence of being photographed in front of them on a camel. The rider sent the picture to a girl back home with the superscription: "Forty centuries look down on me—including the present."

One night he drove out alone for a creepy and impressive call on the Sphinx. "All about was the desert and above it the purple sky and the white stars and the great negro's head in front . . . with its paws stretched out, and the moonlight turning it into shadows and white lines. . . . It was just as if I had been the first man to stumble across it, and I felt that I was way back thousands of years and that the ghosts of Cæsar and Napoleon and Cleopatra and the rest were in the air."

Port Said, with a wicked reputation not lived up to, thought the reporter who had covered New York's Haymarket. American cocktails at sea at the moment of Cleveland's inauguration, Davis, the host, informing all hands that a great man was being made President.

Athens, "a small town but fine." Memories of Pan and Aristides the Just and St. Paul. It made the traveller wish he had brushed up on his Greek history. Constantinople, reminding him that at college he used to sing:

> The Sultan better pleases me.
> His life is full of jollity . . .

but not recalling much of his history course. Still the deferred education of Richard Harding Davis had progressed miles. He was learning now as a reporter learns—by observation at first hand. Geography from travel, history from its monuments, anthropology by meeting strange peoples.[5] Everywhere he had made friends. He had cruised to shores studded with settings for short stories and novels: Tangier—*The Exiles* and *The King's Jackal,* Cairo—*The Writing on the Wall,* Constantinople—*The Grand Cross and the Crescent.* But he was glad to board the Orient Express. It ran to Paris—wind-up of the Grand Tour, city of the Latin Quarter and *La Vie Bohême,* and the capital of art.

III

Davis took quarters near the house where Alfred de Musset had lived and from his balcony gazed romantically across the street at a Fair Unknown with sleepy black eyes who wore a black bandeau about her alabaster brow, a diamond pendant at her lily-white throat, and a pink-and-white wrapper. The fair one remained unknown. Davis wove fancies about her. She would go nicely in a story.

He must find out about Art. It was the duty of a reporter who was preparing to write *About Paris* for *Harper's Magazine* and make the series into a book. Nor did Art mean only artists' models. Those demoiselles were to be observed and the Davis French strained to produce, *"Mademoiselle, comme vos yeux sont tristes."* But that would do.

Kenneth Frazier, risen from artist for the *Lehigh Burr* to portrait painter, accepted nomination as a guide. He made a conscientious effort to show his college chum the best pictures

---

[5] Davis found "something very fine about the religion of Mohammed."

in the galleries and ended by being shown those Davis liked, invariably canvases with dramatic themes. What did technique and chiaroscuro matter, if the artist had caught a thrilling moment in an epic? Gibson, living in the Latin Quarter, was another art Baedeker and boon companion. He and Davis, tall, fine-looking Americans, strode towering through the Gallic ateliers.

William Rothenstein, the English artist, served also, taking Davis to Whistler's salon where the caller found everybody "unobtrusively polite," even Whistler. Davis, admiring Rothenstein immensely as an exponent of art and perpetrator of *bon mots,* bought a sketch of himself and several pastels from the artist who was thus enabled to pay his debts. That, however, failed to hamper the artist's ironic impressions set down in *Men and Memories.*[6] Davis he thought handsome, richly dressed and moneyed—the common delusion of the foreigner in regard to any American purse—and he "spoke as though he were a famous writer."

"I knew nothing of his writing," the disciple of the works of Wilde and Verlaine pronounced, "but he was clearly a robust flower of American muscular Christianity—healthy and wealthy, and, in America, wise. His particular friend was Charles Dana Gibson, the popular creator of the type of which Davis himself (it was he) was a radical example. . . .

"Richard Harding Davis had never met any artists like Conder and me; he was respectful of our dazzling intellects; but he regretted that we were not, like himself, noble and virtuous. We puzzled him sadly; he even at times had doubts in regard to himself, but these doubts, when in the morning before his glass he brushed his rich, shining hair and shaved his fresh, firm chin, and called to mind the sums his short stories brought

[6] *Men and Memories* by Sir William Rothenstein. London, 1931.

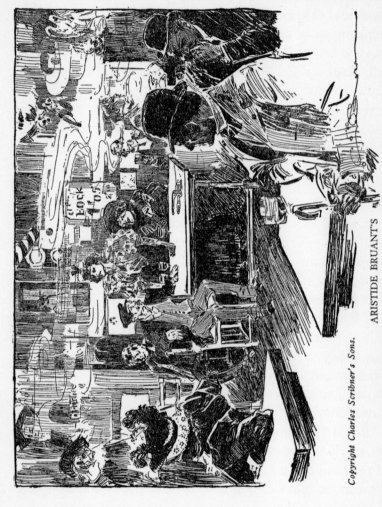

ARISTIDE BRUANT'S

Davis, in the foreground, sketched by Gibson at a Paris café.

him, proved fleeting as last night's dream. I liked Davis. I was touched at his wanting to make me a better and seemlier person, a sort of artistic boy scout springing smartly to attention before laboring on the good, wholesome work of art I was to achieve each day."

Beneath the sarcasm were some revealing bits of characterization. Davis did set himself up as a judge of other people's morals, even of his friends, and incurred the usual resentment. His principles, said one, stuck out and stuck into you. Some, like Rothenstein, considered him a prude. Others forgave him because he was so straightforward and too capable of frankly enjoying life himself to seem the dour reformer; because he obviously acted from affection and highminded motives; because he had the outspoken courage of his convictions. Yet there were moments when these friends felt like King Arthur's knights—ready to encourage Sir Galahad to go questing for the Grail so that the atmosphere of the Round Table might be freer and easier for a while.

Paris was in for some chiding from this uncompromising critic. He watched the arms of the Moulin Rouge turning and decided they were too often grinding down health and virtue and souls. When the rejected lover of an actress brought bullies from Montmartre to hiss and stone her, Davis gathered two Englishmen and rallied to the rescue. He was shocked at French callousness after the assassination of President Carnot and disgusted when a battalion of militia in the funeral parade was routed by the noise of a collapsing stand. He dared the heresy of condemning Yvette Guilbert, "the most artistic and the most improper of all the women of the *cafés chantants.*" The graphic Guilbert did not tax even *his* French. He knew very well she was singing songs "beneath the morals of a medical student."

Davis was glad no young American girls were taken to hear her. He was distressed so many of them were being brought over on title hunts, titles which looked well in New York but had to be worn—and their worthless owners endured—abroad. He and Gibson never tired of crusading against that type of American investment. Although they plied their pens with all their might, the tide of international nuptials trade rose until 1895, the banner year for heiress-export which saw the Marlborough-Vanderbilt, the Castellane-Gould, and the Paget-Whitney weddings.

Nor could the American colony in Paris escape Davis spankings. He mercilessly told on those voluntary exiles who were not wicked but only liked to be thought so; its men posing as the friend of this or that married woman and the lot of them lacking the nerve to carry silly affairs to the end.

Too much tinsel evil, too many wastrels, too much flippancy and leisure in the city of the Seine for energetic, forthright Mr. Davis. Now that his chronicle of it, admirably illustrated by Gibson, was done, he was off to towns more to his taste, to New York and Marion and London.

IV

Davis could never stay away from his country for long. He might miss too many of the marvellously interesting things that were happening to it. Mighty forces had wrought transformations during his absences: the Panic's deflation, the Klondike's inflation, the World's Fair welding. The all-conquering bicycle was rolling over the face of the land, pathfinding for the automobile, spreading back-to-nature gospel. Open-air breezes were supplanting fans and the graceful languor of the ballroom. From the front seat of a bicycle built for two, a girl—even the girl wearing a derby and bloomers—could glance back with winning coquetry at the beau furnishing most of the balance and propulsion; could start him humming, "Daisy, Daisy, give me your promise true." The Athletic Girl was coming into her own at last.

Cycling Norfolk jacket, cap, knickers, and stockings became the traveller back from foreign parts. He could mention that a spill from a bicycle was nothing to a tumble from a camel in Egypt or a mettlesome steed in the Bois de Boulogne. Or he could discourse charmingly to a maiden on Constantinople, seated appropriately in the scimitar-decked, draped-divan Turkish corner of her correctly appointed home. A fair one dining with him at Delmonico's might learn that the newly returned traveller was urging the management to install sidewalk café tables looking over Madison Square in order to acquire a truly Parisian atmosphere. And ladies invited to tea at the Davis domicile were admitted by an East Side youngster, uncomfortable but impressive in a page's choke-collar jacket studded with brass buttons,—a bit of old London.

The author of *Gallegher and Other Stories,* on its way to sell more than 50,000 copies and spoken of in the same breath with *Trilby, Ben Hur,* and *David Harum,* was undoubtedly a catch. American womanhood in particular and in general approved of him, and that approval was worth having, since it was bestowed by a new power in the land. Dana Gibson, keen social satirist, sensed it. His series in *Life,* "When Our Betters Rule," was prophetically picturing beauties presiding in pulpits and ambassadorships, Madam Presidents and Madam Secretaries in cabinet meetings; Vassar girls, lovely creatures in jerseys and moleskins, triumphing over a football team of mere men. The Irresistible She, the Titaness as Thomas Beer dubbed her, was daily demonstrating her increasing sway as censor over the manners, morals, and literature of the United States. New-crowned queens of opinion graciously observed that Davis's manners were correct, his morals clean, and his stories free from indecency.

Life was bright. He dined with Sir Henry Irving, Mark Twain, Whitelaw Reid, William Dean Howells, and Richard Watson Gilder, as one celebrity with others. His mother dedicated a book to him. "I feel thrills of pride when I see us sitting cheek by jowl on the newsstands," he wrote her. Still there must sometimes be a cloud in any sky. Davis suffered a severe attack of sciatica and was laid low for weeks. Throughout his life that painful affliction descended intermittently to cripple his fine physique.

When he recovered he sailed back to London to be Irving's guest at a dinner for Bernhardt and Rejane and to drive home at dawn with Ellen Terry and her daughter, royal in cloaks made from Irving's robe of cardinal red. He met at a luncheon Oscar Wilde whom he recalled unpleasantly lecturing at Philadelphia in velvet knickerbockers and with sunflower to plant *Bunthorne* for D'Oyley Carte before the American production of *Patience*. Now the clashing temperaments of the English esthete and the direct American struck sparks as Wilde indulged his penchant for baiting Yankees.[7]

"So you are from Philadelphia where Washington is buried?"

"Nonsense, he's buried in Mount Vernon," Davis answered abruptly.

Wilde, miffed, switched the talk to a new French painter. "Do let's hear what Mr. Davis thinks of him," he purred. "Americans always talk so amusingly of art."

Said Davis: "I never talk about things when I don't know the facts."

[7] The anecdote is from Beer's article in *Liberty*.

Wilde's rapier wit flashed back: "That must limit your conversation frightfully."

Years later after Reading Gaol had brought degradation and inspiration, an English doctor came to Davis in Paris and asked his help for Wilde, starving in his exile. The Davis generosity responded with an envelope stuffed with franc notes. He was not a man to hold a grudge.

V

New York-London steamer lines had become almost a shuttle for Davis. It was time to leave the beaten track. Why not visit Honduras, suggested a fellow diner at Delmonico's one evening. The exiled Louisiana State Lottery, largest gambling concern in the world, was newly established there and reaching out into the United States for its golden profits of yore.

Davis looked up the history of the Lottery, found how for years it had "put its chain and collar upon legislatures and senators, judges and editors, when it had silenced the voice of church and pulpit by great gifts of money to charities and hospitals, so giving out in a lump sum with one hand what it had taken from the people in dollars and half-dollars, five-hundred and six-hundred fold, with the other. How it had persuaded Generals Beauregard and Early to lend it names made glorious in a lost cause and preside over its drawings. It was driven from the country now and the mails closed to it by Postmaster General Wanamaker, but it had not surrendered. It was shipping tickets by express and Davis could read its crafty advertisements in his theatre programs. "Conrad! Conrad! Conrad!" they proclaimed, adding that a person of that name ran an ice company and, incidentally, a lottery in Puerto Cortez, Honduras, where bids for supplies might be addressed to him.

"There's a story in that!" Davis exclaimed, and early in January, 1895, he sailed with two kindred spirits, Somers Somerset, younger son of an English noble family, and Lloyd C. Griscom, then on the threshold of a distinguished career as a diplomat.

There were many stories in that. His *Three Gringos in Venezuela* became a travel book and not an exposé, for the United States shortly closed avenues of access to the Lottery. But out of this journey to Central and South America came *Soldiers of Fortune,* laid in Cuba but plotted on muleback on Venezuelan trails; *Captain Macklin*; that jolly farce, *The Dictator*; a splendid short story, *The Consul,* and others. These opened a new locale for American writers, the bullets-and-bananas school of fiction.

The Three Gringos made a wild, crazy lark of the trip. They were young and foolhardy and they waded rapids to stalk alligators, played tag with sharks in the surf, and put on an amateur bullfight in a village arena. Davis snapped his camera at the bull charging him. One, Jeffs, the swashbuckling adventurer serving as their guide, conceived the idea of testing them with an ambush. He slipped away in the moonlight, hid behind a rock beside the trail, and when his patrons came up, let out a series of yells in Spanish and opened up a fusillade over their heads. The Gringos tumbled off their mules, grasped carbines, and spattered his rock with so much lead that he shouted for mercy. "We thought it was a sentry of brigands," Davis wrote home, "and were greatly disappointed when it turned out to be Jeffs."

Riding over mountains and through jungles, Davis would twist around in his saddle and spin the growing plot of *Sol-*

Somers Somerset   R. H. D.   Lloyd C. Griscom

THREE GRINGOS IN VENEZUELA

CHARLES DANA GIBSON AND R. H. D. ON COMMODORE
BENEDICT'S YACHT, *ONEIDA*, 1893

diers of Fortune to Griscom jogging along behind. "And then the mining engineer does this and the girl says that"——. Griscom listened fascinated. A good many thousands of readers would later be experiencing the same emotion.

They bearded swarthy *presidentes* in their tropical palaces and collected medals and orders which Davis donned with boyish delight. What grist to the mill it all was—inland villages or coast towns like "Porto Banos" of *The Dictator.*

> "Porto Banos, south-east coast, 300 elevation,[8]
> A former colony of Spain, ten thousand population.
> Only two per cent of them can even read or write,
> And less than that do any work—the rest just loaf and fight.
>
> The ruler is a president and he is self-elected.
> He remains in office for as long as he's protected.
> The only place of worship is a ruined Spanish mission.
> It's full of yellow fever but there is no prohibition."

They ranged from jollifications with the officers aboard American men-of-war to immense amusement in the scratch ceremonies of welcome arranged for Somerset by punctilious British consuls. There was the occasion when the inhabitant of an isolated hut in Venezuela, hearing the introduction, "I'm Davis," came through nobly with, "Not Richard Harding Davis!" But Davis grew homesick, as he always did, and the expedition sailed back in March.

When he arrived in New York he read in the paper that John Drew was playing in Harlem. The returned traveller and explorer grinned and wired that he was organizing a relief expedition and would lead him out of the wilderness in safety. He followed it with other messages in the best Livingstone-Stanley tradition. "Natives from the interior of Har-

[8] From Frank Craven's lyrics for *The Girl from Home,* a musical comedy version of *The Dictator.*

lem report having seen Davis Relief Expeditionary Force crossing Central Park. All Well." "Relief reached Eighty-fifth Street. Natives peacefully inclined. Awaiting rear column led by Griscom. Save your ammunition and provisions." And one more just before the curtain fell: "If you can hold the audience at bay for another hour, we guarantee to rescue yourself and company and bring you all back to the coast in safety. Do not become disheartened."

Davis and his band, booted, spurred, and armed, and with two colored men costumed as African warriors, burst through the stage door. Drew, thankful the performance was over and his curtain down, met them with Maude Adams by his side.

"Mr. Drew, I presume," Davis declaimed.

"Mr. Davis, I believe," laughed the actor, "I am saved!"

VI

People talked of the luck of Richard Harding Davis. They avowed that horses won races because he bet on them. He wrote a short story on that theme, a yarn about a struggling author whose hunches gleaned a greenback harvest at the track, and Davis himself seemed to be *The Man Who Could Not Lose*. He might have become a great gambler but horses, cards or the stock exchange held little appeal for him. It was the chances a boy takes for sport which attracted him and, above all, he was ready to risk even his life to get a good story.

Every year he demonstrated more convincingly that fortune guided his pen. The envious and the failures grumbled that they never knew the like of it. They readily forgot the hard training which had given him his nose for news, his ability to sense and anticipate the timely and to be on the spot before a trend set in or an event happened.

His books on the Mediterranean and England had caught at the flood a wave of foreign travel by Americans. And here was the *Three Gringos* coming out just after President Cleveland had laid down the law and the Monroe Doctrine to Great Britain in the Venezuela-British Guiana boundary dispute amid a buzz of war talk and sudden interest in South America. Several paragraphers jested that Davis's book had inspired the President's message.

There was something of a "break" in that. Nor was the kindly goddess who balances on a wheel by any means through rolling around to Dick Davis's doorstep. Mlle. Yvette Guilbert, who took up pages in *About Paris,* was playing in New York. Duly censored for her audiences of Puritanical Yankees and hence slightly disappointing, she nevertheless charmed them. Davis, attending a reception at Mrs. Reginald De Koven's, sat on a cushion on the floor in front of his hostess while a playlet was finished. When the lights went up, he noticed her companion, a tall, red-haired, magnetic woman in a gown cut like a kimona. Whereupon he was presented to Yvette Guilbert whom he had scolded so in print for singing naughty songs.

She spoke to him in English. "It is not comfortable on the floor, is it?"

The debonair Mr. Davis rose to the occasion.

"I have been at your feet for three years now, so I am quite used to it," he announced gallantly.

During the applause, he boldly asked some one to tell her in French that he had written a book about Paris and was going to mark it and send it to her.

"No," said Guilbert. "Send me the Van Bibbere book. M. Bourget told me to meet you and read it. You are Mr. Davis, are you not?" Then she offered to give him French lessons and he felt he owned the place.

It was all priceless publicity for R. H. D. Success seemed to breed success. The up-and-coming *New York Journal* was after him to act as its correspondent. Hearst pressed him to cover the Yale-Princeton football game, but Davis was unwilling and politely refused to undertake it for less than $500 which he regarded as a prohibitive figure. The publisher took him up and startled him into acceptance. It was a record price for a single piece of reporting, but a good bargain. Demand for the edition containing Davis's story of the game quickly exhausted it.

The pleasure of sports reporting was dimmed by anticipation of the appearance of his short novel, *Princess Aline*. Davis had enjoyed writing it more than any other of his books— this charming romance of a noblewoman, an American girl, and a successful young artist who emerged in the illustrations as a Davis-Gibson Man at his handsomest. *Princess Aline* had stepped out of a photograph in one of Davis's foreign magazines to become his heroine. Not many months after she won her way in fiction, her original swept into world news.

Princess Alix of Hesse-Darmstadt read the cablegrams, was about to wed Nicholas, heir of the late Alexander III, and be crowned with him at Moscow as Czar and Czarina of all the Russias. In other words, *Princess Aline,* having lost *Morton Carleton* to a Gibson Girl, was fulfilling the stern sad destiny of royalty.

The luck of Richard Harding Davis was not altogether an empty phrase.

CHAPTER SEVEN

THE PASSING OF PRINCESS ALINE

I

CHARLEY DAVIS, American Consul in Florence, Italy, by grace of Cleveland, was entertaining his brother Richard and their friend, Augustus Trowbridge,[1] in the spring of 1896 when a cablegram from New York arrived. Mr. William Randolph Hearst desired the services of Mr. Richard Harding Davis once more. Would the correspondent turn from quarterbacks to kings and for a sum named cover the imminent coronation of the Czar of Russia for *The Journal*?

Dick Davis considered the offer and decided that crownings should come much higher than football games. A polite refusal had worked wonders the last time Hearst tried to hire him, and a scornful one might do more. Back flashed a withering reply:

"They don't run penny buses to Moscow."

The astute publisher, remaining unwithered as usual, raised the figure; he required a Big Name and results and would pay what they cost. Even then Davis hesitated; he knew no Russian and practically no French and foresight warned him he was bound for Babel. *The Journal* clinched its correspondent only when Trowbridge, a fluent linguist, agreed to go along as interpreter.

The pair had scarcely arrived in Moscow before Davis realized he had chosen an indispensable aide. "Trowbridge," he wrote Charley, "flatters, lies, threatens, and bribes with a skill and assurance that is simply beautiful, and his languages and

[1] Dean of the Graduate School, Princeton University.

his manners pull me out of holes from which I could never have risen. With it all he is as modest as can be, and says that I am the greatest diplomat out of office, which I really think he believes, but I am only using old reporters' ways and applying the things other men did first."

There was need for all the tricks of the trade. This was a big story, this elevation of a new ruler over vast Russia, and at any moment the explosion of a Nihilist bomb might make it a bigger story yet. "The opposition," as a newspaperman calls his competitors from other papers, was appalling. Here were gathered first-string correspondents from all over the world and most of them would be working under pressure of time and striving to score a "beat" over the rest. Out of the 300 present, ninety had hopes of securing intensely coveted admissions to the small chapel where the coronation ceremony would take place. The press was allowed only a dozen representatives there and just two or three of those places would go to Americans. Only two wires ran out of the ancient capital to carry the scores of despatches which would be filed in a rush by clamoring journalists.

Davis, working in strange territory, had never faced so difficult an assignment. He buckled down to it with all the energy and ability and ingenuity at his command.

Installed in a hotel suite originally engaged for Mrs. Hearst, Senior, who had decided not to come to Russia, Davis and Trowbridge had a splendid vantage point for observing the parades and processions. The two young men, alone in such palatial quarters, were suspected as bombers and their rooms searched nightly by the police. Davis refused to rent any of their ten grandstand windows but in a lordly manner invited friends to look from them. Then the two, weighted down by money belts, sallied forth to the telegraph bureau and made themselves so solid that they obtained a private entrance to the office of the chief. Crossing of palms being an old Russian custom, they fought the devil with fire. They could not risk being handicapped in the race for the wires.

It was all like a game of whist and poker combined, Davis thought, and they were bluffing on two flimsy fours. "There is not a wire we have not pulled, or a leg, either," he wrote, "and we go dashing about all day in a bath-chair, with a driver in a bell hat and blue night-gown, leaving cards and writing notes and giving drinks and having secretaries to lunch and buying flowers for wives and cigar boxes for husbands, and threatening the Minister with Cleveland's name." Davis simply must get into that chapel and every influence he could think of was brought to bear.

The ladies were for him as usual. Princes, grand dukes, and ambassadors were persuaded to lend a hand. U. S. Minister Breckinridge wrote letter after letter. The special American Ambassador, Gen. Alexander McDowell McCook, on whose daughter the wily Messrs. Trowbridge and Davis were dancing attendance, obligingly exerted influence. "Every man, woman, and child in the visiting and resident legation is crazy on the subject of getting Davis into the coronation," complained a rival correspondent.

But it was Trowbridge who finally swung it. That first-class factotum had been his comrade's encyclopædia for Russian background. He was ready with answers when Davis asked such questions as: "Who was Ivan the Terrible and why was he terrible?" Now he was a walking reference to the Almanach de Gotha, calling on the powerful acquaintances he had made in the course of his studies abroad to help in the storming of the chapel. By a stroke of luck one of these was Prince Wolkonsky, the Grand Master of Ceremonies.

He besieged that glittering official. Was he aware that Richard Harding Davis was no mere journalist, but an essayist, a famous writer of *belles lettres,* the American Paul Bourget, in fact? That he would describe the coronation not primarily for any ephemeral news-sheet but for *Harper's Magazine* where it would go ringing down the ages? The Prince was impressed and ordered the personage brought to call on him.

Trowbridge returned in dismay to his "famous writer of *belles lettres*" who could speak only enough French to translate that phrase or inform the Prince, *"Comme vos yeux sont tristes."* He could never live up to the reputation given him at that rate. The linguist went to work on him and soon, Davis, clever mimic and actor, had memorized ten numbered French sentences.

With these, the two schemers went to call on the Master of Ceremonies. Trowbridge stood behind him. The Prince addressed a question in rapid-fire French to Davis. Trowbridge stealthily held up three fingers. Davis in a passable accent parroted Sentence Number Three. Another question. Eight fingers. Out rolled Sentence Number Eight. The ten sentences were still holding out when Davis received his welcome dismissal.

Trowbridge remained to ask how Prince Woronsky had liked his friend.

"Il est très bien," the Prince approved, *"mais un peu taciturne."*

The conspirators were still laughing when the coveted blue badge for the chapel arrived. It was for Trowbridge but he instantly turned it over to Davis. Women cheered the news, kissed Davis and each other, and men crowded around to congratulate him.

II

He who would shortly crown himself Nicholas II, Czar of Russia, was about to enter Moscow in all his state. The squares and streets of the thronged city resounded with the national anthem, magnificent basses swelling through its stirring organ harmonies. Religious exaltation for a moment transfigured the sad faces of the moujiks. Here and there the approaching cavalcade drew furtive looks of hate, masked quickly as the watchful police thrust the crowds back against the walls.

Davis and his friends watched from their windows, heard the blare of trumpets and the tread of squadrons and battalions which lives in the barbaric beat of the music of the *Marche Slav.* Leading the ranks of his glittering nobility and his massed columns of troops, a small, bearded figure in uniform rode reluctantly toward his throne. The reporter's eyes observed Nicholas but the man's eyes were waiting for some one else.

Then she came in her gilded coach, she who had been the Princess Alix until only a few weeks ago when she was snatched from her little German principality to mourn at the bier of Alexander III, wed his heir, and hasten from a brief honeymoon to this, her new realm. The watcher in the window leaned forward and his heart beat fast. His *Princess Aline* had come. He thought he never had looked on any one so beautiful, so sweetly girlish. He could have sighed with *Carleton,* "Ah, to think, that such a lovely creature as that should be sacrificed for so insignificant a thing as the peace of Europe when she might make some young man happy!"

She came to fulfil the destiny of a princess, that inexorable fate on which Queen Victoria had regally pronounced during Davis's last visit to London. An equerry had graciously informed him that the Queen and her daughters had much enjoyed reading *Princess Aline.* "How did they like the conclusion where the Princess doesn't marry the commoner hero after all?" Davis asked with a smile. "Of course," the equerry vouchsafed loftily, "they realized that no other conclusion would have been possible."

Great tear drops glistened on the cheeks of the Princess, as if she could gaze down the dark, tragic road before her. Her coach rolled past. So Dick Davis bade a heroine hail and farewell.

III

There was a great early morning bustle in the hotel suite as Davis arrayed himself for the coronation. Dressing the part of distinguished visitor as well as correspondent, he donned silk stockings, culottes of black satin, swallow-tailed coat, and tricorn-plumed hat. The chambermaid entered to catch sight of him standing on a stool before a tall mirror to put the finishing touches on his grandeur and was completely entranced with the spectacle. Murmuring, "Beautiful! Beautiful!" she approached to stroke his silk-stockinged calves in the excess of her admiration. Trowbridge howled with glee to watch Davis swearing and kicking to escape.

They drove to the scene, a *laissez passer* in the coachman's hat clearing the way. All was ready for any contingency. Trowbridge, stationed in the Kremlin square, had two 2000-word "leads" for the coronation story already prepared by Davis: one for an undisturbed ceremony, the other in case of a bombing. A signal from the chapel would start him in his race to the cable office with one or the other.

The correspondent in court costume vanished into the

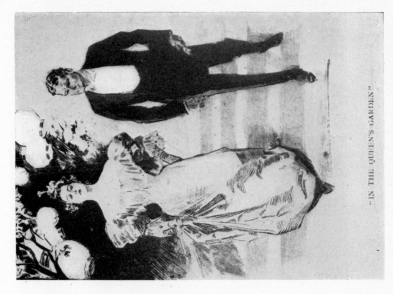

"IN THE QUEEN'S GARDEN"

R. H. D.—GIBSON'S MODEL FOR THE HERO
IN *PRINCESS ALINE* Harper & Bros., 1895.

R. H. D. IN LONDON NEAR THE TURN
OF THE CENTURY

FINLEY PETER DUNNE, R. H. D., AND JOHN FOX, JR.

R. H. D. IN HIS MARION, MASS., HOME

Chapel of the Assumption. For six solid hours he stood in that packed assemblage and scribbled off copy held on his tricorn hat, while the priests wailed and chanted amid clouds of incense and the gleam of myriad candles on cloth of gold. At last the heavy crowns pressed down on the brows of the Czar and Czarina and Davis emerged to wave his signal over the heads of the crowds to his courier. Lead Number One and all was well. Trowbridge rattled off in his carriage, raced by a rival in a hack happily nabbed by the police. He filed the copy and returned to the hotel where Davis with a towel wrapped around his head was turning out the rest of the story. He finished and applied to his sore eyes the lotion which kind ladies had scoured the town to procure for him. Back at the cable office, the chief apologized to Trowbridge that some messages of other correspondents were ahead of the rest of Davis's. That must be a mistake, Trowbridge insisted, since this story was continuous and should be sent without interruption until completed. If the chief would step out of the room for a moment, he would arrange the cable pile in proper order. It was so managed.

The Journal was out early with the story of the coronation[2] and Managing Editor Julian Ralph cabled his congratulations. One might have thought Richard Harding Davis had been

---

[2] Newspapermen blame Davis for failure to cover the Kodynka disaster which occurred a day or two after the coronation. A multitude of 500,000 townsmen and peasants had massed around the Kodynka plain to obtain free coronation souvenirs: food and vodka, sweets, memorial mugs, and painted handkerchiefs. When the signal was given, the crowds rushed the souvenir booths, swept aside the miserably inadequate police. Two thousand men, women, and children were crushed and trampled to death and many thousands more injured. In partial extenuation of Davis for missing this big story the following facts may be mentioned. He was ignorant of the language. He had covered the assignment for which he had been sent and he was not a regular Moscow correspondent. A rigid censorship suppressed all news of the disaster in order not to cast a gloom on the remainder of the festivities and that censorship was still largely unpierced by reporters when Davis left the city the day following the calamity. "I was disappointed at missing the accident at Moscow. It must have been more terrible than Johnstown," he wrote his brother.

crowned over in Russia, so large was his picture spread on Page One. *The Philadelphia Press,* also using the story, ran his name in the top deck of the head. What pleased him most was the check for $500 sent Trowbridge by *The Journal* on Davis's representation of his friend's invaluable help.

IV

Davis's article on the coronation for *Harper's* headed the book titled *A Year from a Reporter's Note Book.* What a crowded year it was! He hastened from Moscow to Budapest for the Millennial Celebration. There *Van Bibber,* that veteran clubman, discovered the finest club in the world, the Park, whose members had searched the world for the best type of ashtray and handbell, the best cook and musician. The amateur guitarist felt his heart being dragged out of him by the Gypsy orchestras, and the Beau Brummel was delighted with this country "where men change from the most blasé and correct of beings to fairy princes in tights and feathers and jewelled belts and satin coats." Sitting across the square from old Franz Joseph, majesty in white sidewhiskers, Davis watched the procession of nobles in costumes of marvellous splendor, unrolling before him a pageant of the history of Hungary.

Back over the Atlantic, black coats and boiled shirts furnished a contrast still striking after the passage of months[3]— President McKinley's inaugural ball. Davis complained of a lack of color but commended the ceremonies for their air of a family gathering where every member-citizen had a share.

One more great parade remained to be covered in the full year, 1896–97, Queen Victoria's Diamond Jubilee. The reporter

[3] In order to place the Inauguration and the Jubilee logically, this chaper departs from strict chronology. Intervening events, the Cuban Insurrection and the Graeco-Turkish War, are dealt with in the following chapter.

knew he was looking on an epochal event such as no man had seen before or was like to see again—this muster of a far-flung Empire to do homage to a woman. The Widow of Windsor passed in a crescendo of loyalty and affection and in her train the miles-long columns of her subjects and men-at-arms. Statesmen and students, bishops and rajahs, British Grenadiers, Borneo and Australian Colonials, Canadian Mounted Police, African and East and West Indian troopers, black and brown and yellow men, they massed before St. Paul's and lifted the mighty volume of their voices in the Doxology. And when at last the stately Archbishop of Canterbury turned from kissing Victoria's hand to lead three thunderous cheers for the Queen, there was at least one American who joined in with all his heart.

CHAPTER EIGHT

FORTUNE OF SOLDIERS

I

THE mighty deeds of the mining engineer of *Soldiers of Fortune*[1] and the sweet surrender of its heroine, confided to Griscom on a Honduran mule trail, were about to become public. Davis had paused in his globetrotting long enough to write the novel which proved to be his greatest financial success.

A guest of Jennings Cox, whose home overlooked the city of Santiago de Cuba[2] and was situated near the iron mines of which he was the American director, Davis wrote his story in the midst of its local color. In this perfect atmosphere, the author summoned his characters to come trooping out of his experience and play their parts in the turbulent "Republic of Olancho." *Robert Clay,* the handsome, intrepid hero drawn from John Hays Hammond, they say, but with a good deal of Davis in him too. *MacWilliams,* his right-hand man, whose original, David Kirkpatrick, was still mining in Cuba. *President Alvarez,* his rebellious generals, and his brown-skinned citizenry—all transplanted from Central America. *Madame Alvarez* with her slumberous eyes, reminiscent of the lady across the street in Paris. Gallant *Captain Stuart* of the body-guard, who might once have served as a subaltern in the Gibraltar

---

[1] Addison Mizner in the *Many Mizners* (New York, 1932) stated that he gave Davis the underlying plot, based on his own adventures in Guatemala.

[2] Mr. Cox had other qualifications as a host *par excellence*—he was the inventor of the Daiquiri cocktail. His residence is now the convent, "La Cruz."

garrison. *Reggie King,* New York clubman, a slightly more purposeful *Van Bibber.* And those attractive, contrasting sisters, *Alice* and *Hope Langham,* both owing something to a fair lady who providentially had been dining at Delmonico's one evening when Davis and Gibson were present. The gentlemen were introduced to the exquisite Irene Langhorne, one of the Virginian family of sisters whose beauty was toasted everywhere, the artist to fall in love with and win a Gibson Girl come to life, the author to become her admiring and devoted friend. She posed for both *Alice* and *Hope* when Gibson illustrated *Soldiers of Fortune,* and it was to Irene and Dana Gibson that Davis dedicated his book.

Thus were assembled the dramatis personæ for a tremendously popular novel. Davis enthusiasts were engrossed from the first chapter when *Clay* met *Alice* at a New York dinner party where a young married woman, attracting attention by telling a story in a loud voice, cautioned a débutante down the table: "Don't listen. This is for private circulation. It is not a jeune-fille story." Whereupon—*O tempora, O mores!*—the débutante "continued talking again in steady, even tones." Readers eagerly followed the characters to the tropics where their destinies developed to the exciting ending, with bluejackets landing from American warships to clinch victory and true love triumphing.

No wonder the novel, skillful admixture of sure-fire ingredients, was a huge success when the Scribners published it serially and in book form in 1897. One printing after another poured out of the presses. The regular edition was followed by a cheap edition, by subscription and foreign editions. By 1899 the book was in its 114,000th and by 1902 in its 135,000th. A computation made in 1932 showed more than 521,000 copies sold.

Great are the rewards of "popular literature" when it is truly popular. Davis received $5,000 for the serial rights to *Soldiers of Fortune*. Royalties on copies of the book sold, according to an approximate but conservative estimate by the publishers, had amounted to more than $50,000 by September, 1932. Dramatic and motion-picture rights swelled that total very considerably, for the story was a hit both on the stage and on the screen.

Nobody could deny that Richard Harding Davis was himself a soldier of fortune in the larger sense, by his own definition, "a man who in any walk of life makes his own fortune, who when he sees it coming leaps to meet it, and turns it to his advantage."[3] The mercenary-minded regarded him with new respect. Apparently it paid to be a favorite author.

Admirers saw him often at the theatre, for the stage was then scintillant with the talent of his friends—Joe Jefferson playing in *Rip Van Winkle,* Maude Adams as *Babbie* in *The Little Minister,* Ethel Barrymore in *Trelawney of the Wells.* Augustus Thomas's *Arizona* and the tuneful scores of Victor Herbert and Reginald de Koven were delighting audiences.

Davis's progress through the theatre lobbies was almost royal, opera hat on leonine head, satin-lined Inverness over broad shoulders, immaculate white gloves, "at least a figurative flower in his buttonhole." No New Yorker, they say, ever wore evening clothes better unless it were Mayor John Purroy Mitchel. The theatregoers watched him enter a box or rise from his orchestra seat to see who was present after the Continental fashion. Some branded him as conceited, not realizing that the man, although he enjoyed his fame, was curiously modest and frequently put on an iron mask to keep from blushing at the attention he attracted. Such was his shyness that Martin

[3] Davis, *Real Soldiers of Fortune.* New York, 1906.

Egan, when his companion, sometimes had to shove him down the aisle. He was in demand for chafing-dish parties after the play and the company lingered late to listen to his gifted story telling.

One evening at an informal musicale, he was asked to play his own setting of "Danny Deever." Entirely undaunted by the fact that Paderewski was present, Davis advanced confidently on the piano, but, once seated, he stared at the keys in a puzzled fashion. Finally he turned to the great Polish pianist and declared:

"I can't find the starting note. I composed my tune on a Steinway and this is a Weber. Where would the note that is under the 'W' on a Steinway be on a Weber?"

His escort made girls "as happy as full dance cards." Being shown New York by him carried the thrill of adventure. He advised a fair Bostonian that if a man ever tried to rob her on a lonely street never to hit him but instantly to jab him in the stomach with her umbrella. It seemed wonderful, thought the girl, to live so dangerously that such a thing might happen.

To live dangerously and not only in a land of make-believe. *Toujours l'audace*—that was life for Dick Davis. He had run risks as a reporter, but he knew it was true that "the good reporter, like the good soldier, must look upon war as the supreme adventure in the great drama called Life."[4]

The war correspondent was the modern knight-errant in his dreams, and for years it had been his ambition to ride by light of the red star under which he was born.

It was Mr. Hearst and *The Journal* who proffered a golden stirrup-cup and opportunity to break a lance-pencil in the Cuban jungles where patriots were struggling to throw off the yoke of Spain.

[4] Finley Peter Dunne.

II

Three thousand dollars and expenses from *The Journal* for one month's work. Six hundred more for an article in *Harper's*. More yet to come when his sketches on Cuba in war time were cashed in on again as a book. Such were the prospective rewards of war correspondence. Davis liked the idea immensely.

His worried family didn't. Their letters mentioned the matter of yellow fever mosquitos and bullets flying through the Cuban atmosphere. He never took fever, Davis soothed them, and the Spaniards were renowned as rotten shots. The family (who might have been reading over the *Three Gringos*) must disabuse themselves of the impression that he was a wild, filibustering, hot-headed young man, for he was nothing of the kind, he said.

His word for that had to be taken. He was already in Key West with Frederic Remington, the artist, and Charles Michaelson, another correspondent, making every effort to cross and join the Cuban rebels in Santa Clara Province.

One black night they tried it in a light launch, were caught in a heavy storm and nearly foundered. The crew struck, put back into port and would not venture again. Nothing better could be arranged than a safe, inglorious steamer passage to Havana, and a tour within the Spanish lines.

General Weyler gave out a pass to this new Yankee correspondent. The grim efficiency of that old soldier did not include strict censorship, although it must have been daily more apparent that the press despatches were inflaming American opinion against Spain. While Davis tried to be impartial at first, those whom he called "yellow kid journalists" made no such effort.

Correspondents lounging at the café tables of the Prado could hear the muffled volleys behind the walls of Cabañas fortress which were the knell of rebels; could imagine that the breeze from Moro Castle across the harbor bore faint echoes of the screams of poor wretches thrust through an aperture to hungry sharks in the waters below. But Davis must see for himself what he wrote. He was off for the fields one dawn to watch the execution of a Cuban patriot.

The ragged, youthful prisoner walked without a tremor to his station, a wisp of smoke curling up from the cigarette between his lips. His name? What did it matter? It was Rodriguez, if the Yankee must know. A command and the rifles of the firing squad were levelled at his back. Davis "observed with some satisfaction" that another file of Spanish troops were in the line of fire. He said nothing, but an officer also spotted it. He halted the imminent volley, walked up behind Rodriguez and laid his hand on his shoulder to move him aside. As the hand fell, Davis, all his vivid imagination centred in the doomed youth, shuddered.

"It is not pleasant to think what that shock must have been. The man had steeled himself to receive a volley of bullets in the back. He believed that in the next instant he would be in another world. He had heard the command given, and heard the click of the Mausers as the locks caught—and then, at that supreme moment, a human hand had been laid on his shoulder and a voice spoke in his ear."

Rodriguez gravely changed his position. Then at last the crack of the rifles and a limp body carried from the field after the marching column. But the eye of a great reporter, before he followed, searched out a symbol to end the requiem he would write. There in the grass where a brave man had stood and died for the freedom of Cuba his cigarette still burned, "a tiny ring of living fire."

In the once beautiful countryside, Davis saw for the first time the horrors of warfare—ruins of homes, churches, and sugar mills—starving, fever-stricken women and children corraled like cattle in the concentration camps. If that was war, he was of the opinion that "it is a senseless wicked institution made for soldiers, lovers, and correspondents for different reasons, and for no one else in the world and it is too expensive for the others to keep it going to entertain those few gentlemen."

There were spies on Davis's trail to keep him from observing too much to the detriment of Spain, but they were tracking a man who had seen William Gillette in *Secret Service* and learned that the thing to do was smoke, keep cool, and be baffling. The correspondent dodged them at Cienfuegos by buying a ticket on a steamship bound for Santiago and abandoning her at sea in an open boat to land and bluff his way through an inspection of the *trocha,* the Spanish barrier of blockhouses and barbed wire which stretched across the eastern end of the island fifty miles through the jungle.

Gallantry and sacrifice he saw but little martial panoply. War was the ghastly business his mother had said. Spain brutally crushing revolt was making a slaughter-house and a pest-hole out of this fair island. It was like a slave-holder beating in the head of his human chattels with the butt end of a whip, Davis thought, and he demanded American intervention in the name of humanity.

Every line he wrote in that cause was fuel to the flame the Hearst press was feeding so assiduously. When his despatch on the so-called "*Olivette* outrage" ticked in over the wire, the flame blazed up bright and yellow back in New York where Mr. Hearst was bent on simultaneously singeing two beards with one brand, the King of Spain's and Mr. Joseph Pulitzer's.

Sensationalism was the fiery weapon in the struggle of those two great barons of American journalism for supremacy, and circulation was the trophy.

The facts of the *Olivette* affair were: Spanish officials, annoyed by the activities of the Cuban Junta in New York, had boarded an American ship in Havana harbor; three Cuban women aboard had been searched for treasonable papers in spite of all protests.

The Journal's headlines over Davis's story exploded in the face of *The World*.

"DOES OUR FLAG PROTECT WOMEN? INDIGNITIES PRACTISED BY SPANISH OFFICIALS ON BOARD AMERICAN VESSELS. RICHARD HARDING DAVIS DESCRIBES SOME STARTLING PHASES OF CUBAN SITUATION. REFINED YOUNG WOMEN STRIPPED AND SEARCHED BY BRUTAL SPANIARDS WHILE UNDER OUR FLAG ON THE *OLIVETTE*."

Even more devastating was the half-page drawing with which Remington, who had returned to the United States some weeks before and knew nothing of the matter, illustrated the story on order. It showed a young woman, nuder than a Remington Indian, standing before several Spanish soldiers engaged in searching her clothing.

Circulation and war fever rose. There was a furious outcry in Congress and an explanation was demanded from Spain.

It was forthcoming from the man who had written the despatch the minute he saw how *The Journal* had handled it. In angry resentment he hit hard at his employer, choosing the most vulnerable spot. He took no chance of his denial lacking prominence. He sent it to the editor of *The World*. Davis's letter was gleefully headlined:

"MR. DAVIS EXPLAINS. THE *"OLIVETTE* SEARCH

OUTRAGE" IS NOW MADE CLEAR. A LETTER FROM
THE WRITER. THE PAPER HE REPRESENTED, NOT
RICHARD HARDING DAVIS, GUILTY OF DELIBER-
ATE FALSEHOOD" (etc.).

Davis declared that his despatch had never said that the
young women were searched by male police officers; that they
were in fact examined by a police matron in the privacy of a
stateroom while the officers were on deck. That point, he
honestly acknowledged, he had failed to make clear. But his
lapse did not justify the construction put on the incident, and
the idea of the women "having stood disrobed before male
examiners was wholly a product of *The Journal's* and of Mr.
Remington's imagination." *The World* clinched victory by
finding one of the Cuban women and securing from her dis-
avowal of any personal indignity. ·

There was one correspondent whom *The Journal* never
would be able to hire again, even should it so desire, at any
price.

III

Wars came thick and fast to employ the new correspondent.
Davis had left Cuba still simmering with insurrection only in
February, 1897, and now in the spring hostilities were brewing
in Greece. Two more wars would call him in the course of
the next three years.

Davis was in London when he heard that the Greeks had
thrown down the gage of battle before Turkey once more.
Would he report the conflict for *The London Times?* He
would have preferred a longer interval of peace and quiet but
the compliment of representing the "Thunderer" was too great
to be resisted. He set out via Monte Carlo, where he nearly

broke the bank, and sailed for Patras in company with Stephen
Crane of *The New York Journal.*

Others of their craft greeted them in Greece. Frederick Palmer, at the outset of a long and notable career as a war correspondent, watched Davis demanding credentials from the
aide-de-camp of Crown Prince Constantine. That resplendent
officer, whose military duties seemed to be confined to training
his bristling mustachios and writing the royal menus, snubbed
the representative of the paper which had tried to curb the
rash martial enthusiasm of his country.

"Really," he announced loftily, "we are not interested in
doing anything for *The Times."*

Davis, arguing belligerently, decided that he had been insulted and that the thing to do was challenge the fellow to a
duel.[5] The classic procedure for challenging escaped him for
the moment but no second could have made his intentions
clearer.

"Come out here in the yard," he invited, "and I'll fight you
with swords, pistols, clubs, fists, Weber-and-Field style, or any
weapon you choose."

The idea of fists—he had heard Americans and English were
skilled in such barbarous combat—was too much for the aide.
He feared for his profile and meekly made out the credentials.
Davis hurried off with John Bass, of *The Journal,* to scour the
country for a battle.

For a long time he thought he never would find one in the
welter of countermarches and strategic retreats. But he en-

---

[5] A few years before Davis had sent a half-serious challenge to E. W. Townsend, of
The Sun, author of the *Major Max* and *Chimmie Fadden* stories. In his character of
the *Major,* Townsend had expressed weariness over a Davis rhapsody on the ceremony of "Retreat" in the British Army; it was done just as well at Governors Island,
N. Y., said the *Major.* The affair blew over with a jest that the place of combat be
an empty stable and the weapons be potatoes. The men remained friendly. On another occasion, Davis named Martin Egan as his second to convey a duel challenge
to a man who he imagined had insulted Mrs. Davis. The man challenged apologized.

joyed himself hugely reciting "Maid of Athens, ere we part," treating the Greek army to wine whenever he met any of it, and lifting his voice in song with generals, mayors, and cable operators. This was a comic-opera war, he thought, with the soldiery in petticoats and gold-braided vests tending sheep with carbines; and on those early impressions he built his farce, *The Galloper,* later made into a highly successful musical comedy, *The Yankee Tourist,* in both of which Raymond Hitchcock starred.

But the scene shifted swiftly to actual warfare, and Davis with his priceless instinct for action was on the spot. When all the other correspondents left Velestinos on a wild-goose chase to Volo, Davis and Bass remained alone in the former town to be the sole press witnesses for eight hours of the infantry and artillery battle which was one of the major engagements of the war.

The sound of cannon brought them rushing out from their bivouac in the deserted home of the mayor. The Turks had crept up under cover of a hailstorm and were advancing across a broad, green plain. Into the wet trenches with the Greek infantry the two correspondents tumbled. For thirteen hours they were under heavy fire, often forced to hug the bottom of the trench, their retreat cut off by cross fire. Davis learned to know the appalling express-train blast of shells and the rustling-silk whisper of passing bullets. One shell struck three feet from him, its explosion filling his nose and mouth with dirt. A bullet drilled the soldier next to him through the chest and all along the trench men dropped. There was no going back through that cross fire sweeping behind them "the way the wind comes around the City Hall in the time of a blizzard." Davis swore, felt his hair rise as each bullet zipped past, but went on photographing and making notes.

Through all that day Davis kept his eyes on a Greek peasant boy fighting his first battle, dazed but valiant. This unknown youngster was the central figure for his story of Velestinos. The historian must paint a large canvas, but the reporter or the novelist who knows his craft selects some vivid individual drama to tell his tale most brilliantly.

Sunset made retreat possible and the filing of exclusive stories. Davis, unwounded, was stricken down by his old enemy sciatica, brought on by the dampness of the trenches. He struggled on until his right leg became useless. They hoisted him on a donkey then and got him aboard a hospital ship among the groaning wounded. By the time he reached Athens he was well enough to make love to the nurses.

The Turks were victorious and Greece was forced to buy peace with an indemnity. Back to London Davis sailed, a veteran correspondent now and measuring up to some of those requirements of the ideal war correspondent which Archibald Forbes, himself a great one, said only Julius Cæsar embodied. Davis lacked the gift of tongues but he had proved himself the possessor of these prime attributes: ability to endure, courage under fire, and an instinctive feeling for the place and day of impending combat.

The campaign ribbons had begun to form line on the left breast of his khaki tunic. Already stories were gathering about this unusual correspondent who even in campaigns knelt down and said his prayers every night and wrote his mother every day. An elegant chap who always carried a dinner coat in his field kit. A reporter whose news sense seemed to be coupled with amazing luck; who strove strenuously to get a "beat" yet generously praised the feats of others. They quoted his favorite maxims such as "He travels quickest who travels alone." Or his own saying: Always stick to the end of a cable. Somebody will always come along to you with a story. And—See war through human beings, not tactics.

Peace gave him a breathing spell of only a year. He spent most of it in London, enjoying life to the utmost with friends of the nobility, the diplomatic set, and the arts. It was Jubilee Year and London was gay. Davis was in the thick of things. Giving luncheons at the Savoy for Ambassador John Hay, the Asquiths, and Anthony Hope. Playing the villain at a copyright performance of *The Little Minister,* with Barrie in a low-comedy part, Mrs. Barrie as the gypsy, Cyril Maude the hero, and Charles Frohman the audience. Carrying Christmas packages to sick children in the London Hospital. Getting lost for hours in a fog with Ethel Barrymore[6] and finding sanctuary in a home where her calling him "Duke" together with his fur coat and the orders on his chest caused a furor, much to his delight. Jolly dinners with Justin Huntley McCarthy and his wife Cissie Loftus, Sam Sothern, Marie Tempest, Seymour Hicks, Forbes-Robertson, and the Ben Websters. Davis complained humorously of the red-and-yellow tulips on the table; unless all signs failed, such Spanish colors would shortly be an unpatriotic decoration where an American was present.

The portents materialized. A flash of flame and a roar and the water of Havana harbor closed over the *Maine.* War with Spain it was. This onslaught of vigor on decadence did not bear the look of a fair fight, but Davis had witnessed suffering and misery in Cuba. With those memories still fresh he was not one to worry over pros and cons. The armed forces of his own country were advancing to end oppression. That was enough. He would go with them.

There was competition for his services as war correspondent

---

[6] What a setting for mystery and murder a London fog might be, Davis reflected, and wrote his story, *In the Fog.*

AT THE SAVOY

A Gibson-Davis gentleman dines with his lady in London.

now. *The London Times, Scribner's Magazine,* and James Gordon Bennett's *New York Herald* secured them. His old paper, *The Sun,* printed an apparently insouciant quatrain:

> O, sweetly Dickey pens the tale,
> And how he loves to pen it,
> And sends it off by wire or mail
> To Jimmy Gordon Bennett.

CHAPTER NINE

SPANISH WAR SCAREHEADS

I

"WHERE's Richard Harding Davis?" demanded *Mr. Dooley,*[1] surveying various strategical dispositions for the war with Spain. "On th' bridge iv the *New York?* Tur-rn th' bridge."

Although the bridge of Admiral Sampson's flagship refused to revolve like a turntable span across a river in accordance with the *Dooley* suggestion, it afforded a grandstand view of the initial hostilities. Davis in establishing himself at that vantage point on the strength of a long wire from Assistant Secretary of the Navy Theodore Roosevelt had displayed his usual journalistic enterprise.

He made friends with and praised all hands from Sampson to the black gang and enjoyed himself thoroughly. Blockading Havana seemed to him like a cruise on a luxurious yacht minus the boredom. Now and then the *New York* chased a steamer and fired a shot across her bow, with the band playing Wagner by way of competition with the cannonading. This was, he wrote home, a merry war; that was the trouble with it. Only once did the battleship clear for action to bombard the shore batteries of Matanzas. Their feeble reply could not compare to the baptism of fire the Turks had given Davis at Velestinos. This sort of naval war correspondence struck him as too much "like reporting the burning of the Waldorf Astoria from Brooklyn Bridge." There seemed little prospect of close-up action while the Navy chased Cervera, the phantom Flying Span-

[1] F. P. Dunne. *Mr. Dooley in Peace and War.* Boston, 1890.

iard whose fancied gunfire was strewing the seaboard from Maine to Florida with nervous wrecks. Better go ashore and join the Army mobilizing at Tampa.

Never was nor will be again such a field day and mob scene of war correspondents as the Spanish War inaugurated at Tampa. Scores flocked in every day until hundreds were present. Almost every newspaper office in the land had seethed with intrigues for the prized post of "our special at the front." Star reporters and artists were in great demand. Rank amateurs and outsiders offered their services, and soldiers and sailors expressed their willingness to do a bit of war correspondence on the side. "Sob sisters" sobbed to go and several determined newspaperwomen captured the assignment and journeyed Florida-wards; the prettier ladies of the press volunteered to enter Havana in disguise and obtain coveted interviews. The very copy boys mentioned that they were especially qualified for carrying messages under fire. An agricultural paper despatched a representative toward the field of combat, and not a few religious weeklies sent observers to record the heathen goings-on of Mars.

The press strove to mask its lack of martial experience by dressing the part. "You never saw such a collection of boots and pith helmets and field glasses in your life," wrote plump, little Acton Davies, a dramatic critic bound for the theatre of war. "It is like a rehearsal for a military melodrama. . . . We are all acting parts for *The Light That Failed.*" Kipling, however, had declined to play a rôle in his own story, although several American papers cabled him invitations to cover the war at his own price. After all, British, not American, imperialism was his forte.

In the mass of reporters, artists, and photographers the veterans who had seen some campaigning or knew a canteen from a condiment can stood out. Davis, of course; his friend Stephen Bonsal, with daring exploits in the Balkans and Africa to his credit; that frail genius, Stephen Crane; Sylvester Scovel, Ralph Paine, Caspar Whitney, James Creelman; big genial Frederic Remington, former Yale football player, H. C. Christy, and Rufus Zogbaum, those fine delineators of soldiers; Jimmy Hare, the indomitable photographer, and others comprising about a score in all. These would head the one hundred or so who finally managed to crowd into Cuba, outnumbering badly needed army surgeons.

The papers served by this journalistic multitude were already in action, though nothing else was. Special copy desks were organized to deal with warfare (as if the regular ones could not have taken it in their stride!). Washington staffs were doubled and trebled. Costs raced with circulation. As high as $500 was offered for a good action photograph. One newspaper employed a band and a lightning artist to attract the crowds to its bulletin board. Proprietors were groaning at copious use of the wires from Florida at a press rate of five cents a word, still happily ignorant of cable tolls which would mount to three dollars and twenty-five cents a word. Enormously expensive despatch boats—one newspaper boasted five—were dashing about the Caribbean. The still unprosperous *New York Times* could not afford one. Expense accounts were filibustered through the treasurers' offices. Scareheads were expanding across papers to their latitudinal limits and could only grow taller and blacker. Printing and distribution speeded up tremendously, and the remarkable record of forty editions in one day was set. One extra after another spilled out of the presses and newsboys were chronically hoarse and weary from the weight of coins in their pockets.

Much of this flood of printer's ink derived from interviews

with Dame Rumor by correspondents who had been marooned two months in Key West before transferring to Tampa. They were ready to cede Florida back to Spain, as they rocked through tedious hours on the hotel porch. "A rocking-chair campaign," Davis called it, donned blue double-breasted coat, white ducks, and natty straw hat, and wished there were some pretty girls around the place.

In a fever of impatience he watched the troops filtering slowly in, the Regulars desperately few, the Volunteers and Militia desperately green but disdaining the services of any stiff West Pointers. Officers, veterans of the Civil War, looked worried. Others, whose thirty years' service had never given them a glimpse of a brigade, looked startled at the sight of so many soldiers in one place. Still no transport sailed, for Cervera remained unbottled. Warriors who, according to post-war songs, had sung "Good-bye, Dolly Gray" had plenty of time to write it again or mail another farewell to that "Bluebell" of whom by now they had expected to be dreaming " 'mid shot and shell." The blaring bands prophesied "There'll Be a Hot Time in the Old Town Tonight." There was, but the heat was only the weather and the old town just Tampa, where profiteers sold water.

Davis was diverted by a serious problem of his own. President McKinley, offering him a captaincy in the army, plunged him into that dilemma which other war correspondents have faced with turmoil of soul. Should he accept or refuse? He could not bear to think of his courage or patriotism being questioned. The love of soldiering was in his blood. Yet there was loyalty to his contracts to be considered, and "swords are not the only weapon in the world. Something may be done with a pen."[2] Anxiously he sought the advice of his newspaper and

[2] Winston Spencer Churchill.

army friends. It was given for refusal and he took it, unconvinced that he was not making a mistake he always would regret.

Gossips on the hotel porch buzzed waspishly. So did a jaundiced group of gentlemen of the press whom Stephen Crane joined at the bar. Crane listened and asked quietly: "Did any of you Indians try to enlist?" There was silence.

Around Tampa the white tents sprouted more thickly. General Miles arrived, as *Mr. Dooley* noted, "fully prepared f'r th' bloody wurruk iv war. He had his entire fam'ly with him, and r-rode recklessly into camp, mounted on a superb specyal ca-ar."

Davis rather neglected the Commander-in-Chief. Lesser but more glamorous ranks claimed his attention. Colonel Leonard Wood, Lieutenant-Colonel Theodore Roosevelt, and their unique outfit of clubmen, cowboys, and athletes—the Rough Riders—had sprung to arms and Tampa. There, the reporter's practised eye recognized, was his story.

II

The Rough Riders at once took up "that strategic position on the front pages from which they would never afterward be dislodged."[3] It was Davis, more than any of the correspondents, who prepared it for them. From the viewpoint of the historian the space he lavished on them was anything but just and impartial, and Gibson's satiric thrust would strike home when he drew a soldier bitterly explaining to a girl: "No, I ain't no hero. I'm a Regular." But Davis was a newspaperman and the gods proffered him first-class copy on a silver platter in these Volunteers who were a society page, a financial column, a sports section, and a Wild West show, all rolled

3 Walter Millis. *The Martial Spirit*. New York and Boston, 1931.

into one and coming under the head of war news. How could he resist?

Dashing, full of *esprit de corps,* ready to charge the foe with or without orders, the Rough Riders were the antithesis of the tradition-bound, dull-if-dependable Regulars. They were Davis's idea of soldiers. They eased his mind of forebodings for the fate of other volunteer regiments, so inadequately trained, rawly officered, miserably armed, equipped, and rationed. Only the fear that he would be giving aid and comfort to the enemy had restrained him from revelations in print which would start "the hell of an outcry from the families of the boys who have volunteered." He and most of the other correspondents agreed that it was no time to emphasize shortcomings.

Observers could turn with vast relief to the Rough Riders whose encampment was soldierly, who had abandoned the heavy army blue for khaki fatigue uniforms, and whose rifles were the best. The army medico and veteran Indian campaigner, Leonard Wood, whose attendance on invalid Mrs. McKinley had won him his coveted line command, had seen to the welfare of his men. Aiding and abetting him was his lieutenant-colonel, the ex-Assistant Secretary of the Navy to whom military channels were no more than elementary navigation.

Davis contemplated Theodore Roosevelt in his new incarnation and knew him for what he was—God's gift to newspapermen. T. R. mentally saluted the power of the press as embodied in R. H. D. There their wagons stalled unhitched. The stars were balky.

For these two positive characters were acquaintances, not friends. Once when Roosevelt was New York City's police commissioner, they had met in front of Delmonico's and fallen into an argument that reached the glaring and finger-shaking stage. Davis had cast defiance in the Rooseveltian teeth and the commissioner had threatened "exposure." The short and ugly word was close to being passed.

Anybody who could write a story like *Gallegher* had his points, in Roosevelt's opinion, but any American who so strongly defended the English was suspect. The apostle of the strenuous life, called dude, lah-de-dah, and even "Oscar Wilde" in his New York Assembly days by his hard-boiled political foes, was prejudiced against the dressy Mr. Davis. Under fire the fellow might shrink into the molycoddle class and none such would be tolerated with the Rough Riders.

As for Davis, he was doubtful if the Lieutenant-Colonel's sound and fury signified anything. The man was decidedly more militant than military. Any officer who dined in public with two of his sergeants, whatever their social connections, must lack the stamp of approval of one noted war correspondent. Sparks of antagonism flew. The Rough Riders were within an ace of being denied, by order of their second in command, the future services of their most talented press agent.

III

The lost and found department of the U. S. Navy reported Cervera's little fleet surprisingly located at anchorage in Santiago harbor. To keep it there a watchful squadron patrolled outside, and Lieutenant Hobson was about to attempt to make assurance doubly sure by sinking the *Merrimac* in the channel. Since the coast now seemed clear for American sailings, long delayed orders for embarkation of the Army were issued at last. As Davis had told General Miles, it was high time.

The troops rushed for transports, Roosevelt and his men seizing another regiment's ship, swarming over the side and standing by to repel boarders in the best buccaneer manner. Davis, still uncertain whether or not the Rough Riders would be relegated to the background, cautiously took passage on the *Segurança* which carried General Shafter and his headquarters. There he and the other first-string correspondents favored with berths were at the fountain-head of news. After due deliberation, the Navy shepherded its straggling convoy out to sea.

When the coast of Cuba loomed up familiarly to Davis's eager gaze, a fellow scribe gratifyingly suggested that a copy of *Soldiers of Fortune* be given every member of the Fifth Army Corps.

"I suppose you mean that the original scenes of the story were taken from this section of the country," responded the glowing author.

So they were and accurately. Yonder at Daiquirí jutted out *MacWilliams's* iron pier on which troops would soon land and toward Santiago rose other landmarks in the tale. Davis was about to campaign in one of his own fiction settings.

But solid fact confronted him less engagingly in the 300-pound person of General William R. Shafter. Davis had suffered in spirit with every look at the commander of the expedition, profuse, profane, and perspiring in a blue woollen uniform topped by a white pith helmet. This fat man, aging and in ill health, had won the Medal of Honor in the Civil War, but now the paladin seemed to be lost in poundage. He simply could not fit a romanticist's conception of a general. Shafter would never seize standard and sabre, leap ashore on Cuban soil at the head of his troops and lead a charge up the steep hill to storm the blockhouse on its top. Such deeds of derring-do would be contrary to the duty of a modern major-general, but he might at least, longed Davis, have looked capable of them.

As the transports hovered cautiously off Daiquirí and the guns of the Navy thundered away at the landscape, commander and correspondents paced the promenade deck of the *Segurança*. Colonel E. J. McClernand, Shafter's adjutant-general, heard Davis address his chief:

"General, I see that the order for disembarkation directs that none but fighting men be allowed in the boats of the first landing party. This will keep reporters back."

Shafter indicated how the hill dominated the beach. If the Spaniards opposed the landing, he would need every American rifle he could rush ashore to make it good. But Davis, who, McClernand thought, did not realize the danger, persisted and tried another tack which had worked in Moscow. He was not an ordinary reporter, he informed the commander, but a descriptive writer and as such should go in Boat Number One.

The General, with the weight of an army on his shoulders, exploded in the face of that necessary evil, the press.

"I don't care a damn what you are," he swore. "I'll treat all of you alike."

"Mr. Davis," wrote McClernand," was offended by the abruptness of the reply and never afterwards, so far as I know, said a kind word about General Shafter."[4]

Launches with strings of small boats were chugging alongside the transports. Davis, who must have realized in his heart the justice of the rebuke he had received, went below to pre-

[4] From Colonel McClernand's contribution to *The Santiago Campaign* published by the Society of the Army of Santiago de Cuba. Richmond, 1927. McClernand thought that Davis's friends sympathized with him and the fact seriously colored their reports of operations. That may be seriously doubted; yet tact with the press would have been worth the trouble. Burr McIntosh remarked that Davis looked at Roosevelt through the right end of his glasses and at Shafter through the wrong end. Davis had no right to expect a personal reconnaisance by the Commanding General at San Juan. But he was too honest to slander through a grudge and historians confirm his estimate that the job was too big for Shafter's capabilities.

pare for the landing. There seemed to be no hurry now and he was still accoutring himself when a boat containing the correspondents pushed off. They stared back as their tardy confrère hailed them from the deck. There he stood in full regalia—felt hat with white puggaree, high, white, composition collar, blue coat, trousers tucked in field boots, field glasses slung.

"We've got to go back for Dick Davis," said Bonsal. The others grinned. They all liked Davis. The boat put back for him.

Spanish inertia and American luck combined that day to save a slaughter. The Spaniards had withdrawn from their position on the heights and no hail of bullets swept the exposed beach. Soldiers weary of the sea tumbled out of the boats onto firm land in a holiday spirit. Davis had two drownings to report as the only casualties.

He joined Roosevelt and his regiment, ashore early as a result of having commandeered somebody else's transportation as usual. The ponderous Shafter might land in due course and mount a form-fitting phaeton or a mule inspiring universal sympathy. One correspondent would not wait to attend him. Davis was bound for the front and action, and all doubt that the Rough Riders would take the most direct route had disappeared.

His instinct proved its sureness. There was a little matter of orders to the effect that General Lawton and his brigade of Regular infantry, already at Siboney, would move in advance. Fighting Joe Wheeler, the little gray-bearded ex-Confederate who was the ranking general ashore, was of another mind. His cavalry division was dismounted but infantry had never scouted ahead of cavalrymen in '61-65. Wheeler, as Davis diplomatically put it, "disarranged" Shafter's original order. Past the unsuspecting Lawton's flank on the morning of June 24 slipped the Rough Riders, with Young's cavalry brigade on a parallel route, hiking toward the trail fork called Las Guasimas.

IV

The June sun smote down and its heat steamed back up from the rich Cuban loam. Marching men sweltered under full pack. Wood at the head of his regiment could hear Davis behind him expatiating on flora and fauna to Roosevelt. The latter, new to the tropics, listened with interest and never an accusation of nature faking.

Ahead the trail plunged into the deceptive shadows of jungle growth. Wood, old campaigner, halted and deployed his men. Slowly they moved forward through the high grass, breaking the barriers of thick creeper vines with blows of their carbines.

Then in the direction of the squad scouting as "point" in advance of Capron's troop abruptly crashed a heavy fusillade.[5]

Davis's field glasses snapped up to his eyes scanning a hill across the valley. A group of Spaniards, unmistakable in cockaded sombreros, leaped into his vision. He showed them to Roosevelt and ran to direct the fire of six sharpshooters on them. A volley answered, wounding and killing men by his side. He crawled back to cover dragging one of the wounded.

Mauser bullets from unseen riflemen swept over him. A white-faced officer fled by to the rear. Davis rose, unhit but staggering, for sciatica had begun to rack one leg agonizingly. He limped forward barely managing to get over the rough

[5] Davis declared that the Rough Riders were caught "in a clear case of ambush" but reversed himself later. Calling it caught in ambush still ruffles Rough Riders. They make the fair distinction that the regiment had been deployed and that the advance troop had pushed a point ahead through the jungle for the purpose of developing the enemy resistance and guarding against surprise of the main body.

LIEUT.-COLONEL ROOSEVELT AND R. H. D. AT TAMPA, FLA.,
AT THE BEGINNING OF THE SPANISH WAR

IN CUBA. THE SPANISH WAR

A war council at General Wheeler's headquarters. Gen. Wheeler and Col. Roosevelt side by side in centre. Gen. Wood in white shirt sitting on ground. R. H. D. seated next to Col. Roosevelt

ground. Past him toward the dressing station strode the Rough Rider's surgeon, a one-time Princeton football star, carrying over his sturdy shoulders a trooper who had been an opponent of the gridiron. The reporter sinking down by the side of a winded Rough Rider heard himself greeted: "I met you at Harvard in the racquet court." Through the trees a guidon fluttered like a college pennant. Cheering as if from a distant grandstand echoed from the right where the Regulars were in action. The scene took on an unreal aspect. It was like some deadly contest on an athletic field.[6]

Khaki-clad figures, crumpled and still in the lush grass, brought the correspondent to a sudden halt. He recognized the body of gallant Captain Capron. "Death had given him a great dignity and nobleness." Near lay a dead sergeant, the young New York clubman, Hamilton Fish. "His very attitude was one of attack, his fists were clenched, his jaw set, and his eyes, which were still human, fixed with resolve."

Davis, bending down to save a keepsake for the soldier's family, found his watch bearing the motto, "God gives." God could not have given a nobler end than this, he thought—"to die in the forefront of the first fight of the war, quickly, painlessly, with a bullet through the heart, with his regiment behind him, and facing the enemies of his country."

Yonder through the foliage Roosevelt was shouting for a charge. Davis straightened up, the exaltation of battle upon him. He hobbled forward under a shower of bullet-clipped leaves, caught up a carbine dropped by a wounded man, and joined some of Capron's troop under command of a second lieutenant. Flame spurted toward them from a tin shack where the Spanish rearguard was making a stand.

---

[6] The paragraphers might have paraphrased the Iron Duke with a line to the effect that the battle of Las Guasimas was won on the playing-fields of the "Big Three."

The correspondent, a non-combatant by the rules of war, could only remember that friends with whom he had played "football and all that sort of thing" were tackling the foe. What if he had refused a captaincy? He was an American and he had to help. He heard himself ordering the lieutenant and his men to charge. Stumbling ahead with their rush, he fired, loaded, and emptied his carbine again.

Rough Riders and Regulars were converging on Las Guasimas. The Spaniards climbing out of their trenches were in full retreat. Fighting Joe, sloughing off thirty-five years in his excitement, waved his troops on to victory with an exultant Rebel yell: "Come on, boys. We've got the damn Yankees on the run!" As the fleeing foe vanished in the jungle and the firing died down, Davis suddenly recalled his civilian status. He found stretcherbearers for plucky Edward Marshall of *The Journal*,[7] desperately wounded but still scribbling away on his story.

Las Guasimas was a milestone passed on the road to Santiago. It was only a skirmish but valor is not measured by the magnitude of its setting. Davis wrote its story simply, movingly. Back home householders answered the cries of the newsboys and crowds poured out of the theatres to seize the extras and forget the stage's fantasy for reality's drama on a distant island. On a vine-clad porch in Pennsylvania a boy read it to his best girl, read unashamed of the tears in his eyes as he seemed to hear the whirr of Mauser bullets and see valiant men in khaki pitching forward into the long grass.

And the writer of the despatch was witnessing a dazzling and gratifying spectacle now, the Roosevelt grin of friendship; was listening to the citation that no one in the regiment had been more help or shown more courage than the correspond-

---

[7] Marshall recovered and lived until 1933.

ent who had gone into the firing line and taken command like an officer. He could have a commission for the asking and in any event must consider himself hereafter an honorary member of the Rough Riders.

That honor and the Colonel's heart-winning accolade of "Bully!" would suffice. Davis having proved himself a fighting man was content to stick to his job and to Roosevelt, promoted to command the regiment vice Wood "kicked upstairs" to a brigadier-generalcy. T. R., good copy, and plenty of excitement would never be far apart. Davis stood by. Thus *Mr. Dooley,* putting words in the Rooseveltian mouth, was shortly able to announce:

"At this time it became apparint that I was handicapped be th' presentce of th' Army an' Navy. A number of days was spent by me in reconnoitring, attended only by me brave an' fluent body guard, Richard Harding Davis."

V

Squat Spanish blockhouses crowned the crests of the sentinel hills which screened Santiago and the sea. Machine gun and artillery emplacements, deep trenches, and cat's-cradles of barbed wire showed in the lenses of Davis's field glasses—ominous signs that a new era of warfare had dawned. Against these, light brigades would charge no more with flashing sabres and thundering hooves. It was well that the American cavalry continued horseless, though Remington was disgustedly threatening to go home and paint fruit. Galloping batteries going into action in the open were doomed.[8]

The storming of San Juan Hill and El Caney gave promise

---

[8] Grimes's Battery tried it on the San Juan crest, using black powder. Spanish fire forced speedy withdrawal.

of being a bloody business. Davis, alive to the hazards and
blunders of the campaign, saw little prospect of a "glory
story." Delay in attacking had given the Spaniards six days'
grace to strengthen their defenses. Cannon to blast a path for
the assault were still in Tampa. Nobody was heeding General
Chaffee's recommendation that new trails be cut through the
tangled growth of the jungle to avoid the two on which the
Spanish guns surely were laid.

Dawn, July 1. Prelude to battle. American infantry, artillery, ammunition pack mules, and ambulances jamming into
the bottle-neck of a single narrow trail. Dark blue uniforms,
black powder, a balloon—invitations to slaughter. Crashing
volleys from the Mausers, accepting. Lead spattering down
like a slanting rainfall as the Spanish sharp-shooters opened
fire from their leafy ambushes in the trees. Chaos and the
bottleneck running red.

Davis pushed into it. In the sharp shadows and sunlight,
scenes unreeled like a swiftly run film, now clear, now blurred
with smoke. A flash of a small boy, stowaway from the transport, riding grandly happy, with the teamster of an ammunition wagon—digging out with his knife a Spanish bullet which
just had thudded into the wagon, to prove he had been under
fire. A glimpse of a sergeant and his brother using an ax to pry
out a shell stuck in the breech of a dynamite gun. The balloon
bobbing up, drawing fire, learning nothing, and ducking down
in silly futility. Roosevelt roaring for the right of way. Dead
men in the bushes and wounded men on the banks of the
stream waiting patiently for first aid.

Davis halted to put a tourniquet on an unconscious soldier
who was bleeding to death. He grasped the feet of a Rough
Rider to help a comrade carry him to the dressing station. The
man at the head collapsed, shot through the chest by a sharp-

shooter in a tree, shot at again as he lay on the ground. The correspondent managed to drag them both under cover.

At last the human cork burst from the bottleneck, and Davis from the Bloody Bend watched figures in blue and khaki creep up the slopes of San Juan and Kettle Hills. In spite of the stuttering machine guns and the evil whistling of shrapnel balls, charges, trumpet calls, streaming banners, and desperate courage still survived. Davis with the soul of a *preux chevalier* could still chronicle the Battle of San Juan Hill in the brave style of Froissart or Joinville.

The slow tide of the dogged advance seemed more wonderful to him than a swinging charge. Breathlessly he followed the snow-white head of General Hawkins leading the Regulars and the flutter of Roosevelt's blue polka-dot bandana. Some of the figures fell and lay still. The rest pressed onward, bending forward as they climbed, rifles at the port. The figures massed, rushed the blockhouses.

"They were very noble; they cared nothing for their lives!" Thus Froissart chronicling a charge of long ago. And Davis, staring up at the last stirring scene on the crest, marshalled similarly glowing words to record it.

"They drove the yellow silk flag of the cavalry and the Stars and Stripes of their country into the soft earth of the trenches, and then sank down and looked back at the road they had climbed and swung their hats in the air. And from far overhead, from these few figures perched on the Spanish rifle pits, with their flags planted among the empty cartridges of the enemy, and overlooking the walls of Santiago, came, faintly, the sound of a tired, broken cheer."

The correspondent lowered his glasses. Well, he had remembered to report, not to charge, this time. He climbed the slope to the trenches. That was where the news was.

VI

The valley before Santiago spread out in a panorama blazing with Spanish rifle fire sweeping the crest. A bullet thwacked into the parapet near Davis. "That hit you?" he asked the soldier by his side. The man grunted no, glanced sidewise and swore with surprise. Davis had not taken his glasses from his eyes. Like his own character, *Chesterton,* the war correspondent, he seemed to bear a charmed life. They carried back James Creelman, shot through the shoulder in the charge, but Davis was vulnerable only to sciatica. Now it dropped him again as if he had been shot. Stephen Crane and Jimmy Hare ran to help him as he lay writhing on the ground just behind the crest. He grinned up at them and waved them away, telling them they made too big a target and pulling himself back to the rifle pits. "Who's your friend?" Hare asked and Crane introduced him. "Gosh!" the little photographer whispered. "They told me he was a four-flusher."

Crane wandered off and stood outlined on the hill like a semaphore obliviously courting death or one of his own red badges of courage.

"Get down," General Wood shouted. "You're drawing fire on my men."

Crane only moved aside. Davis, who knew his hatred of pose, called to him: "You're not impressing any one by doing that, Crane."

Crane blushed and hastily crouched down and Davis crawling over laughed: "I knew that would fetch you." "Oh, so that was it," said Crane.

But he was soon up again, fascinated with the smoke and flame running along the line of Spanish entrenchments in the valley. Davis, sighing resignedly, climbed to his feet, seized him by the shoulders and forced him to the ground. As he did so, a bullet knocked off his hat and another chipped the leather case of his field glasses.

For two days the rifle pits were held. Davis considered it a precarious position, cabled *The Herald* as much and was accused of treason by the opposition press. But meanwhile Cervera had steamed out to meet his fate, and a procession of flags of truce heralded the surrender of Santiago. Davis, covering the brief and tidy conquest of Porto Rico, put his third war behind him.

VII

He came home to the celebration of victory, home to meet not only praise but considerable sarcastic criticism of what he had written and was writing. He had seen many men die who need not have been sacrificed and he would no longer keep silent. Some day his country would fight another war and she must not bungle again so frequently and so tragically, must not face it so pitifully unprepared for command, in training and supply. He raked the authorities over the coals for every inefficiency from black powder to lack of tobacco for the troops and of such supplements to their rations of hardtack and bacon as canned tomatoes.

Editorial writers, paragraphers, and reviewers of the opposition hooted at him for an infantile and ignorant "military expert" with no more knowledge of warfare than he might have obtained from reading Cæsar or covering a football game. No tomatoes for our soldiers? No *pâté de fois gras?* No baths? they chortled. What hardships! Now the cruel war was over, they urged that Mr. Davis go back to England to

renew his lessons in ease of social behavior to duchesses or sit
to Mr. Gibson for more pictures if he doubted there were
enough already.

It hurt but what did it matter if he had done his duty, as he
saw it, in speaking out? Thousands who had seen the war
through his eyes remembered his despatches with admiration,
and he would never lack a paper to send him to any future
conflict he chose to cover. His book, *The Cuban and Porto
Rican Campaigns,* was popular, and he was at work on two
short stories: *The Derelict,*[9] that yarn of a correspondent and
Cervera's dash to sea, and *On the Fever Ship,* a masterly depic-
tion of a returning soldier's delirium.

Most welcome of all was the respect of the men with whom
he had been under fire. There was the testimony of a Regular
officer: "I thought that Davis was a parader, until I bunked,
faced fire and ate beans out of the same can with him in
Cuba." Now I want to hear nothing against him in my presence. And there was Roosevelt—higher on the ladder of the
White House because of the aid of the Davis pen as a rung—to
fight the war over with, and the Rough Riders who counted
their correspondent as one of themselves. They would not forget
the man who had charged with them, carried their wounded,

[9] Of this story Franklin Clarkin wrote for the author of this biography the following fine analysis:

Some of Davis's fellow-correspondents in Cuba were critical of *The Derelict.*
They found in it "misleading allusions," "inexact references to persons," not allow-
ing for the circumstance that it was fiction and that, while it integrated and general-
ized to present a total picture, it did not pretend to be history. His characters in the
tale are composites. One recalls that there was on the blockades of Havana and
Santiago and the push through the Siboney chaparral a correspondent who was
brilliant, one who drank hard, one who was caddish, one who saw the battle of
Santiago and wrote the earliest description and one who was sunstruck in a land
battle and whose account had to be written from his lips by a comrade who signed
and got credit for it, while the sun-smitten man received a harsh cablegram from his
office for a supposed dereliction that had been really heroic devotion to duty. The
true Harding Davis, the expression of a gentlemanliness of heart which one remembers as his characteristic, came out in the climax where the derelict sees the man he
had made being dined and celebrated and would not spoil the party.

and sat beside stretchers in the hospital tents to write letters home for them.

In New York and Marion girls flocked about him, eager girls in flaring white skirts, trim shirtwaists, stocks and straw sailor hats. They clamored for the story of the war with Spain. No one but Richard Harding Davis would do to describe it— one always thought of the two together. He told them and he could tell a story marvellously. The fair audiences hearkened to the handsome, sunburned young bachelor and were thrilled, martially and romantically. It was a great life.

CHAPTER TEN

GALLEGHER—ENGLISH EDITION

I

A PRETTY girl once confessed to a curious critic that she liked books by Richard Harding Davis "because I want to know his men and because I would love to be like his girls."

It was a high compliment from a personal as well as a literary viewpoint, since Davis's fiction was so frequently autobiographical. His heroes were Dick Davis dramatized a trifle more than in life. His heroines were ideals out of his dreams. If mortal maidens were striving to materialize *Hope Langham* out of *Soldiers of Fortune, Edith Morris* from *Princess Aline, Patty Carson* from *The King's Jackal,* and *Helen Cabot* and *Marion Cavendish* of *The Lion and the Unicorn,* proud, courageous, high-spirited, lovable Gibson Girls, one and all,—if such were the models for fair young readers, what more could a bachelor author ask in this vale of chance and compromise?

As for those men of his whom girls would like to know: *Robert Clay, Morton Carleton, Archie Gordon,* and the rest, it was vain for an acrimonious satirist to put them on trial and challenge:

"Do you believe that a man can embrace a girl with one arm, hold a mob in check with the other, and start in motion with both feet simultaneously two boulders to crush a revolutionary army at the foot of the mountains?"[1]

"Well, pretty nearly," would have been the trusting and

[1] From *The Literary Guillotine.* New York and London, 1903. Anonymous.

tremulous answer of the ladies of the jury. For men were men in Davis's pages and his own adventures seemed to emulate the feats of his stalwarts.

Women sought to capture him in one way or another. There was an intense Russian charmer for one. "She still pursues me," he wrote home lightly but with an undercurrent of alarm. "As she has no sense of humor and takes everything seriously, she frightens me. I am afraid she will move in any moment. She has asked me to spend the summer with her at Paris and Monte Carlo, and at her country place in Norfolk, and bombards me with invitations to suppers and things in the meantime. She has just sent me a picture of herself two feet by three, with writing all over it and at any moment, I expect her to ring the bell and order her trunks taken upstairs."

She might as well have tried to seduce Sir Galahad who, however, would have enjoyed the process less and avoided her less dexterously.

And there was the actress whose often proven lures failed so flatly to entangle him in a *liaison* that she was moved to demand of a friend if there was anything the matter with that fellow Davis.

Advances more maidenly were as futile. For Davis was at bottom one of the shyest of men. He had in his heart taken chivalrous and knightly vows and he kept them. Girls who knew him best recognized that he was no Don Juan. An accomplished cavalier and squire of dames he was, with a splendid "line." Now and then he fell desperately in love or thought he had. Either through his own changes of heart or declinations by the fair ladies to whom it was offered, these affairs progressed no farther than courtship. He reverted to marrying off dozens of characters in novels and short stories, while he personally looked before he leaped.

"The trouble with me is that I care too much to make Platonic friendship possible, and I don't care enough to marry any particular woman," he made *Carleton* remark in *Princess Aline*. "That is, of course, supposing that any particular woman would be so little particular as to be willing to marry me. How embarrassing it would be now, if, when you were turning away from the chancel after the ceremony, you should look at one of the bridesmaids and see the woman whom you really should have married! How distressing that would be! You couldn't very well stop and say: 'I am very sorry, my dear, but it seems I have made a mistake. That young woman on the right has a most interesting and beautiful face. I am very much afraid that she is the one.' It would be too late then; while now, in my free state, I can continue my search without any sense of responsibility."

Yes, you might so easily pick the wrong girl. *Clay* had been in love with *Alice Langham* before he saw the error of his ways and her sister *Hope*. *Alice,* as *MacWilliams* had told him, was too careful. She had no illusions and no sense of humor and a woman with such deficiencies was bound to become monotonous. "You can't teach her anything, you can't imagine yourself telling her anything she doesn't know. The things we think are important don't reach her at all. They're not in her line, and in everything else she knows more than we could guess at."

Marriage certainly was a matter for caution, an affair of "awful joys and responsibilities."

"A young man runs two chances of marrying the wrong woman," mused *Stuart* in *Miss Delamar's Understudy*. "He marries her because she is beautiful and because he persuades himself that every other lovable attribute must be associated with such beauty, or because she is in love with him. In this

THE GREATEST GAME IN THE WORLD—*HIS MOVE*
A drawing by C. D. Gibson with Davis in mind.

THE WEAKER SEX. VII

He takes a hand at bridge and has difficulty in keeping his mind on the game, with the
result that he repeatedly trumps his partner's tricks. A drawing by C. D. Gibson
in which he again made use of his friend, Davis.

latter case, she gives certain values to what he thinks and to what he says which no other woman gives, and so he observes to himself, 'This is the woman who best understands *me.'*

"You can reverse this and say that the young woman runs the same risks, but as men are seldom beautiful, the first danger is eliminated. Women still marry men, however, because they are loved by them, and in time the woman grows to depend upon his love and need it, and so she consents to marry the man for no other reason than because he cares for her."

Stuart in the story anticipates the married state by sitting alone in his apartment and conversing with a large photograph of his sweetheart. The lady in the picture seems to betray distressing ignorance of such fascinating subjects as geography and rifles. The conversation lags. The picture doesn't wish to go to a hot old theatre. It doesn't care to have any of its "husband's" pals tramping in, either. *Stuart* falls asleep and next morning leaves for a hunting trip to Abyssinia. Undoubtedly the author who conceived that ingenious idea tried it himself on the poster of the Russian lady or others of the various portraits gracing his rooms.

Then there might arise such terrible questions as the *Bishop* in *The Other Woman* had asked his daughter's suitor. If he had only thirty days to live with no responsibility here or hereafter, would *Latimer* still choose his daughter? The young man in that fine story of Davis's could not answer yes nor could he return to the other woman.

Davis at thirty-five was still unmarried. Life and his career were so engrossing that he seemed to have little time to consider matrimony beyond its literary aspects. It was just something that happened on the last page of his novels.

II

The piping times of peace, provided by the latter part of 1898 and 1899, did not pall on the correspondent, home from the wars. New York was brisker, livelier than ever. He could take a walk up the Avenue (there had been "a story in that")[2] and in Central Park were to be met lovely ladies voluminously draped in modish black riding habits. He could make a bridge of his hands for a small booted foot and lift its wearer into the saddle, responding to an appealing helplessness that independent young things in breeches would never display in later years with their disdain of masculine aid. He could saunter into his publisher's and disrupt the work of the staff by telling stories; or confer on advertising, a supplement not so necessary for an author whose "personality went into even more editions than his books."

There were football games to watch in company with his idol, Walter Camp. Or occasionally he would stroll into the Waldorf bar, a magnificent shrine of Bacchus where sixteen bartenders practised their art before a gleaming pyramid of glasses of traditional shapes. The rapid-fire rattle of shakers and the popping of cork barrages was never stilled during the cocktail hour. Clover Clubs, rickeys, foaming, plebeian beers and every beverage on which the alchemy of nature and the ingenuity of man could collaborate paraded across the polished mahogany.[3] Snacks from the most sumptuous of free lunches spaced and speeded the procession—thirsty canapes, lusty cheeses, slices of Virginia ham, and luscious Russian caviar.

[2] *A Walk Up the Avenue,* is in *Gallegher and Other Stories.* New York, 1891.
[3] Indebtedness for the moist and memorable background of this section is acknowledged to *Old Waldorf Bar Days* (New York, 1931), by Albert Stevens Crockett, veteran newspaperman and long the esteemed press representative of the famous old hotel.

Davis with some such comrade of Cuba as John Fox, Jr., might order a "Santiago Sour" or a "Hobson's Kiss" but surely never a "Shafter Cocktail."

A bronze bull and bear shepherding sacrificial lambs surmounted the massive refrigerators in the centre of the bar and gave token that here was Wall Street's favorite way station on its route home to Murray Hill. Under their auspices J. P. Morgan quaffed his daily "Manhattan" and Bet-a-Million Gates conservatively downed his crackers and milk. E. Berry Wall, King of the Dudes, outshone the prosperous brewers and suave wine agents combining business with pleasure. Buffalo Bill might be seen imbibing some firewater or Mark Twain piloting a potion down his gullet. Davis might meet such celebrated newspaper proprietors as Colonel William R. Nelson of *The Kansas City Star* or Marse Henry Watterson of the *Louisville Courier-Journal,* but he would encounter few reporters. The Waldorf Bar was too distant, elegant and costly for Park Row.

Evenings might find him in his favorite haunt, Delmonico's. Once—the story is Thomas Beer's—seated alone in a corner of the bar, he heard some one ask if Stephen Crane, who had just left, had tried to get himself shot in Cuba. A hulking photographer gabbled that Crane was dying anyway from disgraceful diseases. A reporter protested and the backbiter offered to fight. Davis rose and ordered the fellow to keep still. The photographer, towering above him, glared and mouthed more filth. Then "Davis, blushing furiously, towed the big gossip out of the place and came back with his customary dignity and a cut lip to ask such men as he knew to forget the affair."

After a strenuous New York winter, Marion, Massachusetts, was a peaceful haven. In the calm of that little town, cooled by breezes from the sea, Davis wrote busily through the summer in a cottage screened by rose-bush hedges bordering the roads. His family were close by and from the neighborhood and the shores of Buzzard's Bay friends gathered for fishing cruises or parties—the Joe Jeffersons, the Gilders, the Cleve-lands, St. Gaudens, Henry James, the John M. Clarks of Chi-cago, with their daughter Cecil. The brunette Miss Clark was a lively girl, fond of sports and of dogs and horses. She pos-sessed genuine talent as an artist. Travel and adventure ap-pealed to her and cloistral conventions for maidenhood seemed as old fashioned as the fading nineteenth century. She was interested in, though not overwhelmed by, celebrities.

There was, it began to appear to Davis, another reason than a World's Fair for trips to Chicago.

III

In spite of the Middle West's attraction, the London "sea-son" of 1899 found Davis in town and entering the social whirl zestfully.

H. J. Whigham, native Briton but Chicago newspaperman, watched his friend answering invitations and writing notes. Prepared to deliver them, a small, trimly uniformed messenger boy waited—an English edition of Gallagher but minus the impudence. Davis, who frequently employed him, glanced over where the fourteen-year-old lad stood, alert and respect-ful. He extended two missives.

"Jaggers," he directed, "take this to the Duchess of —— and this to No. —— St. James Square and"—he picked up another letter and his eyes twinkled—"take this to Miss Cecil Clark, Prairie Avenue, Chicago, U. S. A."

The friends saw Jaggers step up and accept the letters with-out batting an eye.

JAGGERS, THE DAVIS MESSENGER WHO CARRIED A NOTE
FROM LONDON TO MISS CECIL CLARK IN CHICAGO

TWO CHARACTERS FROM *THE BAR SINISTER* AND THE AUTHOR
Jimmy Jocks to the left, *The Kid* on the right.

R. H. D. AND THE FIRST MRS. DAVIS AT ZANZIBAR

"Yes, sir. Very good, sir."

Davis stifled his laughter. "Can you go to Chicago?" he asked.

"Yes, sir. Whenever you say, sir."

By Jove, he'd let the imperturbable little fellow do it! Such instant and unquestioning readiness deserved a reward. Immensely amused, Davis launched on the subjects of route, expense money, and arrangements. As he talked, the whim appealed to him more and more. It was like an episode you might read in a love story. Now he, the writer of fiction, was making it happen in fact. What would critical editors who were always harping on credibility say to this?

There could be a bet on it, a wager that Jaggers would beat the dilatory regular mails; the odds were he would. Davis handed over the letter and two more addressed to his brother and sister. William Thomas Jaggers took them, saluted smartly, and marched out.

Davis declared he had no idea the affair would become known. But several days after Jaggers had slipped away from London, the pride of the boy's father let the secret out. Soon it was all over town. Cables flashed it across the Atlantic. The betting spread. Every one from friends to waiters in the clubs begged Davis for bulletins on Jaggers's progress. Speculation was rife on the contents of the letter to the girl in Chicago. Surely, ran the rumors, it contained an engagement ring or at the very least a proposal. It held neither,[4] for such matters already had been broached to the lady without success. The letter, however, was proof that its sender had not accepted her answer as final.

In the vast buzz of interest aroused in England and America mingled notes of censure. Some questioned the taste of

[4] On the authority of Mr. Whigham who was present when the letter was sent.

the stunt. Others refused to believe it was entered into on the spur of the moment. They knew their Dick Davis, they said, and his liking for the public eye, and you couldn't tell them that this was not the best piece of author's publicity that had been pulled off in many a year. One jester who signed himself "Karl" published hilarious stanzas in the lilting metre of *The Ingoldsby Legends* in Davis's old paper, *The Philadelphia Press*.

> Lord save us,
> Dick Davis,
> Don't try to deprave us,
> Yet what in the mischief is this that you gave us?
> O, Dick, is it wise
> For a man of your size
> To flaunt us
> And taunt us,
> So you advertise?
> You impute that our postmen are gray-coated laggers,
> The mail is too slow—and affecting the swaggers!
> And so you must send your epistles by Jaggers.
> Oh, Richard, oh please,
> We beg on our knees
> That you'll not let the English come over and seize
> Our post office dignified, stately and grand,
> And cart it right bodily off to the Strand.
> Now honest,
> Dick Davis,
> You really unnerve us
> By slighting the mail for the messenger service;
> Just think of the tons and the tons of the mail
> For Jaggers to carry—he's really too frail.
> It's all very well for the poor little rascal
> To carry one letter from Darby to Paschal,
> But as for a lot,
> Why, Dick, it's all rot,
> Though Jaggers himself is a wide-awake tot,
> Were both of his shoulders as big as your head—
> (Excuse me, that phrase isn't very well bred,
> But then it expresses what others have said)—

If his shoulders were big as your cranium, Dick,
He couldn't be really one-hundredth as quick.
    Are we to divine
    That over the brine
Came panting our Jaggers in March, '99,
With no thought of breaking a record or two,
But merely, Dick Davis, to advertise you?

Jaggers beat the mail handily by several hours and in eighteen days, with 8400 miles behind him, was back in London to be met by cheering thousands. A real duchess pinned a real gold medal on him, and the Queen herself was graciously moved to receive him at a garden fête.

Davis would have taken delight in the indomitable little messenger's triumph even if the letter he placed, along with a bunch of violets, in Cecil Clark's hands had gone unanswered. But Miss Clark knew that it had been prompted by a sincere desire to please her; that it was the sort of boyish thing Davis would do naturally. The letter won a reply and later a cable suggesting he come back.

They were married in Marion on May 4, 1899. It was a jolly wedding. Ethel Barrymore was maid of honor, Cissie Loftus McCarthy matron of honor, Charley Davis best man, and Gibson, Griscom, and John Fox, Jr., groomsmen. A toy figure of Jaggers fittingly occupied the centre of the wedding cake, and that young mercury soon arrived from England to fill the post of "buttons" in the household of the bride and groom.

IV

Van Bibber once was a guest at a winter houseparty at Southampton where the hostess was the doting owner of a Scotch collie named Duncan. That annoying animal chose to run away and poor *Van Bibber,* snug indoors, was forced to head the search to impress the lady. After plowing through the snow all day he was ready to play *Macbeth* if he ever found the beast. The story's title was *Love Me, Love My Dog.*

It was one fiction rôle Davis had never considered playing in life, but now he was married to a girl who was a fancier and exhibitor of dogs—even an authority on several breeds. He rose to the occasion and became decidedly doggy, while his friends observed the new enthusiasm with interest. "Dick until he married Cecil used to pass dog after dog," Dana Gibson smiled. "Now he practically sleeps with 'em. Maybe he'll take up canaries next."

Kennels, populated at times by as many as thirty-five barkers, were attached to the Davis menage. Jaggers, drafted to take charge of them, was incautiously referred to by his employer in the course of an interview with a group of reporters as "my kennel-master." The term was exact and had been used without assumption, but it sounded high and mighty and un-American to the press. Davis was kidded mercilessly in news columns and editorial pages.

Still the literary result of these dog days was worth far more than they cost. Davis, making a serious study of matters canine, followed the dog shows with his wife, absorbing all the craft of the ring. It was her keen judgment which picked out the splended snow-white bull terrier named Edgewood Cold Steel for the glint of his fighting eyes and The Kid for his affectionate nature. She gave up a tailor-made suit, peak of the mode though it was, to pay the $125 for The Kid.

Frank Dole, the seller, was talking over the football days with the former Lehigh halfback he had watched as Pennsylvania's coach. Switching to The Kid, the dog expert remarked:

"You know, not that I believe it, but they say in Canada that The Kid's grandmother was a black-and-tan mongrel."

Dole always remembered the look that flashed over Davis's face at his words—a queer, dreamy, half-smiling, there's-a-story-in-that expression.

So was born the tale, *The Bar Sinister*. The Kid trotted into its pages to fight for a drunken master, win upward to show championships and find his unpedigreed mother at last. Davis, bringing off the difficult feat of telling it in the first person, speaking for The Kid, produced a yarn which ranks as one of the dog-story classics. From the battling bull terrier to his comrade, *Jimmy Jocks,* the toothless old bulldog who buried bones from force of habit and in case a friend should drop in, every line testifies to a love for dogs no less genuine for its recent acquisition.

More familiar than the clamor in his kennels, the barking of the dogs of war summoned Davis again.

CHAPTER ELEVEN

THE BOER ANGLE

I

DAVIS's war correspondent's kit grew with his reputation, winning renown in the profession as particularly complete and comfortable. For the Boer War, calling him in January, 1900, he assembled the following personnel and equipment.

Three Kaffir servants "who refuse to yield to my sense of the picturesque and go naked like their less effete brothers." One of them did nothing but polish the Davis boots and attend to harness.

Three ponies, two oxen, and a Cape cart.

A puppy picked up starving and fed on compressed beef tablets.

A green tent with tape window panes, ventilators, pockets inside, doors that looped up, and red knobs.

A bathtub, a folding bed, two tables, two chairs, two lanterns, and——

That unusual item, a wife.

Sharing her husband's exciting adventures, even to the extent of being under fire, appealed to Mrs. Davis infinitely more than a regular rôle as the girl he left behind him. The journey to South Africa became their wedding trip but British regulations prevented her accompanying him farther than Cape Town where she remained in the company of the Rudyard Kiplings[1] and other friends. Davis rode on to join Buller's column in the field.

[1] Davis often expressed warmest admiration and affection for Kipling, but Conrad influenced his writing more.

This war sorely confused his loyalties. Three years before he had at first condemned Doctor Jameson's raid; then under the persuasive eloquence of John Hays Hammond, doughty partisan of the imperialistic Rhodes, Davis had reversed himself and written a pamphlet in sympathy with the viewpoint of the British South African settlers.[2] His affection for the English always pulled him strongly, yet his heart, so often ruling his never deeply analytical head, now told him that the Boers, like the Cubans, were fighting for independence; that British arms sought only to fling a far-flung empire farther. A stone-and-glass-house comparison with the United States' annexation of Porto Rico and the Philippines, not to mention Hawaii, occurred to him no more forcibly than to the mass of his countrymen. He reflected American favoritism for the Boer as the underdog.

"Although throughout the war," wrote Charles Belmont Davis, "my brother's sympathies were with the Boers, and in spite of the fact that the papers he represented wanted him to report the war from the Boer side, he persisted in going at first with the British forces. His reasons were that he wished to see a great army, with all modern equipment in action, and that practically all of his English friends were with the British army."

So the correspondent independent enough to dare defy the desires of two such newspaper autocrats as Lord Northcliffe of *The London Daily Mail* and Bennett of *The New York Herald* requested his credentials at General Buller's headquarters. It was a fateful decision. Mutual irritation began almost at once, British assertiveness and the same quality in Davis clashing. When he rode with Buller and his staff, he returned salutes given them, a grievous error for a civilian. Censorship

[2] *Doctor Jameson's Raiders.* New York, 1897.

of despatches to prevent military information reaching the enemy seemed exaggerated in strictness to a writer unused to it. Censors were harder to endure than copyreaders. The latter might cut only the worst of a story; the former often deleted the best.

Trim in a neat khaki uniform, the blue bandana badge of Roosevelt and the Rough Riders worn as a puggaree around his felt hat, Davis followed the drive for the relief of Ladysmith. He was as well turned out as any of the smart British officers, but gone was the old comradery of Oxford and London. He could not forbear criticizing the blundering tactics of Her Majesty's Generals which were shelving them, one after another. Much of the Empire was joining in the indignant clamor, but the added voice of an outsider was not welcomed. The waste of lives in frontal attacks on kopjes held by Boer sharpshooters was too like history repeating Bunker Hill for a Yankee to deplore acceptably.

And yet Davis never stinted his admiration for dogged British valor. Not from Kipling himself could have been expected a more vivid picture of the relentless advance across the Tugela River Basin. Davis, seeing Epsom Downs on Derby Day shifted to the African veld and unnaturally brilliant in the glare of the sun and the flash of bursting shells, wrote his despatch as he accompanied the column.

"Hundreds of teams of sixteen oxen each crawled like great black water-snakes across the drifts, the Kaffir drivers naked and black, lashing them with whips as long as lariats, shrieking, beseeching, and howling, and flinging themselves upon the oxen's horns to drag them into place. Mules from Spain and Texas, loaded with ammunition, kicked and plunged, more oxen drew more soberly the great naval guns, which lurched as though in a heavy sea, throwing the blue-jackets who hung upon the drag ropes from one high side of the trail to the other. Across the plain, and making toward the trail, wagons loaded with fodder, with rations, with camp equipment, with tents and cooking-stoves, crowded each other as closely as cable cars on Broadway. Scattered among them were fixed lines of tethered horses, rows of dog-tents, camps of Kaffirs, hospital stations with the Red Cross waving from the nearest and highest tree. Dripping water-carts with as many spigots as the regiment had companies, howitzer guns guided by as many ropes as a May-pole, crowded past these on the trail, or gave way to the ambulances filled with men half dressed and bound with the zinc-blue bandages that made the color detestable forever. Troops of the irregular horse galloped through this multitude, with a jangle of spurs and sling-belts; and Tommies, in close order, fought their way among the oxen, or helped pull them to one side as the stretchers passed, each with its blue bandage stained a dark brown crimson."

With the first word that the advance had raised the siege of Ladysmith, Davis filled his saddlebags with tobacco and galloped ahead of the main body of the army. Others could flash the news of the relief—he must look on the men who had made so gallant a defense. He rode into the strangely hushed town, his heart wrung at the sight of the gaunt, fever-yellowed faces. He passed out cigars, accepted with gratitude half hidden by British restraint. With tears in his eyes, he witnessed the entrance of the cheering relief column, while the starved, haggard garrison stood to arms to receive its deliverers and cheered them back in husky whispers. Two battalions of the same regiment, parted five years before in India—one of the Ladysmith garrison, one of the relief—broke ranks to pound each other on the back. In the spectacle of brave men saluting brave men, Davis could almost forget the Boers and their cause.

II

But not for long. The prospect of a delay of weeks in further British operations increased his desire to see the war from the other side. It was irregular procedure, but the authorities consented to and even facilitated it, willing to get rid of an uncompromising critic. Rejoining his wife in Cape Town, they entered Boer territory via Lorenzo Marquez.

A writer could ask nothing more striking in contrasts than that of the Boer commando and the British war machine. The bearded patriarchs and their sons, unkempt, slouching, and stolidly Dutch, were far from a Davis model soldier, but they handled a rifle as familiarly as that other article of their kit, a Bible. An aura of embattled farmers and the Spirit of '76 hung over them. As an added filip to his copy, he found a foreign legion in the Boer ranks: Italians of Garibaldi's red-shirt army, Swedes, Danes, Germans with university *schlager* scars, Russians, an Irish-American contingent who called themselves an ambulance corps for passport purposes, and cowboy scouts. Only Roosevelt and the Rough Riders were lacking. These Boer allies were soldiers of fortune, he felt, fighting without gain to "save the independence of a free people."

Davis's enthusiasm made him a headlong advocate. "As I see it," he wrote, "it has been a Holy War, this war of the burgher crusader, and his motives are as fine as any that called 'A Minute Man' from his farm or sent a Knight of the Cross to die for it in Palestine."

The Boers, aware that they had acquired a powerful press reinforcement, interposed no objection to Mrs. Davis's going to the front. The correspondent and his wife rode toward the fighting beyond Ventersburg, admiring the pastoral simplicity of the camps, the singing of evening hymns, and the politeness of the burgher soldiery who raised their hats as Mrs. Davis passed. Picking up an interview with President Steyn en route, they hurried on toward the Boer forces retreating before Lord Roberts's column. News that the British were only two hours away failed to deprive them of a night's rest at Ventersburg. Next day they almost were caught between the lines but managed to extricate themselves and camp out on the veld. The following morning they climbed a hill to gain a fine view of a British attack. When the Boers left the hill as untenable, the two interested observers transferred to another where shrapnel was bursting in the foreground.

Davis reminded his wife that he had kept his promise—she was under fire for the first and last time. "Pshaw!" remarked Mrs. Davis and calmly took five minutes to tighten her horse's girth before they rode to a third hill which the Boers already were abandoning. They were warned that it was no place for a woman and the correspondent joined in urging his wife to keep back. She dismounted and walked up the hill after him. "We showed her the shells striking back of her and around her but she refused to be impressed with the danger," he wrote home. "She went among the Boers begging them to make a stand very quietly and like one man to another and they took it just in that way and said, 'But we are very tired. We have been driven back for three days. We are only a thousand and they are twenty thousand.' Some of them only sat still, too proud to run, too sick to fight! When the British got within 500 yards of the artillery, I told her she must run."

The couple took flight at last. Pausing in Ventersburg, they looted a cook (they anticipated they would need one in Pretoria), collected a dog and cat and loaded up the lot in a cart. Davis, having left in his hotel room a note reading, "I'd leave my happy home for you," for whatever British officer would occupy it, mounted and the cavalcade left at a gallop. Paced by the terrified Kaffir driver of the cart, they covered thirty miles in five hours.

III

Out of Pretoria came the most unlucky despatch Davis ever wrote. It cost him the loss of a possession he prized most highly: many of his English friendships.

British officer prisoners of war, confined in a Pretoria schoolhouse, had in Davis's opinion behaved in a most unsportsmanlike, ungentlemanly manner in drawing offensive caricatures of Boers on the walls and destroying the school children's copy books. When he visited them, he considered their conduct toward his Boer officer escort as rude and "cheeky."

"Their chief offense, however, was in speaking to and shouting at the ladies and young girls who walked past the schoolhouse," he wrote. "Personally, I cannot see why being a prisoner would make me think I might speak to women I did not know, but some of the English officers apparently thought their new condition carried that privilege with it. I do not believe that every one of them misbehaved in this fashion, but it was true of so many of them that their misconduct brought discredit on all. Some people say that the young girls walked by for the express purpose of being spoken to; and a few undoubtedly did, and one of them was even arrested after the escape of a well-known war correspondent,[3] on suspicion of having assisted him. But, on the other hand any number of older women, both Boers and English, have told me that they found it quite impossible to pass the schoolhouse on account

[3] Winston Spencer Churchill escaped from the Pretoria prison.

of the insulting remarks the officers on the verandah threw to
one another concerning them, or made directly to them. At
last the officers grew so offensive that a large number of the
ladies signed a petition and sent it to the Government complaining that the presence of the Englishmen in the heart of
the town was a public nuisance. It was partly in consequence
of this, and more probably because the number of the prisoners
had increased so greatly that there was no longer room for
them, that they were removed from their comfortable quarters and sent to the camp."

Conduct unbecoming officers and gentlemen, Davis branded
it. His high sense of chivalry could not condone it. Young
Britishers cooped up for months might call out pleasantries to
pretty girls passing by (he was in dead earnest when he said
that in their place he never would have spoken without a
proper introduction) but if, as his information convinced him,
remarks had passed the bounds of badinage and became insulting, it was inexcusable. War propaganda, bitterness against
an enemy, and feminine fancy might be suspected of playing
a part in inspiring the story and his own pro-Boer prejudice
of influencing his acceptance. Yet the facts as related to him
admitted of sufficient verification, in his judgment as a well-
trained reporter, to print. Though denials were made, he let
the story stand in the book containing his articles on the war.[4]

It took courage for Davis to make charges he believed reflected on the honor of British officers. That others might not
take the affair as seriously as he never entered his head. He
only knew that his knightly code demanded he act as he did,
regardless of consequences.

Davis had capped a series of severe strictures on the British
and he paid the price. One friend turned his picture to the

[4] *With Both Armies in South Africa.* New York, 1900.

wall; one ironically praised his Boer War fiction. Others
snubbed him. He half expected to be met by a mob the next
time he visited London and he did experience difficulty in obtaining tickets for the coronation of Edward VII because of
the feeling against him. Although his sensitiveness magnified
the extent of the aversion, the beloved city would never again
seem to give him its former warm-hearted reception. It
dawned on him, as it might on a hurt youngster, that you could
not always tell what you honestly believed to be the truth and
stay popular.

IV

By a dash to China, Davis could have covered his fifth war
in three years, the Boxer Rebellion. Joining the American contingent of the Allies, he might have seen the storming of Pekin,
the relief of the legations, and the sack of ancient palaces—a
story packed with drama and color. But he was tired and as
embittered as his sanguine nature could be. He travelled from
Africa to France and took ship for New York.

The ship news reporters met him at Quarantine. Those cynical inquisitioners, who examine a Big Name more strictly than
an Ellis Island inspector does an immigrant, who ransack mental baggage more mercilessly than a Customs man a trunk, had
swapped yarns on the Davis foibles coming down on the cutter.
They interviewed him, listening without enthusiasm to the tale
of his difficulties with the British. Let him plead his own cause,
swing his own publicity. From the "working press" a newspaperman no longer under city-room harness receives scant professional courtesy.

Davis insisted that he still was a reporter; that the world,
not a district or a city, was his "run"; that he placed his copy
with magazines because they paid better. Old-timers on news-

paper staffs, men still doing leg work or toiling as galley slaves on the copy desks, retorted that he was a mere dilettante writer. Journalism ranks with acting and authorship as a green-eyed profession. Envious newspapermen, asked what they did not like about Davis, sometimes frankly confessed: "His success."

A succession of cub reporters, however, worshipped Richard Harding Davis and tried to emulate him. Alexander Woollcott, remembering his own cub days, recalls how the young college graduates with the scribbler's urge planned to give some newspaper two or three years of their time; then shake off the dust of the city room, and, in the manner of R. H. D., adventure in South America, return, write fiction and succeed gloriously. In later years fledglings, eyes on the Woollcott model, would be prepared to break right into the game as dramatic critics.

Men rising from the ranks became Davis's lifelong friends when they received from him letters of warm and generous praise for able pieces of writing,[5] whether he knew them personally or not. One adherent, coming to his defense against the anvil chorus, declared:

"They called him conceited—and he was. But it wasn't the kind of conceit they meant. Rather, it was the bumptious, unaffected conceit of boyhood, the happy appearance of strength and resource."

Davis's attitude was not uppishness, Franklin Clarkin, a newspaperman, explained after knowing him for years. "His

[5] Irvin Cobb, landing his first story in *The Saturday Evening Post*, treasured Davis's letter of congratulation. Albert Stevens Crocket did the same with a note lauding his report of an Olympic Marathon. Winston Churchill's first novel, *The Celebrity*, whose top-lofty hero was erroneously supposed to be drawn from Davis, once encountered him on a train from Marion. They were strangers, but the older man introduced himself and Churchill nervously admitted his identity. Davis by his cordiality toward the younger writer showed his disbelief in the charge that *The Celebrity* satirized him.

gifts had made him sought after. He appreciated distinction—even in himself. He could have understood the socialist, Bertrand Russell, who confessed a weakness for 'meeting Italians who have names known to me from Renaissance history.' But Davis was a more inclusive connoisseur of what was illustrious. Lacking all the Thackerayan attributes of snobbery, he had none of its false standards of value. The ordinary, the commonplace, did not exist for him; but any distinction arising from exertions, on any level of life, could stir his emotions—the office boy who pulled off a scoop for his paper, the East Side rough who risked himself to do a rescue, the casual soldier of fortune achieving a moment of splendor, the disdained street dog who could win a fight or a blue ribbon, the brilliant derelict who wrote the most glorious story of the Spanish War for an unconscious rival and, never telling, let him get the reward and the renown."

Certain qualities always continued to keep the legend of the Davis hauteur alive: his sensitiveness, his acute fear of being bored, his dramatizations, his adornments. He was a pioneer wearer of a wrist watch which drew a gibe as "a bracelet with a watch in it." For formal occasions he pinned on his campaign ribbons and his foreign medals and orders with unconcealed pride; on one such evening a wit fingered the glittering array with apparent awe and gently inquired, "Swimming?" So they might have been (though they were not), for the wearer in his youth had saved several lives in the surf at Point Pleasant. Never toplofty about his decorations, Davis took jokes about them in good humor. In *Soldiers of Fortune,* he made his hero explain a medal from the Sultan of Zanzibar. That potentate, remarked *Clay,* "gives them away in place of cigars and he happened to be out of cigars the day I called." Davis resented only implications that his badges were not authentic.

He could not restrain his curiosity as to what was said about him, either good or evil. A woman friend walking with him one afternoon saw him stop at a newstand, buy a copy of *Town Topics,* read the meanly jeering paragraph on himself which that scandal sheet frequently printed, and throw the magazine in the gutter with the remark: "That's over for the week."

New York, that critical and distracting metropolis, did not keep him long after his return from abroad. Its tempo which had so often stimulated him in the past had accelerated amazingly. Hansom cabs by the hundreds swung through the streets. They poured in and out of the Park Avenue tunnel with its barnyard exhalations like an endless caravan. Along with dangerously scorching bicyclists, they taxed the amateur traffic directing talents of the gray-helmeted bluecoats of the "Finest," who found automobiles were the least of their troubles. Mobs of messenger boys scurried across between the vehicles, answering call bells in many residences innocent of telephones.

Sidewalks, encroached on by stoops, were thronged with pedestrians who, masculine and feminine, had two characteristics in common: haste and high collars, the men's stiffened by starch, the women's by whale bones. Soles swished ceaselessly on the cement as the current flowed on and on, slippers pinching women's feet as usual and striding men suffering equally in the leathern grip of "toothpick" shoes with which Cinderella's sisters would gladly have revenged themselves on the Prince. Padded shoulders and derbies, swelling bosoms, bowed and befeathered millinery, riveted by long hat pins to pompadours based in turn on humble "rats"—these bobbed along on the surface of the restless, rushing tide. In the New York of 1900 the town of the leisurely *Mr. Van Bibber* had vanished forever.

Here was little calm for the pilgrim weary from following

the red star through Europe, the Antilles, and Africa. Davis hurried off to Marion to write in the study of his cottage, its walls decorated with his framed credentials as a correspondent; with a photograph of Roosevelt autographed, "To my fellow on the firing line"; with one of Anthony Hope, its inscription conveying the compliments of *Princess Flavia,* heroine of Hope's *Prisoner of Zenda,* to *Princess Aline* in a verse reading:

> "Excepting myself, there never was seen
> A prettier girl than the Princess Aline."

It was restful and pleasant to work among such mementos, but a month or so sufficed to revive a longing for the helter-skelter, fascinating city. No wonder New Yorkers hurried— there was so much happening and they hated to miss anything.

Certain lights were burning brightly there, lights which had lured Dick Davis since boyhood, the lights of the stage. They were glowing more irresistibly than ever these days, for they were illuminating plays of his own.

CHAPTER TWELVE

DRAMATIC PAGE

I

"You will never live through the first night of your first play but once," the young playwright hero of *The Lion and the Unicorn* was told by a noted dramatist congratulating him on the stage after his first success.

Davis himself had been fascinated by the sensations he described in that story of his. How could a book you wrote possibly inspire the high exaltation that was yours when you witnessed a play from your pen? "Instead of a page of black type, you see on the stage real people doing the things black type can only suggest," he declared in a *Collier's* article. "You see a house, at least one room of a house, of which you were the architect; you see 'skeleton' armies, wearing your uniform, fighting for your flag. You see vice punished, virtue rewarded just as you arranged it should be."

If your book made readers laugh or sigh, you never knew it. While in the theatre, there was the fun of leaning on the velvet railing back of the orchestra and watching the audience troop in, or, maybe, hearing them chuckling as they went out. You sat with them, marked where they coughed or fidgeted with their programs and heard their friendly, kindly laughs— which gave you a healthy, delightful feeling.

"It is the comradeship of the show business that counts," Davis maintained. "The pleasure, which you are sure is mutual, of having a strange usher whisper, 'It looks like a big night tonight.'" And there was going behind to get your letters from a Japanned tin mail-box, smelling the fireproof scenery and the grease-paint, listening to the orchestra tune up, and sitting in the star's dressing-room on an iron-bound trunk, that throne of thrones. To the new-fledged playwright it was all wonderful.

He always had loved the stage since he stood in the wings as a youngster in Philadelphia, met the great actors of his parents' generation in his home, and browsed through his father's unique library on the theatre. His bent to write for it—nearly everything he wrote was essentially dramatic—revived after he had made his name in other fields.

Like so many things in life he wished for very much, his chance to be a playwright came to him.

E. H. Sothern, the talented young English actor, needed a curtain-raiser. His friend Davis heard of it and submitted a dramatization of a short story, one of his saga of *Rags Raegan,* tough lad of the New York waterfront. Sothern liked it, worked on it with him, and was ready to play the title rôle if only he could overcome one formidable obstacle. While he could manage a rich Cockney dialect, the *Raegan* part called for pure, unadulterated Boweryese, decidedly "another language." But the resourceful author met the emergency. He took the actor for a call on a leading citizen of the Bowery he had known in his days as a reporter.

The friendships of Dick Davis, so often accused of snobbishness, ranged from crowned heads to cauliflowered ears and one of the gems of the collection was Steve Brodie. Ever since he jumped from the Brooklyn Bridge into the East River in 1886, Brodie had been famous.[1] He had trusted to gravity, not gen-

---

[1] There were those who doubted that Brodie performed the feat at all. They said he simply leaped from the boat that picked him up. But none of the sceptics expressed his doubts to Steve's pugilistic face. (At least half a dozen persons a year jumped from the bridge in its earlier days from either mercenary or mortuary motives.)

ius, declared his press, and swooped to conquer. Proudly he wore the degree of B. J. (Bridge Jumper) which he had conferred on himself. "Steve Brodie—he took a chance" had become part of the national folklore, and a favorite slang term for accepting a risk was "to take a Brodie." Basking in renown, Brodie had founded his fortunes first as the drawing card and then the owner of a Coney Island dime museum and a Bowery saloon, as well as of a string of tenement houses.

Steve received Sothern and Davis at his saloon, 114 the Bowery, where he sold Bowery whisky at Broadway prices. Spade-shaped face, powdered shaven chin, diamond glittering in yellow-and-green shirtfront, shallow derby tipped forward over one eye and cigar cocked in the other eye's corner, Brodie was *Raegan* to the life. Probably he was the original of Davis's character; in any event he could speak for him.

When his inquiring guests asked his assistance on their problem of theatrical research, Brodie cordially complied. Only a year before—in 1894—he had himself donned the buskin, enacting the leading rôle in a melodrama featuring his saloon, his bridge jump, and his native tongue.[2] He was, as his biographer emphasized, noted "for helping people of all classes—bums, ruined sporting men, distressed women, newspapermen temporarily in need, and actors." Since his present callers came under that category, he escorted them on a tour of "joints," one of which inspired a setting for the play. Next he obliged by giving a reading from the script in his best Bowery accent.[3] Sothern cleverly catching it was free from all suspicion of using the King's English on the opening night.

The Disreputable Mr. Reagan,[4] calling on Sothern for a vir-

[2] *On the Bowery,* starring Steve, was a repertory favorite for several years.
[3] Carpers insisted that Brodie's dialect was only a weak imitation of Chuck Connors'. But Brodie's quaint speech induced *The New York World* to send him on a tour to Europe whence he sent back correspondence couched in rich Boweryese.
[4] Spelling of the name was changed on the playbill.

tual monologue, with only a child playing opposite and two detectives entering at the climax, was enthusiastically received. Even the august William Winter, dean of reviewers, approved, commenting that while the situation was grossly improbable— a criminal giving himself up to save a starving child—it was good theatre; and that Sothern's touching and accomplished acting of the rôle showed a mastery of soliloquy.

Van Bibber was the next character to come to life behind the footlights. Robert Hilliard dramatized Davis's story, *Her First Appearance,* under the stage title of *The Littlest Girl.* Appearing as the elegant young clubman in that knight-errant episode in which he restores a child actress to her wealthy, estranged father, Hilliard played it more than 4100 times in the United States and Great Britain. He revived the piece in 1921 when the fine flavor of the 'Nineties in its costumes and properties[5] was doubly effective.

Both those playlets first appeared in 1895 and seven years passed before the theatre offered Davis any more real encouragement. Managers seemed as determined to turn down his plays as editors were to accept his books and stories. Like his playwright character, he might have been asked: "But I thought you made such a lot of money by writing?" and have answered as *Carroll* did: "I do—that is, I could if I wrote the things to sell; but I keep on writing plays that won't."

One of his scripts was bought but never produced. Another was dropped because he obstinately refused to make changes. It was that literary gold mine, *Soldiers of Fortune,* which proved to be the foundation of his stage fortunes.

James K. Hackett spotted the novel as first-rate play material, but he refused to allow the author to make the dramatization even when Davis offered to bet him the customary $500

[5] See Chapter Five.

advance that his work would be worthy of production, and in addition proposed that if he won, the money count as first payment on royalties. Hackett withdrew and Davis, his confidence in his ability as a playwright somewhat shaken for the moment, submitted his story to the experienced Augustus Thomas, who made the stage version and directed it. Henry B. Harris produced the play in February, 1902.

In the dramatic qualities of the original story, Thomas had ideal material. The play, splendidly acted by a cast headed by Robert Edeson as *Clay*[6] and Guy Bates Post as *Captain Stuart,* opened in New Haven and registered an unqualified hit. Cries for "Author!" after the final curtain brought Davis out on the stage. Always shy of speaking in public, he was at a loss until over the footlights he caught sight of a friend from the Harvard Law School who had invaded Yale territory in honor of the occasion. That young gentleman having celebrated in advance was gently snoring in his first row aisle seat. Davis looked down, grinned, and remarked that he hoped most of the audience had enjoyed his play in spite of the fact that it had put one of his best friends sound asleep. The laugh he drew was loud enough to wake the slumberer.

The play, like the novel on which it was based, was a mint. Davis, stimulated and more experienced, took down others of his books from the shelves and dramatized them.[7] *The Lion and the Unicorn* yielded *The Taming of Helen. Ranson's Folly,* story of Army-post life in the West, made a play which enjoyed a long run. Again the author heard himself called on for a curtain speech but lacking inspiration from Harvard this

---

[6] Edeson's forte, recalled a recent Theatre Guild program, "was to portray the strong, manly man, preferably from the great open spaces, who worshipped humbly at the feet of pure maidenhood. Self-sacrifice was his long suit—and his big emotional scenes were the delight of the matinée girls of the early nineteen-hundreds. He was the perfect Richard Harding Davis hero."

[7] H. C. Quinby's bibliography of Davis lists all his dramatic works.

time he beat a hasty retreat from his box and slipped into a seat in the gallery where he joined in shouting enthusiastically for the author. A cheering spectator next to him leaned over encouragingly.

"We'll keep this up," he vowed, "until we get the author out."

"I'll yell plenty," Davis agreed, "but I doubt if the fellow will show up."

Ethel Barrymore, whose guardian Davis had been appointed following her parents' deaths, dutifully complimented him by both producing and acting with her brother John in the one-act *Miss Civilization.* In that rather slight drama of a robbery in a Long Island country home, a posse of railroad men and the law burst in to the rescue in the nick of time, and the leading lady, having heroically outwitted the criminals, came down with the curtain in a good old-fashioned swoon over the arm of the chief of police. *Miss Civilization* was translated into several languages, becoming a particular favorite of Spanish actresses who played it on fête nights in South American cities.

II

A Davis first night on Broadway became an ultra-fashionable event. "The way to get into real high society is to go to a R. H. Davis play," declared an anonymous newspaperman, penning a Sunday feature on the opening of *The Taming of Helen.*

Produced by Charles B. Dillingham and starring Henry Miller as *Philip Carroll,* that comedy had been "tried on the dog" in Toronto in January, 1903. Before taking it to New York, the author generously transported the company to Marion to give a complimentary performance for the townsfolk.

THE WEAKER SEX. VIII   A cartoon by C. D. Gibson
after a Davis inspiration.

He goes to the play, but finds it impossible to become interested in the piece.

Although Davis and John Drew marched the cast through town in the manner of a circus parade, the play was reservedly received by the stern and rockbound New England audience. Four nights later, on the stormy evening of March 30, the curtain of the Savoy Theatre rose for the New York run.

The feature writer on hand to chronicle the occasion was of the school that enjoyed poking fun at Davis, as became evident from the first paragraph. Whenever Davis saw himself referred to as "Dickey," he groaned and knew he was in for a spoofing. Along with him, the society audience was the butt of the humor of the Sunday piece, illustrated with pen-and-inks of celebrities present. Its scribe, assuming the character of a young clubman, depicted it as the gala affair it was.

"All the fellows in our set turn out when Dickey Davis has a new play," he bubbled. "We will all be there every night, for Dickey Davis is such a doosid clever chap that we can't understand him all at once. It was such beastly weather that some of the chaps said they wouldn't leave the club for anything else but a Dickey Davis play."

There were so many shining shirt fronts in the pit, he observed, that it made the place look like a cellar full of geese. All dress suits and not a dinner coat in evidence. "A dinner coat is what the fellows not in our set call a 'Tuxedo' just as they call a frock coat a 'Prince Albert.' Fancy!"

The audience, not the play, was the thing. As was only proper, there were Gibson Girls all over and all paired off with Davis men. For were not Gibson and Davis chums—"Gibson, the creator of those big, goddessy American girls who travel abroad and never marry anything under the degree of a Duke, and Davis, the creator of the Davis Man, who is always a war correspondent, or a civil engineer or an author or something else classy?"

There were Mr. and Mrs. Charles Dana Gibson in a stage box with Mrs. Davis. Charles Belmont Davis, of *Collier's,* occupied a front seat, and Stanford White was visiting around. The observer noted Freddy Gebhard, the Borden Harrimans, Mrs. Whitney Warren, Stuyvesant LeRoy, Reggie Ronalds, Mr. and Mrs. Allen Wallace, Miss Anna Sands, Robert Potter, Gordon Fellows, and so on; in fact, many on the roster of the "400." Surely to be expected that night or later were John Jacob Astor, Robert J. Collier, Berry Wall, Arthur Paget, Foxhall Keene, the Meadow Brook Hunt, Mr. and Mrs. George Gould and the Lakewood set, the Ardsley golf set, Reggie Vanderbilt and H. K. Twombly, and the Morristown exclusives. "In short, to be seen at a Richard Harding Davis play is as imperative as to attend the Horse Show."

The second-act curtain fell and "Dickey," very nervous, in response to an ovation made a speech giving credit to every one but himself. Then the final curtain and the fashionable assemblage chattered their way out into the lobby. Three hundred carriages jammed the snowy streets for blocks, causing altercations with irate tram men who were blocked for an hour. Elder ladies and gentlemen were whirled off to Del's or Sherry's for supper, while "we of the younger set," finished the "clubman"-reporter, "betook ourselves to the Racquet and Calumet clubs to discuss what a terrific fellow Dickey Davis is. What?"

In spite of the fanfare of its opening, *The Taming of Helen* was not a hit. The short novel on which it was based offered too slight material for a play, and the critics panned it. Davis, reading the reviews, asked with a grin: "Was that the Flatiron Building that fell on me?" Still, with its road tour, the comedy made enough money to be rated as mildly prosperous.

III

Davis might have been content with dramatizations by himself or others of his published works. They gave him the thrill he sought from the theatre, and using book material over again as a play was good literary economy. He continued to think of himself first as a war correspondent, then as a writer of fiction, and as a playwright only by avocation.

It was the reviewers' hostile reception of a novel that stung him into bending all his energies to original playwriting.

On *Captain Macklin,* published in 1902, he had spent more time and effort than on any of his books. He considered it his best and there could be no surer proof of his belief in it than its dedication to his adored mother. Although he had gone back again to Central America and its revolutions for his locale, *Macklin* was no conquering superman but a character of real originality, a human, fallible young adventurer. "I tried," Davis confessed, "to make a hero who was vain, theatrical, boasting, and self-conscious, but still likable."[8]

All his admiration for soldiers of fortune, who never vainly came to him in want, shone in the pages of this book. Jeffs of Honduras—he of the *Three Gringos*—"the best fighting man of foreign birth that ever bore arms in Central America," was the prototype of *Macklin.* The appealing figure of *General La Guerre* was drawn from General McIver,[9] a fine old veteran of many battles under many flags. The story remained

---

[8] From a letter to Arthur Bartlett Maurice, quoted by C. B. Davis in *Adventures and Letters.*

[9] "A side of Mr. Davis's personality that never was noticed publicly was the odd, chivalrous interest he took in the wrecked gentlemen adventurers of whom he wrote," ran an article in *The New York Evening Post.* "No such wastrel ever went uncared for if Davis heard he was in trouble. When the old soldier of fortune who was the original of Davis's greatest character, General La Guerre, in *Captain Macklin* —perhaps the most vital character he ever drew—died in a furnished-room house in

faithful to type throughout. At its end, *Macklin* does not settle down and marry the girl at home but, true soldier of fortune, sails for Indo-China to fight in another war under his beloved leader.

Davis had done something new, something different, and he was proud of it. He looked anxiously for that shower of reviews from a clipping bureau which every author awaits with bated breath. The pink-tabbed cuts of news print were never more disappointing. "Mr. Davis's hero is a military cad, and Mr. Davis cannot see it." The verdict was almost unanimous.[10]

Nothing seemed ever to have hurt so much. He suffered a strong revulsion from fiction writing—it hardly seemed worth while if you did your best and it counted for so little. There was no war for him to cover just when he would have gone most eagerly. This was the curious, paradoxical result of the adverse reviews of *Macklin:* they drove him to writing uproariously funny farces.

The Dictator was a tremendous hit. There was nothing sardonic or embittered in its humor because its author lacked those qualities. Derived from the hairbrained adventures of the *Three Gringos* and dealing with the dilemmas of Americans in the "Republic of San Mañana," it was full of clever twists and hilarious situations. Charles Frohman, who declared he never had produced a play with so many laughs, gave it an excellent cast headed by William Collier and John Barrymore and including Nanette Comstock and Thomas Meighan, later to star in motion pictures. Staged in this country in 1904 and

New York, practically of starvation, leaving nothing but a trunkful of medals and orders, swords of honor, and faded uniforms, it was Davis who stepped forward and did what could be done, and in private almost wept at the thought that he had not known of his old friend's plight, until too late to save him." Davis, who had written McIver's biography in *Real Soldiers of Fortune,* served as his literary executor.

[10] Mr. Maurice, then editor of *The Bookman,* was one of the few critics dissenting from the adverse decision against *Macklin.*

DAVIS AND RAYMOND HITCHCOCK (BY THE CHAIR) AT A REHEARSAL OF *THE GALLOPER*

The correspondent repairs his kit.　　　DAVIS IN MANCHURIA, 1904　　　He mounts for a news hunt.

the next year in England, with Marie Doro as leading lady, Collier revived it successfully in 1911. At that time he had already played more than 1000 performances. One of the Taliaferro sisters trouped with it in Australia. Two musical comedy versions of the play also were performed.[11]

Money rolled in and Davis spent it as freely as it came. It added another filip to life to be pointed out as a prominent playwright among his other distinctions; to be known as a chap with a grand sense of humor. He had written highly amusing stories, notably the yarn about the man who tried to take three dancing bears back to nature. But what was more fun than standing in the shadows at the back of a box and listening to a great audience roar with laughter at a farce you had written? Only one year after the appearance of *The Dictator,* he was ready with another.

Not even the dignity of war correspondents could escape this time. The merry scenes of the earlier days of the Græco-Turkish War when he was vainly searching for a battle in a classic Arcadia of wine, song, and petticoated peasantry flooded back into his memory to form the plot of *The Galloper* (1905). Raymond Hitchcock as a comedy correspondent played the lead in that jolly farce on the mistaken identity theme. Davis did not halt at poking fun at himself.

"Does your gentleman friend write for a newspaper?" "No. He writes for *The London Times,*" ran a bit of the dialogue. Another hit near home could be discerned in a character who came to report the war with five servants and thirty-two pieces of luggage and who boasted he had covered ten wars and eight revolutions and helped crown six kings, four savage and two tame.

Two years later Davis converted this farce into a musical

[11] *Captain Kidd* in London, 1910, and *The Girl from Home* in New York, 1920.

comedy, *The Yankee Tourist,* which again starred Hitchcock and was even more of a hit than the original. The lyrics were by Wallace Irwin and the music by Alfred G. Robyn.

Vera the Medium, dramatized from his short novel of that name,[12] was one of Davis's failures. It did not interest the public demanding, in that sentimental day, that a heroine and hero should have all the virtues. As in the case of *Raegan,* the playwright made every effort to give it an authentic setting. To the delight of Hugh Ford who was directing, the author brought around a swami with the un-Oriental name of O'Reilly. By his knowledge of the tricks of the trade, an apparatus of mirrors was rigged, enabling *Vera* to "materialize" as the ghost of the millionaire's wife. But neither the skilful stage business nor the acting of the beautiful Eleanor Robson[13] could save the piece. It was, as Davis admitted to the star, a bad play unredeemed by his struggles in rewriting it. And, he begged in his courtly way, would a great artist and a great lady, whom it had been his rare privilege to know, forgive him for foisting that young person, *Vera,* on her?

But the fickle fortunes of the theatre had been magnificently generous to Dick Davis. At one time he had three shows on Broadway and the golden shower of his royalties heaped up as high as $3000 a week.

[12] Into the plot of *Vera,* Davis wove threads of various experiences. *The Evening Sun* in his day had crusaded against trickster clairvoyants. While on a visit to Geneva, N. Y., in 1907, he observed how the authorities of Hobart College barely managed to dissuade a wealthy donor, influenced by mediums, from founding a spiritualistic institution for women. Thus William Smith College became a regular college for girls, its educational system allied with that of Hobart. (The author is indebted to Thomas M. Johnson, a Hobart alumnus, for this story.) The hero of *Vera* was a star on the Hobart baseball team and *Vera* was a Geneva girl.

Evangeline S. Adams, the astrologer, in *The Bowl of Heaven* (New York, 1926) told of the visit of a young man with the build of a prizefighter and the mind of a hawk who provoked her into a warm defense of her profession. After she had finished, he dropped his incognito. It was Davis in search of material for *Vera.* He presented his photograph autographed "To Miss Adams, from one who has respect for you as a woman but no respect for Astrology."

[13] Mrs. August Belmont.

IV

As a playwright, Davis's affection for and association with the stage became more closely bound than ever. Between him and its people, generous, sentimental, and dramatic on or off the boards, was a deep spiritual kinship and sympathy. He was never asked in vain to write a sketch for The Lambs club gambol. Proposed by Thomas Bailey Aldrich and seconded by Grover Cleveland, he was elected to The Players, that unique club of actors, authors, and artists founded by Edwin Booth at Number 16 Gramercy Park, New York City. It was one of his favorite rendezvous in spite of a most unhappy experience which befell him soon after his election.

In a Fourth Avenue bookshop, Davis had made a real find: a copy of the playbill of Ford's Theatre on the night that Lincoln was shot by John Wilkes Booth. Elated over his acquisition, he hurried over to The Players, the last place for displaying any reminder of the appalling crime committed by the founder's brother. Davis in his enthusiasm did not pause to think. He entered the clubhouse and proudly showed the playbill to a dimly seen man descending the dark stairway. It was Edwin Booth.

The stage itself seldom offers a more richly dramatic moment. With his own hands Booth had thrust all his actor brother's costumes in the furnace of his theatre—had done everything in his power to banish grimly haunting reminders of the murder which had engraven his family name forever on one of the blackest pages in history. And now in The Players, his own home where he had gathered his friends in a club to save him from solitary brooding, he was not secure. It was as if Greek furies relentlessly pursued an innocent man for kinship with an assassin. A great tragedian seemed doomed to play his tragic rôle through life.

Booth sadly but magnanimously accepted the stammered apology. This thoughtless action by a young man he had known from boyhood, whose mother and father were his old friends, could not have been other than an accident. But Davis's sensitive nature was deeply shocked by his distressful deed. Almost stunned by the realization of what he had done, he was helped to one of the club rooms and put to bed by fellow members.

V

Between the opening of *The Dictator* and the production of *The Galloper,* The Russo-Japanese War intervened in February, 1904. The warships of the mighty Muscovite, battered by the torpedoes of modern Samurai, were limping back into Port Arthur harbor, and the war correspondent clan already was gathering in Tokio. Davis heard the old call of the red gods.

The lure of the stage was strong, but this combat of strange antagonists in the yet unvisited Orient was stronger still. It was both the smell of powder in the nostrils of an old war horse and the flash of a travel folder before the eyes of an inveterate globetrotter. And his friend, Robert J. Collier, to whose magazine he long had contributed, offered him $1000 a week to represent *Collier's* at the front.

The curtains of Broadway must be held for the promise of a greater drama in the Far East.

CHAPTER THIRTEEN

ART SUPPLEMENT—JAPANESE SCREENS

I

WAR correspondents are privileged spies, Lord Wolseley had pronounced, and the Japanese had taken him literally and acted accordingly. As with other military arts adapted from the Occident, they had tightened up censorship to a pitch of novel and twentieth-century efficiency. Correspondents escaped being shot at sunrise—that was one of their privileges—but they were being politely and firmly prevented from seeing and writing any news which might filter through to the advantage of the Russians.

Willard Straight, drafted from the Customs Service to report for the Associated Press, had with his insight into the Oriental mind early perceived the functioning of the new order of things. Before Davis had left the United States, Straight had sketched in his diary[1] a keen description of the troubles of the foreign newspapermen gathered in Tokio.

"The air of the Imperial Hotel was a bright blue from early morn to golden sunset," he wrote. "Famous journalists, veterans of countless campaigns, were held up, bound hand and foot by the dapper little Orientals whose attitude throughout has been greatly wondered at and most profoundly admired. There was Knight of *The Telegraph,* who lost an arm in South Africa, Melton Prior, the artist of *The London Illustrated News,* O. K. Davis, with Richard on the road, Palmer of *Col-*

---

[1] From Herbert Croly's *Willard Straight.* New York, 1914.

lier's, Bass of *The Chicago Herald,* Martin Egan of the Associated Press, Collins for Reuter, and a host of others less notable but equally discontented. The situation was unique in the annals of journalism. A government holding the rabid pressmen at a distance, censoring their simplest stories, yet patting them on the back, dining them, wining them, giving them picnics and luncheons and theatrical performances and trying in every way not only to soften their bonds and to make their stay a pleasant one, but siren-like, to deaden their sense of duty and their desire to get into the field."

And Davis speeding across the continent to San Francisco, again accompanied by his wife, was picturing himself on a holiday trip! His letters to his mother glowed with anticipations of the land of cherry blossoms. Yokohama and Tokio realized them. He almost hoped, he now wrote, that the authorities would not let him go to the front for at least a week so that Cecil and he could sit around in tea houses, served by bowing geishas. His mother need not worry about his safety, for he heard that the Japanese were keeping correspondents two or three miles in rear of the fighting.

The Japanese were doing far better than that—they were keeping them in Tokio. Not even the press contingent assigned to the First Army had yet left, and Davis by his late arrival was relegated to the Second. With two *Collier's* men already attached to the former group, his chances of joining it were nil unless he supplanted one of them.

Jimmy Hare, the photographer with the look of a miniature Uncle Sam and the disposition of a bantam rooster, had no intention of surrendering his place to a writer. "A photographer 'as to be on the spot. A newspyperman can use 'is h'imagination," he piped up in his racy Cockney, with a grin. Davis, though he carried a camera as an adjunct of an up-to-date reporter, knew he could not compete with Hare's news photography. Few could.

But the Davis conscience was troubled by the large sum being paid him for days of inaction. It led him to suggest an exchange with Frederick Palmer, also of *Collier's,* who had been assigned to the First Army. Both men had long war-service records. Davis had won Palmer's regard by one of those considerate deeds of his that made so many remember and like him. He had forwarded a copy of the other's article on the storming of Tientsin in the Boxer Rebellion with a word of praise and the remark that editors usually forgot to mail such copies to correspondents in the field. But Palmer, first on the ground, was naturally unwilling to step aside without stepping out entirely.

"I'll go home and you can have this job, but it might be dangerous to make a substitution at this time," was his answer. Davis saw the other man's point and dropped the matter. With his innate fairness, he wrote home that Palmer's resignation "would be a loss to the paper that I do not feel I could make up."

There was some consolation in the fact that all of the press was in the same boat—or rather, out of any boat bound for Manchuria and the seat of war. Misery had the company it loved and it was good company. Lloyd Griscom, one of the *Three Gringos,* was American Minister to Japan and he had his secretaries came bearing bouquets to Mrs. Davis. An old comrade of arms in Greece, John Bass, was in Tokio with his wife. Some of the Britishers were a trifle stand-offish to Davis on account of his Boer War stories, but to most of the correspondents he endeared himself. John Fox, Jr., was a loyal henchman and Davis constituted himself one of the self-appointed guardians of the lovably erratic future author of *The*

Trail of the Lonesome Pine. Martin Egan remembers the night when, calling on the Davises, an argument on religion was finished by his bantering remark to Cecil Davis, "Thank God, you and I are pagans." His host, profoundly religious, rebuked him mildly when he left for his hotel. Several hours later there was a knock on his door. It was Davis who had walked a mile and a half through the snow to apologize for having, as he feared, hurt his friend's feelings.

Numerous dinners and other functions forced some of the correspondents to borrow evening clothes or have them made in a day by clever Chinese tailors. Davis of course had come prepared and was always perfectly *en regle.* The Japanese general staff had appointed some of its foreign university men as an entertainment committee and they worked night and day to lull the restlessness of the gentlemen of the press. Odd moments were filled in by rounds of the bars where the rustle of a ten-yen note would start a crap game.

But the members of the Fourth Estate assembled in Tokio were star men with reputations to sustain. The Japanese might serve course after course of lotus and still fail to make them forget for long that they had been sent to cover a war and so far had fallen down on the story.

Tension increased as they were put off with one excuse after another. Then the departure in April of the correspondents assigned to the First Army cleared the atmosphere somewhat. Mr. Collier's $1000-a-week man bade them a melancholy farewell.

II

You may trace the story of the bitterness Davis was being forced to taste through the issues of *Collier's* for the spring and early summer of 1904. Among the fiction and the gorgeous double-page drawings by Remington and Gibson begin to appear the war articles of Palmer and Hare's fine photographs. On the lower half of left-hand pages run articles on spring festivals in Japanese temples and the like beneath the by-line: "By Richard Harding Davis, *Collier's* Special War Correspondent in Japan. The Japanese War Office has issued a war correspondent's pass to Mr. Davis and assigned him to the second column. Until this takes the field, Mr. Davis will write of events in the Japanese Capital."

Weeks, months passed and no column with which Davis's pass was good took the field. He and his wife settled down in a house, went sight-seeing and attended the races where he won his bets as usual. Still he "wrote of events in the Japanese Capital" and wrote of them perfunctorily, since the only events he cared about were happening in Manchuria. The zest of the one-time eager traveller through the Mediterranean had vanished. Even his article on the caged women of Yoshiwara, the Tokio red-light district, was flat. John Fox, writing for *Scribner's,* was far surpassing him, sensing the charm of the land of blossoming shrines almost as Lafcadio Hearn had felt it, penning delightful dialogues with a little Japanese maiden, a Geisha novice, and being with difficulty dissuaded from the quixotic idea of adopting her and sending her to school.

Davis sought distraction in the company of his friends. There was a group of jolly young fellows just out of college, including William H. Hitt, Gerald Morgan, and Louis Hinrichs, who had come over for a post-graduate course in war observation. Some of them had been rounded up in Ping Yang, Korea, and sent back to Tokio by the Japanese. They and some of the older men were formed by Davis into a society with the motto, "Ping Yang for the Ping Yannigans"; they struck medals for themselves and gave lively parties.

Coming to the rescue of Jack London, off in Manchuria with Kuroki's army, kept him busy for a time. London, as two-fisted as his fiction, had knocked down a thieving Japanese groom and involved himself in serious difficulties.[2] Davis never had met London, but it sufficed that a fellow American, a fellow newspaperman was in trouble. When word of the emergency reached him, he kept the wires busy with messages to Roosevelt, and the President mediated as successfully as he would later at the Portsmouth, N. H., peace conference. London on his way home stopped to thank his benefactor who advised him that his feeling of bitterness against "the wonderful little people" would wear off and he would remember only the pleasant things.

By the middle of July the philosopher was ready to eat his words. He and the other censored, cooped-up correspondents went raging about Tokio, filing protests at their legations. They were met by what Fox called "the Oriental suavity of the gracious representative of the Stars and Stripes"—meaning Minister Griscom whose considerable diplomatic talents were taxed to the utmost. He and his government appreciated that the Japanese were within their rights, yet nothing he could say could bring Davis to accept the new order of things and bow unprotestingly to the autocracy of the military censor.

For Davis had been brought up to believe in the power of the press. That power as embodied in himself was being flouted. He was conscious of his reputation—that he was a personage. Franklin Clarkin heard him quite artlessly inform a Japanese officer who seemed unimpressed by his credentials: "I am a bigger man in my profession than you are in yours!" Now he had borne all the polite Eastern evasions he could stand. At a weekly conference on war news where the cor-

[2] From Charmian London's *The Book of Jack London*. New York, 1921.

R. H. D. IN MANCHURIA

PLACE CARD FOR A DINNER AT THE AMERICAN
LEGATION IN TOKIO

respondents were told what so often had proved to be a lie: that they would be sent to the front next week, Davis rose in his wrath. In plain words he told the presiding Japanese general his opinion of such tactics.

Irritation mounted as Davis regarded his kit[3] which by this time had reached a state of superiority never previously attained. Not only did there seem no prospect of his using it, but Japanese quartermasters to whom he displayed it had, according to his accusations, copied several of its items without paying royalties to the patentees.

The Russians might have recruited in Tokio a foreign legion of desperate journalists who now had been held up four months and missed the battles of May and June. "In simple kindness," Fox wrote,[4] "the Japanese might have said: 'This is the business of the Japanese and Russians alone. Over here we do not recognize the ancient, God-given right of the newspapers to divulge the private purpose of anybody. We believe that war correspondents are harmful to the proper conduct of a war. Frankly, we don't want you and to the front you can never go.'"

Polite promises, devious ways, and maddening delays had been the method preferred by Nippon. But toward the end of July the screen was moved aside at last and the correspondents attached to the Second Army loaded aboard a steamer bound for Manchuria. It hove to three days off the Elliott Islands and the passengers solaced themselves with swimming. The sun glistened on Davis's fine body flashing down from the top rail on dives for coins—and getting them. Even that amusement

---

[3] For this campaign, the kit included a patent folding chair and water bottle, a German Army cooking apparatus, towels, cards, books, pipes, tobacco, and a six-shooter. Six shots, remarked Davis, are enough, for if you don't hit the other fellow with those, he hits you and you need no more.
[4] From *Following the Sun Flag*. New York, 1905.

was stopped by an officer as contrary to transport rules, rules which were meant to apply only to the soldiery.

III

The *Heijo Maru* made port and Davis with his colleagues stepped ashore on Manchurian soil into the midst of a tumultuous melange of Chinese coolies, Japanese soldiers, mules, donkeys, ponies, and horses. Over the racket the boom of the big guns at Port Arthur carried the inspiration of a real story at last. The Japanese had promised them they should see the fall of the forts, reason enough, affirmed the disillusioned Davis, to believe they should see nothing of the kind.

Fox watched him keep his temper through a trying scene on the docks. As soon as he had finished loading a cart with his baggage, a Japanese officer approached and threw everything out, including his camera and other fragile articles. Davis obtained permission from another officer for his interpreter to load a second cart and the job was done in spite of blistering curses from the objector.

The next day the correspondents were ordered northward away from Port Arthur. Davis was too bitterly disappointed to take any satisfaction in his prophecy. Through the millet fields, under the clouds of red dust raised by the marching columns ahead, rode the cavalcade of reporters. Fox during intervals when the squealing stallion he bestrode was not running away with him gazed admiringly at the glory of the campaign ribbons across the chests of Melton Prior, dean of the corps, the veteran Burleigh, and Davis. Wiry little Clarkin, tall, dapper Willmott Lewis of many tongues,[5] William Brill, Lionel James, and others, English, American, French, and Italian, spurred on eagerly. Perhaps there was action ahead after all.

[5] Sir Willmott Lewis, now Washington correspondent for *The London Times.*

Their spirits rose as they pitched camp beneath the Manchurian moonlight. Champagne corks popped and Lewis's fine baritone rang out in "Absinthe Frappé" to the accompaniment of the Davis guitar.

For eleven days they pressed on. Once they were caught in a terrific downpour and ordered back by an indifferent Japanese major to a village in which they had wished to take shelter when they passed through. Davis helped the older Prior through the dark and wet. They were marooned there two days.

Shepherded and censored at every step, calling their correspondent's brassards "The Red Badge of Shame," they were allowed a distant glimpse of the battle of Anshantien. The disgruntled reporters stood on a hill and with the aid of their field-glasses made out rings of shrapnel smoke floating over a pass miles away. A noiseless, odorless, rubber-tired, perfectly safe battle, Davis disgustedly dubbed it—the only one he ever witnessed "that did not require you to calmly smoke a pipe in order to conceal the fact that you were scared." The press swore sulphurously and collectively and most of it lay down and went to sleep.

"Our teachers, the three Japanese officers[6] who were detailed to tell us about things we were not allowed to see . . . were hurt when they found that none of us was looking at them or their battle," Davis wrote. " 'You complain,' they said, 'because you are not allowed to see anything and now, when we show you a battle, you will not look.'

"Lewis, of *The Herald,* eagerly seized his glasses and followed the track of the Siberian railroad as it disappeared into the pass. 'I beg your pardon, but I didn't know it was a battle,'

[6] Davis's *The Notes of a War Correspondent* under the chapter head, "Battles I Never Saw."

he apologized politely. 'I thought it was a locomotive at An-shantien Station blowing off steam.'"

An indignant round robin addressed by the correspondents to the commanding general drew the answer that they would be permitted no closer view of combat. While the Japanese advance swept all Russian opposition from the road to Liao-Yang, the war reporters, well to the rear, passed over the abandoned battlefields. On the ground of one engagement Davis found the body of a young Russian. As he had done in other wars, he searched the soldier's knapsack for a keepsake for his family; found a letter from his sweetheart. Clarkin, who heard the interpreter read it, tells the story.

"In terms of considerable delicacy she broke their betrothal. To this moving missive the soldier had attached her photograph, showing a face sensitive yet strong, keen yet dreamy, beautiful in the brilliant Caucasus way. Such mementos it is usually deemed a kindness to return when possible to whatever friends or family of a slain soldier to which the finder may have a clue. 'But what,' argued Davis, 'is my duty? What is the greater good—to send these treasured relics of the dead to his one-time sweetheart, or not?' It was a sort of conflict between ethos and pathos. Davis still had the mementos in his pocket when he left Manchuria for home."

There was the plot-germ of a fine short story, but Davis never wrote it. All his thoughts and hopes were concentrated on a chance to retrieve himself and earn his salary. Surely a major battle would be fought at Liao-Yang and he would manage to see it somehow. Questioned, the Japanese major in charge of the correspondents dashed his expectations. Liao-Yang, he declared unblushingly, already was occupied by the troops of the Mikado, with the Czar's army in full retreat.

Davis in spite of his experiences for the last four months

believed him. Sadly, hopelessly, he, Fox, and two British correspondents left the army and took the road for the coast.[7]

He might have hung on and with that grim persistence, which was one of the first lessons he had learned as a reporter, have stuck to his story till he got it. He might have dodged his "keepers," as Hare and several others did. But in that dark, frustrate hour, the intrepid spirit of risk and resource, the once unerring instinct for action, were gone from him.

He reached the coast without adventure; walked into the cable office at Chefoo to wire *Collier's* he was coming home. The Chinese operator smiled up at the big correspondent writing his despatch.

"I congratulate you," he announced.

For a moment Davis did not lift his eyes.[8] He felt a chill creeping down his spine. He knew what sort of a blow was coming, and he was afraid of it.

"Why?" he asked.

The Chinaman bowed and smiled.

"Because you are the first," he said. "You are the only correspondent to arrive who has seen the Battle of Liao-Yang."

The chill turned to a sort of nausea. Davis knew then what disaster had fallen, but he cheated himself by pretending the rumor was unconfirmed.

"There was no battle," he protested. "The Japanese told me themselves they had entered Liao-Yang without firing a shot."

The cable operator was a gentleman. He saw the American's distress, saw what it meant to deliver the blow with the distaste of a physician who must tell a patient he cannot recover. Gently, reluctantly, with real sympathy, he said:

[7] Davis reached the coast without adventure, but Fox, a Harvard man, was arrested as a spy by a Japanese Yale graduate. In the ensuing intercollegiate ruction, Harvard was thrown for the loss of a night in jail, but broke loose in a clear field the next day.

[8] This episode, except for transposition of pronouns, is given verbatim as Davis related it in *The Notes of a War Correspondent*.

"They have been fighting for six days."

Davis went over to a bench and sank down. By a lie, by the space of three days, he had missed the greatest battle since Sedan.

"So our half-year of time, money, of dreary waiting, of daily humiliations at the hands of officers with minds diseased by suspicion, all of which would have been made up to us by the sight of this one great spectacle, was in the end absolutely lost to us," he wrote. "Perhaps we made a mistake in judgment. As the cards fell we certainly did."

But the man had backbone. He could stand up under a heavy blow and take it. The officers of the *U. S. Cincinnati* entertained no whiner but a merry guest that night. While the officer of the deck ignored the uproar and watched a suspicious star, the wardroom rang with song. Davis was leading " 'Way Down in My Heart I've Got a Feeling for You" which provides plenty of grand close harmony.

CHAPTER FOURTEEN

NEWS AND FEATURES

I

Back in his own country, Davis not only wrote news; he was news. Interviewers flocked out to Mt. Kisco in the New York suburban area where he had moved his hearthstone from less accessible Marion and built a comfortable, roomy house, with kennels, a stable, and even an artificial lake. Though a thirsty cow, friends joked, might drink up the lake, it was nevertheless an impressive and baronial adjunct of Crossroads Farm which eventually comprised 300 acres and cost $100,000. A writer who could undertake such an outlay in 1905 was as much news as the man who bit the dog.

Davis was wielding one of the most golden pens of the period. His literary output continued to command top prices, and the rewards of authorship were increasing yearly. Endowed by the fairy godmother, Advertising, magazine editors were paying $1000 per short story to a double quartette of Big Names: Richard Harding Davis, Booth Tarkington, Jack London, John Fox, Jr., Owen Wister, and Frances Hodgson Burnett. Davis, boyishly delighted with his rate of from twenty to twenty-five cents a word, wrote Martin Egan, still in Japan: "Think of getting fifty cents for writing 'for instance'!"

Six short stories a year were his average output, but checks for special articles swelled his income, royalties rolled in from new and old books, and the theatre box offices paid constant tribute. Augmenting them was the sale of extra rights to his novels and stories, particularly for motion-picture production.

Such stipends (one hundred dollars per story, with a modest percentage of receipts) proved the movies to be "still in their infancy" as treasure trove for fictioneers and dramatists.[1] Yet it was like finding money.

The more Davis made, the more he spent. In him the industry of the ant and the improvidence of the grasshopper were joined. "I don't mind working," he used to say, "but I hate like hell to save." Besides the drain of his unostentatious extravagance, he never could refuse a loan to friend or even an acquaintance, down on his luck. Men released from prison to start life over again appealed mightily to his charity, and his love for children made him open-handed to settlement and Boy Scout work.

Crossroads Farm, fond as he grew of it, could not hold him for long. The city with its crossroads to all points of the compass summoned him to the pursuit of copy, adventure, and the not almighty but greatly alluring dollar. New Yorkers would catch sight of his debonair figure enshrined in a stately electric hansom rolling to dock or station. A straw hat with one of the new, swank colored hatbands crowned the well-shaped head, strong hands reposed with dignity on a cane, and heaps of the latest style leather luggage surrounded the traveller. One month he would be bound for the Caribbean to cover the Isle of Pines for *Collier's*. Another would find him sailing for Spain to see Alfonso properly, if impermanently, enthroned. Back over the cable would tick an account of the ceremonies and woe betide the editor who cut or rearranged his articles, for the tables were turned on the copy desk now.

Duster and goggles might be his costume on other travels

---

[1] Davis did not live to see the day when movie rights to a novel brought $25,000 or better; when plays which were stage failures recouped by sale to the screen; when authors treking West in the Hollywood gold rush were paid large salaries for stories never used. But his estate benefitted considerably from sales of film rights to his stories.

and his conveyance the big, red, undependable automobile which inspired his novel, *The Scarlet Car*. Once visiting Ethel Barrymore in New Hampshire, he met Winston Churchill again. Churchill was engaged in exactly the sort of task that appealed most to Davis: living up to one of his own books. That splendid novel, *Coniston*, having smitten machine politics hip and thigh, its author, after two terms in the legislature, was further practicing his preaching by running for Governor on a reform ticket. Davis, always aflame at the prospect of a crusade, immediately offered his services, but Churchill, who knew his State and its people, regretfully declined. Himself originally a summer resident, he recognized that the entry of another outsider—and a swell from New York at that—would be poor strategy. Davis could only read of the candidate's campaign and its stirring climax when Churchill's lead on the eighth ballot united the railroad factions against him and their reinforcements slipped through the State House skylight to defeat the creator of *Jethro Bass*.

II

Political prudence in New Hampshire could silence Davis. Social prudence in New York could not—not when the name of a dead friend needed defense. The risk was all his own and few were willing to share it. Fair-weather companions of the victim now branded an ogre, a satyr, a violator of homes and innocence were flatly denying having known him. Or they were slipping away to Europe or California to avoid contamination from the infamy heaped on the murdered Stanford White.

The sensational story Davis read in his newspapers was front-page stuff for days by every journalistic canon. Action, names, sex, setting, dramatic irony—it boasted them all. St. Gaudens's virginal Diana on the tower of Madison Square Garden presiding that night of June 25th, 1906, over a *crime passionel*. A dull show in the roof theatre dragging through a song by the comedian, "I Could Love a Million Girls." Muffled shots and a commotion among the cabaret tables. New York's most celebrated architect killed in a building he had designed by a wastrel millionaire who swore he fired to save his wife's honor. Then the trials in courts and the press—"a slaying of the character after the slaying of the man"—with White's memory besmirched and degraded to win an acquittal for his murderer on an insanity plea.

Davis with his Puritanical strain and White, the true Bohemian, never had been intimates. Yet they held in common a love of life, a spirit of generosity, and kindness to beginners in their arts. And the writer cherished a profound admiration for the man who had done more than any other "to restore New York to health . . . after it had waked up one morning with a horrible brownstone taste in its architectural mouth."

The imprint of White's genius was on the city Davis loved. To gaze at the Garden's tower, to pass through the Washington Arch, to enter The Lambs or The Players and other clubs or homes was to pay tribute to that genius. The covers of magazines carrying stories by Davis were after White's designs. Beyond the honor due achievement, Davis's sense of justice and fair play demanded he take up arms in behalf of one who could not answer his slanderers.

A public, inflamed by accounts of the trial testimony to consider Stanford White a monster, read aghast the article which *Collier's* valiantly printed. That Richard Harding Davis, "knight of decency," should dare praise the dead architect and declare that he was as incapable of meanness as of great crimes seemed altogether shocking. The author spoke out stoutly. "I have never known an attack to be made upon any one as undeserved, as unfair, as false, as the attack upon White."

Years would bring others willing to clear a blackened reputation, but Davis's defense so soon after the event was an act of rare moral courage. He suffered the consequences. A storm of opprobrium from the bigots and the ignorant broke over him. A library in New Jersey threw his books out in the gutter, while the headmaster of a prominent school for boys warned his pupils to beware of *Soldiers of Fortune* and *Princess Aline* "as foul emanations of a depraved romancer."

III

A new target far more worthy of public indignation soon presented itself in King Leopold of Belgium whose exploitation of rubber plantations in the Congo was raising a worldwide clamor. Charges of atrocious cruelties practiced on enslaved blacks were rife, and the ever-crusading *Collier's* sent Davis to investigate. He accepted with the understanding that he could not give the task the time its thorough performance deserved. His articles, consequently, while timely did not penetrate beneath the surface. Davis's book based on the trip, *The Congo and Coasts of Africa,* is his least interesting travel work, but he could be proud of a short story by-product. *A Question of Latitude,* describing the deterioration of a young Boston Brahmin under the spell of Africa, is a finely imaginative piece of writing, modern in technique.

Except as it caught his fancy as a fiction writer, the charm of the Dark Continent eluded him. Even the hippopotami he shot rose up and plunged back into the river, refusing to become trophies. He was glad to return to London and New York where birds of gorgeous plumage he had sighted in the jungle were perched on vast Merry Widow hats, where skin daringly revealed through peek-a-boo shirtwaists was white, and civilized husbands spent long half-hours hooking up the backs of a wife's evening gown. New York called him for the opening of *The Yankee Tourist;* London for a winter spent in the artist Turner's house in Chelsea, where Sargent came to listen fascinated to Davis's conversation and advise Mrs. Davis in her painting. Cuba demanded another visit. To military manœuvres near Boston he gave tone as a veteran war correspondent.[2] Was it anything like the real thing? all the younger reporters kept asking him, and when Davis, pleased as Punch with his prestige, assured them it was, they were doubly keen for the assignment. There he rode again with the old commander of the Rough Riders, General Leonard Wood, and pledged his lifelong support to that inspiring leader's doctrine of Preparedness. Any good cause he could serve was a Godsend to him in the dark and troubled days now upon him.

IV

Almost all of Richard Harding Davis's love stories ended happily. Words he had written idealistically remained only fiction and would not come true for his own love story.

It was an estrangement of long standing between him and his wife, said his brother, which resulted in their separation early in 1910. The breach, final and complete, seemed to lend color to the contention of the critics who insisted that the heroes and heroines of Davis's books were impossibly innocent young people without parallel in real life. Gouverneur Morris answered the detractors. "R. H. D. never called upon his characters for any trait or virtue, or renunciation, or self-mastery of which his own life could not furnish example."

[2] By-products were a short story, *Peace Manœuvres,* and a one-act play based on it.

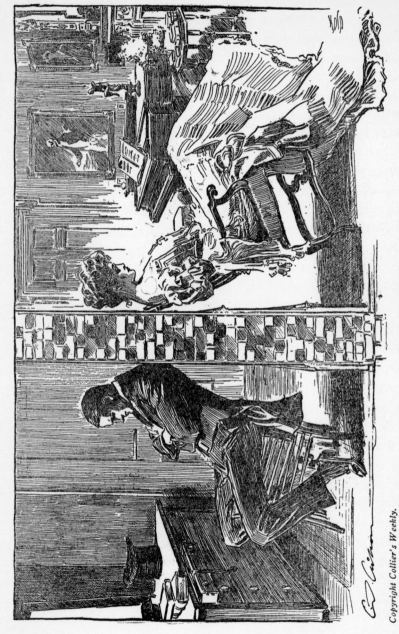

THE PARTY WALL

A cartoon by C. D. Gibson utilizing the Davis profile.

For ten years, bonds which, declared friends closest to Davis, were only those of friendship, of mutual fondness for adventure and travel, of respect for each other's talent, had held him and his wife together. Such platonic comradeship could no longer endure as marriage.

The estrangement and the step of separation, so grave to him, exacted a heavy toll of Davis. These years were replete with sorrows. He had lost his father and now his mother died during a visit at Crossroads Farm. Under the succession of blows his temperament showed its fortitude. His brother thought he never had seen a man make so courageous a fight. A staunch faith sustained him and he wrote in his diary: "Early going to my room saw red sunrise and gold moon. I seemed to stop worrying about money. With such free pleasures I found I could not worry. Every day God gives me greater delight in good things, in beauty, and in every simple exercise and amusement."

He did not slacken in his work, keeping himself at his writing for discipline. His friends rallied to him. "He who had given friendship to so many people needed a little friendship in return." It was given him fully and gladly.

Not until the dawn of belief that life still held romance for him did Davis seek to make the separation absolute by divorce. His wife, acquainted with the circumstances, acceded willingly. Mrs. Davis obtained the decree in Chicago in an amicable suit filed on a desertion charge.

V

Three Twins, the musical show at the Herald Square Theatre, had been playing to capacity, with speculators exacting as high as five dollars for a choice seat. One of their best customers was a distinguished playwright who night after night

occupied a seat in the front row. He had not written a line
of the libretto nor had he any connection with its production,
but he never had attended any play of his own with such fervid
regularity and enthusiasm. Like every other man in the audience who had seen *Three Twins* before, Dick Davis waited
for the moment when a girl with bright eyes and a tiny mouth
which pouted one instant and flashed a smile the next, danced
on in her black Pierrot costume with its big white pom-poms
and bow tie broad as a sash.

None who saw Bessie McCoy dance[3] ever forgot the picture
of grace and sparkling vivacity she made, the charm she wafted across the footlights. It was her show and the song she sang
in her husky contralto always would be hers, too. It was sweeping the country and everybody was singing the tuneful lyric
about the bogey—

> "Yama, Yama, the Yama Man,
> Terrible eyes and face of tan"——[4]

Bessie McCoy sang it as she danced and they encored her again
and again.

The New York newspapermen, voting the Yama Yama Girl
a good fellow, organized the Ten O'Clock Club which met on
the stage after the show. One night Frank Ward O'Malley,
star reporter of *The Sun* and boulevardier of Broadway in its
heyday, removed the club's chief attraction to have supper
with him at Churchill's. O'Malley's homely, genial, map-of-
Ireland face lit up with pleasure when he saw his friend Davis
enter with Granville Fortescue.

"Here comes a man who wants to meet you. Be nice to

[3] Bessie McCoy was her stage name. Her real name was Elizabeth Genevieve
McEvoy.
[4] "The Yama Yama Man." Words by Collin Davis, music by Karl Hoschna.
Quoted by permission of M. Witmark & Sons.

From a photograph by Moffett, Chicago.

MISS BESSIE McCOY AS THE YAMA YAMA GIRL

Augustus Thomas selects a location at the iron mines.
R. H. D. on his right.

Hope Langham and *MacWilliams* hold up traffic
at the Juragua mines.

MAKING THE MOVIE OF *SOLDIERS OF FORTUNE*, SANTIAGO DE CUBA, 1913

him," the reporter urged his guest. Presenting Davis, he asked:
"You've seen Bessie in *Three Twins?*"

"Yes," Davis answered. "I saw her tonight for the eighteenth
time."

It was a splendid cue line but the actress gave most of her
attention to Fortescue, Rough Rider veteran and dashing cav-
alryman. She had heard so long of Richard Harding Davis as
an author, she was ready to class him with Dickens and Thack-
eray. Davis, however, had a trusty ally in O'Malley. Called the
greatest reporter of his time,[5] his name was indelible on the
brilliant morning *Sun* roll which listed Arthur Brisbane, Julian Ralph, O. K. Davis, Edward W. Townsend, A. E. Thomas,
Frank O'Brien, Edwin C. Hill, Samuel Hopkins Adams, and
Lindsay Denison. And O'Malley owned to an immense admiration for Davis as a master in their craft and as a man. His
esteem was reciprocated. A copy of Davis's book, *The Red
Cross Girl,* in which the reporter hero wrote a piece that was
"the kind of a story that made Frank O'Malley famous," was
a prized possession of the little Irish-American.

The congenial party left Churchill's for the Larry Mulligan
ball at Terrace Gardens, the uproarious and bellicose Tammany function which O'Malley covered year after year, always
using the same lead:

"All roads led to the Terrace Gardens last night, where the
Larry Mulligan Association held its annual high carnival.
Champagne flowed like water. Amid garlands of flowers and
the sweet strains of the light fantastic, leading Tammany
statesmen, the city's more prominent wine agents and song

[5] In its obit. on O'Malley, who died in 1932, *The New York Herald Tribune* said:
"Few reporters ever abandoned their profession in such a cloud of glory as Frank
Ward O'Malley. His news-sense, his genial satire, and the easy grace of his writing
were staple material for the prefatory lectures delivered to cub reporters of the last
decade by their editors. The O'Malley legend became as vigorous and hardy as the
legend of Richard Harding Davis."

pluggers, and the elite of the Bowery danced the hours away with their lovely ladies."

Then would follow a list of the injured, as for a railroad wreck:

Burke, Eddie: Third and fourth chins scarified by high-set diamond ring.

Eastman, Monk: Compound fracture of brass knuckles. Removed to Police Headquarters where Mr. Eastman was identified as unknown.

Donovan, Trailing Arbutus Biggie: Other eye also closed. Removed to Considine's, to Churchills, to Jack's, to etc., etc., etc."

Bessie McCoy, Davis, and Big Tim Sullivan served as judges of the dancing contest, care being taken to choose prominent persons as less likely to experience the violent displeasure of the losers.

Davis lost no time. The next evening he appeared backstage in his best *Van Bibber* manner and called at Miss McCoy's dressing room. Her mother and Louise Frey, her companion, heard him launch the first of a long series of proposals of marriage. The lady thus honored thought he was mad. She danced on the stage to sing about another queer fellow, the Yama Yama Man—

> If you don't watch out
> He'll get you without a doubt,
> If he can.
> Maybe he's hiding behind a chair,
> Ready to spring on you unaware.
> Run to your mama,
> For here comes the Yama Yama Man.

But Davis continued in evidence. He followed his flowers in nightly pilgrimages to the theatre. He sounded her praises even in the important pages of *Collier's* where in an article on critics he managed to proclaim that with the rest of the world he was kneeling at the feet of the Yama Yama Girl. *Three Twins* closed and Bessie McCoy continued stardom in *The Echo,* with a score by Deems Taylor. Pierrot became a sprightly toy soldier, blond wig pert under paper hat, wooden sword in hand, dancing with a teddy bear. Nightly still a front-row aisle seat held a worshipful occupant, chin on hands, hands in the yellowest gloves to be bought, hands on cane. Through the duly thrilled chorus would run the whisper that Richard Harding Davis was out front again. Which word, reaching the star, would draw the ultimatum: "Make him go away. He makes me so nervous I can't work." Delivered by usher, the command would be obeyed. The exile would take a dignified but flourishing departure only to return later.

The Echo took the road to Philadelphia, with Davis in close pursuit. John Fox, Jr., present in that city for a similar reason, for Fritzi Scheff was playing at a neighboring theatre in *The Mikado,* would compare notes between the acts with his old friend and fellow star-gazer.

"How's your house tonight, John?" Davis would ask.

"Fine. How's yours?" Fox would return.

"Ours is $20 better than last night."

Ziegfeld bought Bessie McCoy's contract with Charles Dillingham and she appeared in his roof show and went on the road with the *Follies.* Through it all the courtship persistently continued. The glamor of Dick Davis's good looks, personality, and reputation had turned the head of many a girl. But the fascinating dancing star had won fame in her own right. Of stage folk for generations, she had made her début at the age of three, strapped on the back of a pony. As a child actress, she had been trouping in Australia when Davis was reporting the Boer War. Finally she had risen through the vicissitudes of vaudeville and the hazards of horses in the Hippodrome to reach a Broadway pinnacle.

The stage which had meant hard work from childhood on could be given up without reluctance. Although she was earning large salaries and members of her family were dependent on her for support, Davis was making plenty of money. She was only twenty-four and while he was forty-eight he was still young. But the opposition of friends, who doubted the wisdom of the match, helped make the course of true love proverbially rough. Also Davis had not yet obtained his divorce, and Bessie McCoy refused to be involved. Her suitor was rejected more often than *Gallegher* had been.

Months of undiscouraged and deep devotion finally turned the scales. One sharp-eyed lady among the thousands breathlessly watching this romance noticed that Bessie McCoy was wearing Rebecca Harding Davis's 1840 cameos and knew that stout heart had won fair lady. Shortly after the granting of the final decree of divorce, they were married on July 8, 1912, at the home of the Gouverneur Morrises. It was like Davis to wish others to share in his joy. That day in honor of his bride he sent 500 mothers and children from the tenements on a steamer trip and outing at Coney Island. *Van Bibber's* similarly generous impulse had gone no farther than to treat little girls in Central Park to innumerable rides in the swan boats, but then he had not just been married.

Crossroads Farm became their home. "And they lived happily ever after." This time it came true.

VI

Preoccupation with his own affairs could not deafen Davis to the call of an old allegiance. The shouting and the tumult of the exciting election year, 1912, rang in his ears like the

cheers and carbine volleys of Las Guasimas in '98. That em-
bodiment of captains and kings, Theodore Roosevelt, was
about to depart from the political battlefield but not without
giving mighty combat. Davis, true to the blue bandana of the
Rough Riders, charged as spiritedly in print as he had in action through the Cuban underbrush. With Palmer, O. K.
Davis, and many other war correspondents and writers, he
volunteered his services in the campaign publicity bureau organized by Will Irwin and syndicating brilliant material which
even the opposition papers were impelled to carry. If the
names of authors which won circulation for national magazines could have swung votes as surely, T. R. would have
marched over the prostrate bodies of Wilson, Taft, and the
third-term bugaboo and stormed the White House triumphant-
ly once more.

Vincent Starrett in the midst of the racket of the Republican
National Convention at Chicago turned toward the man next
him on the floor and knew Davis from his portraits. He
watched the older man survey the incredible scene with a sort
of whimsical amusement, touched with cynicism; in particular the antics of a delegate shouting for recognition in a thin,
piping voice and accompanying his demands by a ludicrous
swaying of his body. Catching Starrett's eye, Davis grinned
and observed: "Funny old boy, isn't he?" And Starrett, like
so many of the younger reporters, was immensely flattered that
Richard Harding Davis, a hero of his, had spoken to him.

But history refused to repeat San Juan, and William How-
ard Taft could not be written into the background as readily
as Shafter. Leaving him the spoils of the Republican nomination, the Rooseveltians retreated to unfurl the banner of the
Bull Moose in that fatal division of forces which spelt Democratic victory. Helping stage-manage the convention, Davis

turned on the band when the organ seemed to be sapping the
ardor of the crowd. Through the nights he pushed his pen
tirelessly and conferred on campaign strategy. Wallace Morgan, the artist, remembered the elegant spectacle his friend
Davis furnished in the late gatherings of newspapermen in
hotel rooms. Immaculate as always in evening clothes proper
to the hour, he would hash over events of the day with his
disheveled colleagues of the press, meanwhile downing numerous whiskeys and sodas but never, as his code demanded,
exceeding or showing any effects.

Having done his duty by the Colonel at home, Davis sailed
for the scene of their foreign service on business of his own.

VII

Soldiers of Fortune was inevitably earmarked for the movies,
and in the fall of 1912 the author and a company sailed for
Cuba to film the story. Augustus Thomas, who wrote the
scenario, Dustin Farnum playing the lead as *Clay,* and William F. Haddock as production director, led a retinue of three
actresses, sixteen actors, two camera men, and a business manager aboard ship and at once began to shoot the scenes laid at
sea.

For Davis it was one of his most entertaining adventures.
Neither the book nor the play gave him the immensely thrilling sensations he experienced when his characters came to life
before his eyes in the original setting of his tale. He watched
Hope and *MacWilliams* drive a locomotive through the jungle;
saw unfolded the tragic love of *Madame Alvarez* who, thought
the gaping Cubans, must be the Queen of Spain herself; delighted in the mustering of "extras" where he made himself
indispensable. Distinguished Cuban families, squads of *rurales,*
and scores of workmen from the mines rallied eagerly at his

request to people his scenes. When the Santiago commandant refused to lend him his garrison, Davis had only to wire the Minister of War at Havana and the entire Cuban army was immediately placed at his disposal. When local arsenals could not supply the rapid-fire gun called for by the scenario, he cabled the U. S. Naval Base at Guantanamo and forthwith the required weapon, accompanied by a petty officer and crew to man it, was forwarded by fast scout boat to the writer who always had been a friend of the Navy. The clicking cameras reeled in the battle "shots" of a motion picture hit. Five earnest "extras" were wounded in the heat of the fray, and *Stuart* was "slaughtered" almost too realistically as excited soldiery fired at close range and blank cartridge wads smote him in the chest.

Farnum, playing the hero, had been unable to resist borrowing Davis's field clothes, so exactly suited to the part of *Clay*. The garments having been registered on the film, their owner was forced to wear makeshifts until the scenes in which they appeared were finished. As Thomas remarked with a grin, the actor had brought evening togs, so the author could don his own and go out at night correctly attired.

Davis and Thomas after a day of movie making sat smoking together in the evening at a café table on the Santiago plaza. "The President's band was playing native waltzes that came throbbing through the trees and beating softly above the rustling skirts and clinking spurs of the señoritas and officers sweeping by in two opposite circles around the edges of the tessellated pavements." . . . It was the romantic background of *Soldiers of Fortune* revivified. Davis broke a long, musing silence. He was coming back to Cuba next winter, he confided, to bring the *Hope* whose real name had turned out to be Bessie.

CHAPTER FIFTEEN
VERA CRUZ DATE–LINE

I

IN the spring of 1914, rash Mexicans arrested a shore liberty party of American sailors and locked them up briefly in the calaboose of oily Tampico. Washington decided the time had come to despatch less notes and more battleships. On April 20, President Wilson asked Congress to authorize the use of armed forces to compel President Huerta to respect our flag— not to mention our investments, added realists. The next morning a New York station redcap, weighted down with a correspondent's kit marked R. H. D., was conducting its owner to a train for Texas and announcing jubilantly: "We is goin' to wah!"

Davis was not so sure. War had not been declared. He suspected more "watchful waiting." Although John N. Wheeler's syndicate serving *The New York Tribune* and other papers was paying him $400 a week to follow up this martial tip, that was only one of the expensive precautions good journalism must take.

The touch of drama which seldom failed him was waiting at Galveston where army brigades were concentrated under General Frederick Funston, with white transports in readiness at the wharves. Davis stepped into the Hotel Galvez to find a dinner preceding a tango dance in progress. It was as if Lord Byron, war correspondent by poetic proxy, had set the stage with sound effects of revelry by night for him. Bright the lights shone o'er fair women in gowns which 1914 called low-neck and brave men in white tropical service uniforms with gilt insignia. A breeze from the Gulf bent the palm trees in the patio and the orchestra played *"Peu d'Amour"* to accompany soft eyes looking love. In mid-dinner an aide appeared, summoning all officers to report. Orders from General Funston, commanding. Embarkation for Mexico at daybreak. The cannon's roar from Waterloo cleared the ball at Brussels no more rapidly.

Davis, filing the story which had broken so beautifully for him, boarded a transport along with Jack London and Vincent Starrett for both of whom he had arranged credentials.[1] The vessel steamed for Vera Cruz which the Navy had shelled and occupied with sailors and marines after two days of stubborn fighting. Now only the Army was needed to revive completely the Spirit of 1846 and march on to the storming of Mexico City.

Soldiers and correspondents landed in the battered city, its atmosphere sternly martial and tense. Sentries challenged vigilantly from street barricades. Beyond town the outposts, lightly held, were on the alert, momentarily expecting attack. But every officer and man, uniformed in khaki or duck, and every flannel-shirted correspondent who entered the town plaza that evening forgot Mexican menaces for the astounding spectacle to be witnessed in front of the Hotel Diligencia.

Under the *portales,* an arcade holding the open-air street café of the hostelry, sat Davis dining in state. He wore what was probably the only dinner coat within a radius of 300 miles. Book propped against a carafe, a cooler containing a pint of champagne at his side, he dined ritually and obviously on in

[1] London had been falsely accused of printing a canard about General Funston, and, as in Manchuria, Davis helped him out of the difficulty. London expressed his gratitude in a typically London sentence: "People can say what they damn please, but Davis is a great, big 'white man.'"

full view. The military, the press, and the populace trooped by gasping. All Vera Cruz was aware that night that Richard Harding Davis was on the scene, ready to observe the conventions and whatever war news might develop with cool detachment.

"It was not an affectation; it was the man," Starrett explained in reminiscences. "At other times he would tramp miles with the best, sleep in his BVD's or uniform and eat off a box. But in town of an evening, he was Mr. Richard Harding Davis of New York, and the fact that Generals sometimes dined with him had nothing to do with the case. He would have entered a dinner coat at six o'clock if he had been alone on Crusoe's island with only a parrot and a dog."

Davis's distinction of appearance, together with a distinction in dress, which, whether from habit or policy, was a valuable asset in his work, made him a marked man, affirmed John T. McCutcheon. "He was just as loyal to his code as the Briton. He carried his bath-tub, his immaculate linen, his evening clothes, his war equipment—in which he had the pride of a connoisseur—wherever he went, and, what is more, he had the courage to use the evening clothes at times when their use was conspicuous."

Regularly every night, duties permitting as they generally did, the custom was maintained. Some evenings General Funston, Admiral Fletcher or Colonel Lejeune of the Marines might be his guest, but usually Davis preferred to dine alone. He would go the lengths of having all chairs but his own removed from the table, and if a bore seemed about to approach, he would scribble busily on a heap of cable blanks and call a boy hired to pretend to file them. For he stood on his right to be alone, even in public, with his own concerns,[2] whether

---

[2] In contrast, Jack London was unable to protect himself by a hard-shell attitude. Friends and acquaintances besieged him continually, giving him little time to himself.

they consisted in planning his next day's work or writing one of his three daily love letters to his wife. He simply refused to be bothered in time he reserved for himself. He would risk whatever impression his exclusiveness gave but he would not risk being bored.

Once the tables were amusingly turned on him. The story is Starrett's.

Davis had recently returned from an expedition into the interior when Oliver Madox Hueffer, a British correspondent, advanced smiling, with outstretched hand.

"Glad to see you back again," he greeted. "Must have had a great time up there."

"Ha, yes, of course," replied Davis who was not in a mood for congeniality. He meagerly accepted the clasp. "But, by George, old chap," he added, "I think I've forgotten you."

Hueffer's expression remained unchanged, his smile grew broader, his handclasp stronger.

"That's quite all right, old man," he conceded generously. *"You* may have forgotten *me,* but *I* shall never forget *you, Mr. London!"*

II

"Mr. Wilson's private war" dragged on through unbelligerent days. Davis, his forebodings realized, wrote an article for *Scribner's,* "When a War Is Not a War." The bombardment and capture of Vera Cruz had struck him as furnishing "an excellent imitation of what once were considered war-time incidents," but Washington apparently knew it was not the real thing. Thereafter occurred nothing more militant than prizefighting, bull-fighting, and dirt-fighting. The armed forces whose use had been authorized by Congress were doing a noble job in cleaning the city of the filth of Spanish centuries, and one exhausted Navy plumber and fitter had been commended for gallantry. Sanitation, however, and mediation, too, palled quickly as news topics.

This second invasion of Mexico sadly lacked color and incident. Not so Dick Davis—he continued to supply both. A timely Baedeker would have mentioned him as one of Vera Cruz's points of interest, one of the sights to be seen. Afternoons riding, with his striker, a former Mexican colonel, fifteen paces to the rear, or playing a magnificent game of water polo in which it took three men to get the ball away from him. Evenings in dinner-coated glory under the *portales* and winning at roulette with his usual good luck. Mornings turned out in impeccable field togs topped by a gray felt hat with blue polka-dot puggaree and carrying a riding crop. Mrs. Nelson O'Shaugnessy, who had arrived from Mexico City with her husband, the American *chargé d'affaires,* teased Davis about that hatband, the Rough Rider symbol he always wore. "It's the loudest thing in town," she said, "and can be spotted at any distance." Davis grinned and launched his repartee: "But isn't recognition what is wanted in Mexico?"

Swank as they were, these were working clothes. Arthur Constantine, admiring their wearer as one of the two or three handsomest men he ever met, put him down also as the most energetic correspondent of them all, up early unfailingly every morning and off for a round of the encampments, never seeming to mind the intense heat. Hiking ten miles under the tropic sun with Frederick Palmer, Davis joined him in shedding coat and collar but resumed them as they approached the Marine post which was their destination. Palmer objected to such style for interviewing a detachment of hardboiled leathernecks.

"Yes, but you haven't my reputation as a good dresser to live up to," Davis retorted.

Palmer, sarcastically: "Why not put a flower in your buttonhole?"

Davis, sedately: "It isn't in regulations to put a flower in the buttonhole of a military blouse. I am a stickler for regulations."

Among his fellow newspapermen, Davis had come to divide interest with any assignment they covered together. He was always a reliable bone of contention. Aloof and arrogant, maintained his critics. Not when you got to know him, his defenders answered; he would share his news with you and give you any help you asked. A fine, silk-lined manner but no bombast, Jack Lait analyzed him—a chap who had seen everything twice—too reserved to laugh or be shocked into any display—even at his greatest ease, a bit lordly and *Van Bibber*. "He had as fine a pair of eyes as any reporter who ever lived," Constantine thought. Not conceited but sensitive and keen about points of honor and the high calling of the newspaper profession, was William G. Shepherd's rating. J. S. S. Richardson called him a good sportsman and a fine chap; John T. McCutcheon, the beau ideal of a war correspondent; and Vincent Starrett, "one of the finest human beings I ever knew."

Conscientious as always, Davis rushed to the outposts at the slightest rumor of action. Once at a line of trenches held by a naval detachment under Lieutenant Adolphus Staton, he found that a sailor sentry had been calling out *"Quo Vadis?"* all night, the tar's strategy being: if he challenged in English, the Mexicans would shoot, while if they answered his Latin demand in Spanish, he would shoot.

"Quo Vadis?" Davis laughed when Staton told him. "Why don't you have him advertise *my* books?"

Answering another false alarm, Davis and other correspondents almost made their own war news when they heard the report of a skirmish at the "front" near El Tejar. Two victoria-loads of eager scribes raced for the scene of alleged action in hot haste. At Los Cocos, the nervous *cocheros* struck and the press was forced to hike through the dust and heat until Davis sighted and hired a hand-car. Pumping that vehicle to the end of the track, the reporters had dismounted and joined a small Medical Corps detachment when they were suddenly surrounded by Mexican Federals. For a moment it was touch and go, with prospects of an American massacre excellent, for only Davis and one other correspondent were armed with automatics. While the medico lieutenant strained his Spanish to convey their non-combatant status, Jimmy Hare and Palmer saved the situation by lining up the Federals for a photograph. Having looked pleasant, the Mexicans forgot to be hostile and furnished friendly escort part of the remaining distance to peaceful El Tejar.

III

Disgustedly, Davis swore he never would budge for another war until both armies had been battling for two months and he was certain they meant it. He was using quotation marks now and describing himself as a "war" correspondent. Yet even in these mark-time hostilities adventure came through for him.

The daring idea of interviewing Huerta in Mexico City originated with an editor safely distant in the United States. He wired the enterprising assignment to his staff man in Vera Cruz who prudently declined the risk. In the interior of Mexico, Americans were being murdered daily. Refugees from

Mexico City brought back the tale of their last bad night in the capital when they manned the windows of the American legation with rifles and machine guns while a mob outside on the verge of attack howled, "Death to the Gringos!" They advised no one to put his head in that lion's mouth.

The editor passed on his Huerta idea to Wheeler whose syndicate also served his paper. Wheeler, knowing the perilous nature of such a trip and reluctant to impose it on Davis as an assignment under their contract, cabled merely asking if he would be willing to go. In two hours he had his answer: "Leaving for Mexico City tomorrow."

That was like Davis, Wheeler recalled; no hesitancy, no vacillation, always willing to take any chance, to endure hardship, if he had a fighting opportunity to get the news. And the managing editor of an opposition paper, shown the cable, conceded: "That man will go anywhere any one else will go. He will not quit on the job just because it is dangerous."

With papers supplied by the British and Brazilian ambassadors and a highly doubtful safe-conduct, Davis set out with Palmer and Medill McCormick. All three admitted to misgivings. However Washington might regard the situation, the Mexicans "in their quaint ignorance," as Davis put it, "fancied we were at war, that they were our enemies, and at any moment might act as such." Nor had their train jogged many miles when it was halted at a village and the correspondents taken off under arrest. Files of soldiers armed to the teeth marched the Americans toward the town jail.

Davis, towering above his little Mexican captors in dirty blue jeans, was flushing with humiliation as he strode in the lead. Over his shoulder he flung back an angry question to his companions. "Isn't it about time we did something?" he demanded.

McCormick hastily cautioned him. "We don't want to be drawn into any *Soldiers of Fortune* stuff, Dick."

Davis's rashness subsided at that. The three correspondents, searched and locked up, argued the chances of their being shot at sunrise. A firing squad seeming too much of a likelihood for comfort, they began to kid the situation in the Anglo-Saxon way.

"You're smallest, Medill," Davis proclaimed jovially. "They might take you first. Then, if they give Palmer and me time to write the story, all would not be lost."

It was not mere bravado. If it came to an execution, Palmer reflected, Davis would most certainly die in the heroic tradition.

"Everything they did to us I had written and copyrighted," Davis wrote lightly of that uncomfortable afternoon and night later.[3] "The serial, dramatic, and movie rights were all in my name . . . but I found acting it much more difficult than writing it." He remembered that his heroes in similar emergencies always defied: "Release me, or I'll bring a warship here and blow your dinky republic off the map!" Obviously that was the wrong line now. It seemed wiser to keep their guards in a good humor.

Dawn brought no firing squad but a command for Davis and McCormick to be sent on to Mexico City, while Palmer, whose papers appeared less plausible, was ordered back to the coast. He trudged off through the sand with an uneasy expectancy of a bullet between the shoulder blades but reached Vera Cruz in safety.

His story and the uncertainty of the fate of his companions stirred the city with excitement. The Army snapped out of its apathy. If the Mexicans shot those newspapermen, it looked

[3] In *Scribner's* for July, 1914.

From a photograph by J. H. Hare.

A GROUP OF WAR CORRESPONDENTS AT VERA CRUZ

Standing on car, left to right, they are: Thomas P. Coates (Hearst Service), Robert Dunn (N. Y. Evening Post); sitting, left to right: Vincent Starrett (Chicago Daily News), Davis, Frederick Palmer, and Kirk Simpson (Associated Press). **Two Mexican boys behind the car.**

BOY SCOUTS AT CROSSROADS FARM, MT. KISCO, N. Y., 1913

Ethel Barrymore awarding prizes, Norman Hapgood is at Davis's right and Mrs. Davis and Ruth Hapgood are at the extreme right of the picture.

like a punitive expedition and real war after all. Correspondents were on the alert to flash "obits." of the dean of their corps and his companion who was a member of one of the richest and most influential families of the Middle West. Wires to Washington hummed. Mrs. Davis and friends flooded the State Department with demands for rescue, much to the diplomatic annoyance of Secretary Bryan.

The efforts of Sir Lionel Carden, the British ambassador, effected the return of Davis and McCormick after twenty-four hours of confinement in Mexico City during which Huerta refused to be interviewed; in fact, to be anything except merciful. Army and press welcomed the pair back to Vera Cruz magnanimously. "I'm awfully sorry to see you back," one officer greeted Davis with a grin. "If you'd only have stayed in jail another day, your wife would have had us all on our way into Mexico." Correspondents scrapped tributes prepared for colleagues dead in line of duty, and, with professional courtesy, let the quick write their own story.

III

In June Davis sailed home on one of the battleships which Secretary Josephus Daniels recently had made dry territory. The mills of the news ground slowly for a while and granted him a few idyllic weeks at Crossroads Farm with his wife. Contentedly he went on with his writing in the comfortable study which had been surreptitiously cleaned while he was in Mexico, much to his dismay when he learned of it, though his wife's letter had added that charts had been made so that every article would be returned to its proper place. He wrote as always with pencil on small sheets of yellow paper, standing at a high desk and occasionally gazing out into the yard in which no laundry could be dried to distract him nor any white flowers with a laundry aspect be allowed.

Bessie McCoy Davis was jealous of the door of the study which shut her out from her husband when he was at work, but she respected that barrier with the discretion which wives of authors learn. She humored various of his foibles, too. He hated patent leather shoes, so she never wore them. When they went walking in the woods, she willingly had changed her dress, at Richard's wish, to one which would harmonize with the foliage. For she could never be grateful enough for all she felt he had taught her—self-control, optimism, and faith in the ultimate goodness of things—the ability to distinguish between commonplaces and sacred places in life. "He gave me," she declared, "those elements of good taste that give rest and charm to life."

Every morning he did his exercises regularly, for he was resolved never to allow himself to grow fat. Now at the age of 50, he could stand stiff-legged, bend and lay his hands on the floor. He still might have posed for the statue of a young athlete—of the weight-throwing rather than the running type. After a cold bath in which he insisted on singing, he ate his breakfast where he was cheerful and went busily to work. As always, he found time to pen notes of praise to other writers.

Afternoons often brought company. Sometimes friends, sometimes the Italians he had gone to warn away from his cherry trees. They ended up in the kitchen where he regaled them with spaghetti and Chianti. Troops of Boy Scouts frequently would be given camping privileges on his place, with the special proviso that they should not approach the house. That condition, impressed on Mrs. Davis, never held for long. The master of the estate would approach her with a sheepish look, remark that a thunder storm was coming up and wouldn't it be well to quarter the entire troop in the attic? And wouldn't Bessie join him and the Scouts in the kitchen while the boys tried out camp cookery on the Davis larder and he played his guitar for them?

Dressing as regularly for dinner in the informality of his home as he had in the war atmosphere of Vera Cruz, Davis would mix his favorite cocktail: one-third French vermouth, one-third Italian, one-third absinthe. A pint of champagne would accompany the meal, with perhaps one highball later. Sometimes the distant tolling of the alarm bell at Sing Sing could be heard—signal that a prisoner had escaped. Davis always said he feared he could not resist helping a fugitive. There had been "a story in that"—*The Naked Man*.

August, 1914. Quiet days at Crossroads Farm came suddenly to an end. Across the newspapers streamed the great banner headlines day after day. Mobilizations, declarations of war, one great nation of Europe after another flinging its armies and its fleets into the battle line. The correspondent packed his kit once more for the war which would be his sixth, his greatest and his last and answered Wheeler's hurried summons to a meeting.

Would he represent the syndicate again? There would be no dearth of news this time. Six hundred dollars a week and expenses. Davis's nod bound the verbal contract which was all either man asked. August 4, the day after Germany invaded Belgium, he caught an emergency sailing of the *Lusitania*. Lights out, her wireless crackling out the momentous message that Great Britain would stand with her allies, the great ship steamed across the sea which ten months later would sweep in through the torpedo gash in her hull and engulf her.

London, familiar yet strange in her mood of grim determination. Khaki battalions mustering to the rousing strains of "Tip-

perary." Correspondents scurrying for credentials with Kitchener's Army. Cables to the State Department begging nomination for the one place to be given an American. Would Mr.
Bryan accredit Richard Harding Davis? He would not—not
the man whose "Mexican escapade caused us some diplomatic
efforts and embarrassment." The place went to Palmer, also
guilty of the "escapade."[4] but never so free with criticism of the
Administration.

No matter. Davis determined to make his passport do and
join whatever army of the Allies he found fighting. He crossed
the Channel to Belgium. The army of that gallant little country was still holding the German hosts at Liege, they said.
Davis hastened on to Brussels.

[4] The issuance of these credentials was so long delayed in London that numbers of
the correspondents named left for the front without waiting to receive them.

CHAPTER SIXTEEN

MARCH INTO BRUSSELS

II

BRUSSELS was still a city of elegance and joyousness in those early August days. The conflict, Davis perceived, had penetrated the daily lives of its light-hearted people only like a burst of martial music. As if he were a spectator at a colorful military masque, he sat at a sidewalk café table and watched soldiers and Red Cross nurses, eagerly awaiting their call to duty, promenade past. Commandeered limousines, cushions piled high with ammunition cases, rolled through toward the front. Pretty girls, begging for the wounded, gaily jangled tiny tin milk cans. Fire, sword, and famine were dim, distant, off-stage. To the Belgian capital, war was glad and glorious, for the guns of Liege still spoke. David held Goliath at bay, and the city in the path of the giant was proudly jubilant.

As if he, too, were playing a fascinating game where the penalties were negligible, Davis sallied forth each morning, unencumbered by credentials. A big yellow automobile bore him and Gerald Morgan, comrade of Tokio days, wherever fighting was rumored. Like coins flung across a board which was the map of Belgium, sometimes they struck a lucky number, a skirmish; sometimes drew a blank. They found it pleasant to stop play at dusk, drive back to town, bathe luxuriously, and dine with Brand Whitlock, U. S. Minister, or Hugh Gibson, secretary to the Legation.

It was on the night of August 18 that a strange group whose wooden shoes and bundles reminded Davis of emigrants from Ellis Island drew him and other diners from the restaurants of the Place Rogier. A crowd swallowed them before he could reach their side. Spreading swiftly from its centre came startling news—"The Germans are in Louvain!"

Davis could not believe it. Only recently he had been west of Louvain and seen no Germans. Next morning he no longer doubted. The street outside his room in the Palace Hotel echoed to the clamor of horns and the rushing swish of the tires of motor cars dashing to the coast and safety. Raucous, harsh, and peremptory, the warnings of the horns and sirens blended into one long, continuous scream. It beat on Davis's ears with steady roar, and it spoke in abject panic. The racing cars shrieked like human beings driven by dread. In their windows the faces of women and children of the nobility, the gentry, and the rich, white with fear, fatigue, and dust, flashed past the watching correspondent.

He went out into the side streets to view the plodding procession which followed after—the pitiful flight of refugee peasantry from farms and homes abandoned to the invader—the young trudging by the side of plow horses dragging carts heaped with precious chattels—the aged and feeble perched on the bales and boxes. Tragedy unrolled its panorama slowly this time. The reporter could mark the tear furrows on tanned, country cheeks, the terror-haunted eyes of the fugitives. "Heartbroken, weary, hungry, they passed in an unending caravan."

Davis tensely awaited the oncoming tornado whose blast had swept this human débris before it into swirling, fluttering, frantic flight. He moved his quarters closer to the American Legation, a refuge of sorts for a neutral observer through the hazards of bombardment and street fighting. He knew that Burgomaster Max and his civil guard were prepared to make a hopeless defense. Honor demanded it, they said quietly. But at the eleventh hour arrived King Albert's order forbidding resistance and sparing his capital from inevitable destruction.

Neither the prospect of battle nor of iron military rule daunted the spirit of Brussels. The German army, negotiations for unopposed entry completed through Mr. Whitlock, now was at the very gates. Two great airplanes droned overhead, casting their cruciform shadows across the streets. Still the café lights blazed through that night, and on the morning of the 20th, the shops were still open and the streets crowded. Davis, utterly admiring the calm with which the city faced whatever fate might befall it, kept anxious vigil as the moment approached when the legions of the Kaiser must appear.

In mid-morning Brussels underwent a swift and sudden transformation.

From his post on the Boulevard Waterloo, Richard Harding Davis witnessed a spectacle more indelibly impressive than the onslaught of storm troops. The story of the entrance of the German hosts must be given in his own incomparably vivid words.[1]

II

"The change came at ten in the morning. It was as though a wand had waved and from a fête-day on the Continent we had been wafted to London on a rainy Sunday. The boulevards fell suddenly empty. There was not a house that was not closely shuttered. Along the route by which we now knew the Germans were advancing, it was as though the plague stalked. That no one should fire from a window, that to the conquerors no one should offer insult, Burgomaster Max sent out as special constables men he trusted. Their badge of authority was a walking-stick and a piece of paper fluttering from a buttonhole. These, the police, and the servants and

[1] From *With the Allies*. New York, 1914. Quoted by permission.

caretakers of the houses that lined the boulevards alone were visible. At eleven o'clock, unobserved but by this official audience, down the Boulevard Waterloo came the advance-guard of the German army. It consisted of three men, a captain and two privates on bicycles. Their rifles were slung across their shoulders, they rode unwarily, with as little concern as the members of a touring-club out for a holiday. Behind them so close upon each other that to cross from one sidewalk to the other was not possible, came the Uhlans, infantry, and the guns. For two hours I watched them, and then, bored with the monotony of it, returned to the hotel. After an hour, from beneath my window, I still could hear them; another hour and another went by. They still were passing. Boredom gave way to wonder. The thing fascinated you, against your will, dragged you back to the sidewalk and held you there openeyed. No longer was it regiments of men marching, but something uncanny, inhuman, a force of nature like a landslide, a tidal wave, or lava sweeping down a mountain. It was not of this earth, but mysterious, ghostlike. It carried all the mystery and menace of a fog rolling toward you across the sea. The uniform aided this impression. In it each man moved under a cloak of invisibility. Only after the most numerous and severe tests at all distances, with all materials and combinations of colors that give forth no color, could this gray have been discovered. That it was selected to clothe and disguise the German when he fights is typical of the General Staff, in striving for efficiency, to leave nothing to chance, to neglect no detail.

"After you have seen this service uniform under conditions entirely opposite you are convinced that for the German soldier it is one of his strongest weapons. Even the most expert marksman cannot hit a target he cannot see. It is not the blue-gray of our Confederates, but a green-gray. It is the gray of the hour just before daybreak, the gray of unpolished steel, of mist among green trees.

"I saw it first in the Grand Place in front of the Hotel de Ville. It was impossible to tell if in that noble square there was a regiment or a brigade. You saw only a fog that melted into the stones, blended with the ancient house fronts, that shifted and drifted, but left you nothing at which to point.

"Later, as the army passed under the trees of the Botanical Park, it merged and was lost against the green leaves. It is no exaggeration to say that at a few hundred yards you can see the horses on which the Uhlans ride but cannot see the men who ride them.

"If I appear to overemphasize this disguising uniform it is because, of all the details of the German outfit, it appealed to me as one of the most remarkable. When I was near Namur with the rear-guard of the French Dragoons and Cuirassiers, and they threw out pickets, we could distinguish them against the yellow wheat or green gorse at half a mile, while these men passing in the street, when they have reached the next crossing, become merged into the gray of the paving-stones and the earth swallowed them. In comparison the yellow khaki of our own American army is about as invisible as the flag of Spain.

"Major-General von Jarotsky, the German military governor of Brussels, had assured Burgomaster Max that the German army would not occupy the city but would pass through it. He told the truth. For three days and three nights it passed. In six campaigns I have followed other armies, but, excepting not even our own, the Japanese, or the British, I have not seen one so thoroughly equipped. I am not speaking of the fighting qualities of any army, only of the equipment and organization. The German army moved into Brussels as smoothly and as compactly as an Empire State express. There were no halts, no open places, no stragglers. For the gray automobiles and the gray motorcycles bearing messengers one side of the street always was kept clear; and so compact was the column, so rigid the vigilance of the file-closers, that at the rate of forty miles an hour a car could race the length of the column and need not for a single horse or man once swerve from its course.

"All through the night, like a tumult of a river when it races between the cliffs of a canyon, in my sleep I could hear the steady roar of the passing army. And when early in the morning I went to the window the chain of steel was still unbroken. It was like the torrent that swept down the Connemaugh Valley and destroyed Johnstown. As a correspondent I have seen all the great armies and the military processions at the coronations in Russia, England, and Spain, and our own inaugural parades down Pennsylvania Avenue, but those armies and processions were made up of men. This was a machine, endless, tireless, with the delicate organization of a watch and the brute power of a steam roller. And for three days and three nights through Brussels it roared and rumbled, a cataract of molten lead. The infantry marched singing, with their iron-shod boots beating out the time. They sang 'Fatherland, My Fatherland.' Between each line of song they took three steps. At times 2000 men were singing together in absolute rhythm and beat. It was like blows from giant pile-drivers. When the melody gave way the silence was broken only by the stamp of iron-shod boots, and then again the song rose. When the singing ceased the bands played marches. They were followed by the rumble of the howitzers, the creaking of wheels and of chains clanking against the cobblestones, and the sharp, bell-like voices of the bugles.

"More Uhlans followed, the hoofs of their magnificent horses ringing like thousands of steel hammers breaking stones in a road; and after them the giant siege-guns rumbling, growling, the mitrailleuses with drag-chains ringing, the field-pieces with creaking axles, complaining brakes, the grinding of the steel-rimmed wheels against the stones echoing and re-echoing from the house front. When at night for an instant the machine halted, the silence awoke you, as at sea you wake when the screw stops.

"For three days and three nights the column of gray, with hundreds of thousands of bayonets and hundreds of thousands of lances, with gray transport wagons, gray ammunition carts, gray ambulances, gray cannon, like a river of steel, cut Brussels in two.

"For three weeks the men had been on the march, and there was not a single straggler, not a strap out of place, not a pennant missing. Along the route, without for a minute halting the machine, the post-office carts fell out of the column, and as the men marched mounted postmen collected post-cards and delivered letters. Also, as they marched, the cooks prepared soup, coffee, and tea, walking beside their stoves on wheels, tending the fires, distributing the smoking food. Seated in the motor-trucks cobblers mended boots and broken harness; farriers on tiny anvils beat out horseshoes. No officer followed a wrong turning, no officer asked his way. He followed the map strapped to his side and on which for his guidance in red ink his route was marked. At night he read this map by the light of an electric torch buckled to his chest.

"To perfect this monstrous engine, with its pontoon bridges, its wireless, its hospitals, its aeroplanes that in rigid alignment sailed before it, its field telephones that, as it advanced, strung wires over which for miles the vanguard talked to the rear, all modern inventions had been prostituted. To feed it millions of men had been called from homes, offices, and workshops; to guide it, for years the minds of the high-born, with whom it is a religion and a disease, had been solely concerned.

"It is, perhaps, the most efficient organization of modern times; and its purpose only is death. Those who cast it loose upon Europe are military-mad. And they are only a very small part of the German people. But to preserve their class they have in their own image created this terrible engine of destruction. For the present it is their servant. But, 'though the mills of God grind slowly, yet they grind exceeding small.' And, like Frankenstein's monster, this monster, to which they gave life, may turn and rend them."

III

It was called the finest piece of reporting of the war, this picture of "imperialism itself coming down the road."[2] The measured beat and swinging rhythm of its sentences seemed to echo the marching tread of all the hordes of history sweeping relentlessly, interminably over conquered kingdoms. Unsensational, brilliant in its selection of telling detail, this magnificent description crowned the career of a great war correspondent. The world was stirred with its first glimpse of the grim, minute efficiency of the mighty German war machine. Davis's despatch fired the public imagination and was quoted everywhere. Fellow correspondents and critics acclaimed it, and it ranks with the living literature of the World War.

While the field-gray columns still were marching through the city, Davis found Harry Hansen, whose fluent command of the German language was already envied by his colleagues,

2 Arno Dosch-Fleurot.

writing in the Palace Hotel. All regular channels of egress and communication out of Brussels had been cut off.

"Is there any way of getting anything out?" Davis asked.

"I don't know of any, do you?" Hansen countered.

"No, I don't," said Davis.

But he was then checking up on ways and means of slipping his account of the German entry through the cordon. By the time he had completed it, he had found a courier, an English boy named Dalton, who, after being turned back thrice, got through by night. "When he arrived in England," Davis related, "his adventures were published in London papers. They were so thrilling that they made my story, for which he had taken the trip, extremely tame reading." On other occasions, John T. McCutcheon stated, Davis used as his messenger an old Flemish woman who managed to pass the German lines as a refugee and carry his despatches through to Ostend.

On toward Mons and the Marne flowed the torrent of steel. Firing to the south, proclaiming its progress, set a pack of importunate American correspondents to plaguing General von Jarotsky, military governor of the city, for passes. Although most of the passes reluctantly granted by him specified "Brussels and environs," their bearers rushed off toward the fighting determined to stretch environs to the limit of Yankee ingenuity.[3]

The correspondents disappeared in various directions using any conveyance available. Davis and Morgan hired a taxicab and drove as far as Hal. There they were arrested, put under guard but abandoned by sentries who preferred the company of their own regiment to that of the prisoners. Following a

[3] On some of the passes the locality-restriction clause was omitted through error. They carried a group including Irvin Cobb, McCutcheon, Hansen, James O'D. Bennett, and Roger Lewis through the German Army and enabled them to see considerable fighting before they were rounded up, given a sojourn in a German prison, and sent out of the country.

marching column, the reporters reached Bierges, which Morgan insisted was clearly out of bounds.

"If we go any farther," he argued, "the next officer who reads our papers will order us back to Brussels under arrest, and we will lose our *laissez-passers*. Along this road there is no chance of seeing anything. I prefer to keep my pass and use it in the 'environs' where there is fighting."

A wise and proper decision, Davis agreed, but he was not yet ready to make it himself. He preferred to go ahead and risk another arrest. Then he could explain to his newspapers that he had returned under compulsion, and that exacting sense of duty of his would be satisfied.

As Morgan in the taxi vanished down the roads to Brussels, Davis shouldered his haversack and set out on foot. In a pocket of his trim English suit rested his passport, its photograph showing him in a military tunic, copied from a British regiment seen in the Boer War, and with campaign ribbons on its breast. Straight and soldierly, he swung along the road, one of His Majesty's officers in mufti by the look of him. Every step took him nearer to Ath and, though he could not know it, the British lines. Soon he was again in the current of the field-gray tide he had described. It streamed past and closer around the striding figure in khaki. Within the next forty-eight hours it very nearly submerged him forever.

CHAPTER SEVENTEEN

SPY STORY

I

THE black muzzles of four automatics stared suddenly down at Davis where he sat against a tree eating his lunch. One of the German soldiers who had stalked this supposed spy from the rear made his aim surer by jamming his pistol into the target's stomach. Both hands, one holding a sandwich, raised high above his head, the correspondent hastily declared that his identification papers were in his inside pocket. Fortunately the most enthusiastic of the captors understood English. They marched their prisoner, pistols still rubbing his ribs, before their colonel.

That officer having just finished an excellent repast was in a genial glow. He gave the enthusiast a drink for arresting Davis, one to Davis for being arrested, and extended his pass to Enghien, two miles on.

The visé advanced him two hundred yards. Again he was halted, his papers examined, and again passed. This time he reached Enghien, whose burgomaster gave him a permit to spend one night there.

"You really do not need this," the Belgian deprecated. "As an American you are free to stay here as long as you wish." Whereupon he patently winked.

"But I *am* an American," Davis insisted.[1]

---

[1] This section necessarily leans heavily on Davis's own account of his spy adventure as published in *With the Allies*. New York, 1914. Throughout, his anxiety to avoid heroics and egotism is evident. His biography need suffer no such compulsion, and his narrative is here supplemented by reading between its lines and from the testimony of friends to whom he told the story less formally.

"But certainly," the burgomaster answered and winked once more.

It was then that Davis first realized he ought to start back to Brussels. Even the Belgians took him for a British spy. There was no telling how much longer German suspicions, already lively, could be lulled.

But he let his opportunity to retreat slip away with the rest of the afternoon and tried to sleep through a restless night, while the now familiar gray river of death and destruction rumbled by beneath his window. At daybreak he sat on the edge of his bed still wondering whether to go on or turn back. But no one had *ordered* him back. Until some in authority did so, until he had made every effort to reach and report the battle that might lie ahead, he could not give up. Vanity, he called it, but it was not that. He had a reputation to maintain. His was that conscience which a good newspaperman early develops from love for the game and from fear of the withering scorn of his city editor. That he might be pushing both his conscience and his luck too far went unconsidered. Perhaps the memory of a battle missed in Manchuria haunted him that morning.

So he struck out again into the gray waves. One of a group of officers he passed galloped after him, demanded his papers. The procedure was growing monotonous, but no casual arrest and release were in store this time.

"I think you had better see our general," said the officer. "He is ahead of us."

Flanked by a lieutenant and a sergeant, Davis found himself taking part in a forced march toward a surprise attack. For five hours he was compelled to push on at the double-quick to keep up with troops who after two days at such a pace now moved like automatons or men in a trance. Soldiers who dropped were lifted to their feet and flung back into ranks. At the halts the whole column sank to the ground exhausted "as though they had been struck with a club." Davis's fine physical condition and his spirit carried him on in spite of the fact that one shoe had collapsed under the impact of Belgian cobble-stones and was cutting into his foot. The environs mentioned in his pass were left farther and farther behind him.

The big automobile, blazoned with the imperial eagle, which came swooping back along the column at the end of the five hours to pick up the weary correspondent, was not a welcome relief. It flashed a danger signal to Davis's brain, as a high-ranking officer, coldly polite, invited him to enter and accompany him to the Division Staff. Immediately the prisoner appreciated that he was drawing too much attention for his situation to be anything but deadly serious. From that moment he began to work to save his life.

Resplendent, omnipotent, the Staff lunched by the road, a race apart from the gray ghosts of the river sweeping by them. One glittering officer, evidently told off as prosecutor, approached the correspondent in dusty khaki. Dark, tall, and handsome, his uniform of light blue and silver braiding and his high boots of patent leather clung to his slimly elegant form. Davis saw that he was to play mouse to the other's cat and that the German relished his part infinitely. In none of his own books could Davis find a villain wickedly fascinating enough to match him, and for a prototype he was forced to borrow his friend Anthony Hope's *Rupert of Hentzau* from *The Prisoner of Zenda*.

Rupert did not mince matters. He was brutally frank.

"You are an English officer out of uniform," he began. "You have been taken inside our lines." He pointed his forefinger at his victim's middle and wiggled his thumb. "And," he finished, "you know what *that* means!"

"I followed your army," Davis explained, "because it's my business to follow armies and because"—a little flattery which was also truth would not hurt—"and because yours is the best-looking army I ever saw."

Rupert bowed mockingly and grinned. "We thank you," he said, "but you have seen too much."

"I haven't seen anything," protested Davis, "that everybody in Brussels hasn't seen for three days."

"You have seen enough on this road," Rupert differed, "to justify us in shooting you now."

For Davis, as he subsequently learned, had taken the road to Ath by mistake and stumbled upon a Germany army corps marching with all speed and stealth to crumple up the British right flank. Any British officer escaping from Brussels and surprising this secret naturally would attempt to rush a warning through to his own lines. Rupert, grilling him delightedly, piled up black evidence against him. Davis's German pass was not signed, only stamped and probably forged. His American passport had been issued in London, not Washington, and in its photograph he wore a British uniform. Earnestly he explained that the uniform had been modelled on one worn only by the West African Field Force in the Boer War. Several English brigades since had adopted and now wore that very model.

Davis a year or so before had written a short story called *The God of Coincidence*. None of its coincidences were stranger than this fluke of his uniform he was relating with his life at stake. Certainly Rupert regarded his explanation as the wildest sort of fiction. He rejected it with the alacrity of an editor.

"Do you expect us to believe that?" the inquisitor demanded, with a superior smile in which the rest of the Staff joined.

"Listen," Davis shot back at him. "If you could invent an explanation for that uniform as quickly as I told you that one, standing in a road with eight officers trying to shoot you, you would be the greatest general in Germany."

That made them laugh, but Rupert was ready with a retort: "Very well, then, we will concede that the entire British army has changed its uniform to suit your photograph. But if you are *not* an officer, why, in the photograph, are you wearing war ribbons?"

Davis argued that the ribbons proved him a correspondent; that only a correspondent could have been in so many wars in which his own country was not engaged. Rupert's reply scored heavily.

"Or a military attaché," he instantly retorted.

Thus the court martial piled up against him one damaging piece of circumstantial evidence after another. Apparently the Staff of the Seventh Division, Imperial Germany Army, never had heard of Richard Harding Davis or his works. That cup, always a bitter one for the popular author, now seemed to contain hemlock mixed with the wormwood.

The fate of the man who in all likelihood was a British spy, yet might possibly be a crazy American, see-sawed back and forth. Finally they brought his trial to an ominously inconclusive adjournment. Rupert, again making his morbid gesture toward his victim's stomach, left him to his apprehensions for miserable hours, confined in a house in Ligne, with a sentry's automatic following every move.

Visited there by a friendly reservist major, who believed his story, Davis tried to send a note for help back to Brand Whitlock. No one could be spared to carry it, the sympathetic officer returned to report, tears rolling down his cheeks. It was plain that the sentiment of the court was swinging toward a firing squad.

Davis, aware that his plight was desperate, proposed his last resort. Let his captors send him back to Brussels with a pass stating that he was to be treated as a spy and shot on sight if he were found off the direct road or failed to make the fifty miles in two days.

Would the Germans let an enemy agent suspect out of their grasp, even if he were headed toward the rear? Davis knew his plan might be scoffed at, but he was going down in a whirl-pool of spy-scare hysteria and he clutched at a straw.

He feared his last moment had come when an angry officer routed him out of his prison at midnight, driving him to corps headquarters at a château. It was, he saw, no place for a man branded a British spy. Word of a British attack somewhere to the south had filled the great candle-lit halls with tumult and confusion. Electric torches blinded Davis as he sat in a gilt armchair waiting his sentence with two guards over him. The shafts of light showed his khaki and guttural voices cursed him. Outside sirens shrieked and men shouted: *"Die Eng-lischen kommen!"*

Drawing-room doors swung open to reveal Rupert of Hent-zau.

"Mr. Davis," he announced insolently, "you are free under certain conditions." They were those Davis had named. "You will start in three hours."

"At three in the morning!" Davis cried. "You might as well take me out and shoot me now!"

"You will start in three hours," he repeated.

"A man wandering around at that hour wouldn't live five minutes. It can't be done," Davis argued.

He might as well have saved his breath. There was no doubt

in his mind that the three-hours idea played no part in the General's order but was Rupert's own happy thought. Yet there was no chance to appeal from it. Rupert, grinning his sardonic grin which seemed to say that an accidental shooting would satisfy him almost as well as a formal execution, abandoned his victim to destiny.

Not daring to disobey, in three hours Davis started back through a black night. Whenever a sentry challenged, he struck a match to show the red seal on his pass. It was all he could do—he spoke no German. Though it was 100 to 1 that a nervous soldier would shoot at the flash of the match, the Davis luck held. Three times he risked a bullet; then took cover in a haystack till it was light. Every detachment which stopped him and read in his pass that he was "to be treated as a spy" if on the road after August 26 was reluctant to wait for that date. Limping along, one foot nearly bare and raw, and dreading he might lose the way, at last he chanced stopping the automobile of a German general. Happily, he had picked a kindly one. Without reading his papers, the general carried him through to Brussels.

Brand Whitlock found Davis slumped deep down in a big leather chair of the American Legation—a sunburned, unshaven fellow, gray with dust from head to foot. "Despite his good looks, his indubitable distinction in any emergency, he looked like a weary tramp."[2] He had been badly shaken,— he freely admitted that never in his five previous wars had he been so scared—but his nerve still was with him. Whitlock remembered with admiration the droll, humorous look in Davis's tired eyes as he told his story.

The indignant Minister escorted his American citizen to German headquarters. There he laid it on thick, giving General von

[2] Brand Whitlock's *Belgium*. New York, 1919.

Lutwitz, the military governor of Brussels, to understand that Richard Harding Davis was no British spy but, on the contrary, probably the greatest writer that ever lived, not excepting Shakespeare and Milton.[3] The general replied that he had read some of the accused's short stories and that he would not have him shot. The spy stigma was ordered expunged from the pass.

It had been a close call. Richard Harding Davis Shot as a Spy[4] nearly had been in the headlines—and they would have been large ones. A powerful pen, undipped in the ink of neutrality since the invasion of Belgium, had been further alienated by the Germans. Consciousness of personal bias might for a time have restrained its owner. But the path which the war correspondent, his usefulness ended in Brussels, now was about to follow brought him to scenes where *furor Teutonicus* was appallingly manifest.

II

There was a less drastic but more diplomatic method of getting rid of bothersome American reporters than shooting them by mistake. The Germans censored and delayed news stories and restricted every move of the correspondents remaining in Brussels. Davis, with Morgan, Will Irwin, Mary Boyle O'Reilly, and Arno Dosch-Fleurot, was soon resigned to accepting transportation on a train bound for the Dutch border. Davis went more willingly because of startling news just received. On the morning of his departure General von Lutwitz announced that Belgian civilians had shot down German

[3] From Hugh Gibson's *A Journal from Our Legation in Belgium.* New York, 1917.

[4] The Germans could have based a strong defense for such action on the British uniform worn by Davis in his passport picture; also the fact that he was out of bounds. Or he could have been reported killed while observing a battle.

officers and soldiers in Louvain; that vengeance would be taken on the city.

"Fifty Germans were killed and wounded," Von Lutwitz informed Whitlock and Davis, "and for that Louvain must be wiped out—so!" His fist smashed into the papers on his table and swept them to the ground.

The train carrying the Americans must pass through the doomed city. Unless some accident of timing or German strategy forestalled it, they stood every prospect of being eye-witnesses of one of the most stupendous spectacles of the war.

From the train window, a panorama of devastated villages and peasants fleeing from the smouldering ruins of their homes set the stage. The train pulled into Louvain at seven o'clock in the evening, and the Germans locked the reporters in their railroad carriage. But the car windows were vantage point enough. "The story," Davis declared, "was written against the sky, was told to us by German soldiers incoherent with excesses; and we could read it in the faces of women and children being led to concentration camps and of citizens on their way to be shot."

The correspondents stared incredulously out of their car windows at the destruction of the nine-century-old city. A drunken soldier reeling past and hearing their English speech threatened them with his revolver. Others clustered beneath their windows, eager to act as showmen for a display of frightfulness. Bayonets gleamed as uniformed figures milled through the station "like men after an orgy." Irwin anxiously thrust pretty Miss O'Reilly back out of sight. For two hours their train, a mobile theatre box, was shunted about the station. They watched the Germans fire house after house, relentlessly, systematically. The red glare of the mounting columns of flame illumined for Davis a drama which was unreal, inhuman.

Outlined against this crimson backdrop appeared a succession of tragic tableaux. Weeping women and children hemmed in by a shadowy army of gray wolves. A line of men marching to face the firing squads. An officer halting it, mounting a cart illumined by automobile headlights and bellowing the guilt of the doomed to warn others of vengeance. Dark ruins swallowing condemned and executioners. Volleys rattling through the roar of the conflagration.

At last their car was coupled into a train which bore them away from that nightmare. It was a weary group of reporters that detrained at Aix-la-Chapelle. They had passed through a terrific strain and for twenty-six hours had been without food, but they brought out with them news which all their profession would envy. Davis's story would prove to be another classic on war reporting, and Theodore Roosevelt, reading his book, *With the Allies,* particularly praised the chapter on the burning of Louvain.

Dosch-Fleurot, who would term Davis's Louvain article the most vivid piece of writing of the war, studied him as they crossed the border together and travelled through Holland to the coast. He long had admired the artist; now he was beginning to like the man. Davis's character both baffled and attracted his companion. A contradictory, lovable, unclassifiable, arrogant soul, he decided.[5] An answer by Davis, when Dosch-Fleurot complained that the Dutch always washed things in dirty water, stuck in the younger man's mind. "Don't look at the dirt," Davis advised. "Admire the picturesque. That's what I do and that is why I am getting $1000 a week and you are getting—whatever it is you are getting."

The correspondents dodged a woman spy in Maestrict— probably the genesis of Davis's story, *Somewhere in France.*

[5] From Dosch-Fleurot's *Through War to Revolution.* London, 1931.

They also missed a piece of news when the police arrested some of them to prevent their learning that the Dutch Prince Consort had brought German officers, friends of his university days, across the line for a party.

Davis was not looking for news just then. He could think only of reaching London where he believed his wife was waiting for him. It would be a crushing disappointment, yet he would entirely approve when he found that Mrs. Davis, who was expecting a baby early in the winter, had deemed it wise to await her husband's indefinite arrival no longer and had returned to the United States.

It was late when Davis, Dosch-Fleurot, and Irwin (the others of the party were not crossing then) detrained in Flushing and boarded the Channel boat. Though obtaining accommodations in that crowded vessel seemed an impossibility, Davis produced keys to three reserved cabins.

"What luck!" Dosch-Fleurot exclaimed.

"Not at all, I wired for them."

"But still, in this crowd."

The resourceful Mr. Davis smiled. "I signed my wire 'Sir Richard Davis!' " he explained.

CHAPTER EIGHTEEN
CRUSADER IN KHAKI

I

FOR a second time Davis unsuccessfully pulled every wire he knew in London to be accredited as a correspondent with the British Army, besieging Kitchener through Asquith and Winston Churchill. He was told flatly that his case was hopeless. Denied the safeguard of credentials, either he could give up an assignment which nearly had cost him his life or he could run again the risks from which he had garnered brilliant stories. Unhesitatingly he made his decision. His contract with his newspapers had not expired. He left London at once for the fighting in France.

The battle of the Marne still was raging as he made all speed for Paris. How narrowly the German torrent had been damned, how close it had come to engulfing him once more, he realized when he reached the city he had cherished and chided as a fresh young traveller in the 'Nineties. It was strangely empty, its animation suspended. The correspondent did not linger but prepared to follow the ebbing tide of invasion.

Let the French, like the British, fume and forbid the front to correspondents. Their prohibition only put Davis on his mettle. With Gerald Morgan and Granville Fortescue, he obtained War Office bulletins decorated with imposing red seals. These the bluffing trio flashed with supreme assurance and took the salutes of one unsuspecting sentry after another, as their taxicab rolled toward the thunder of the guns at Soissons.

Northward from Meaux, Davis's fine reporter's eyes stored

their picture of the desolation spread by the battling armies in collision, retreat, and pursuit. The magnificent poplars which lined the white highways "looked as though drunken woodsmen with axes from roots to topmost branches had slashed them in crazy fury." German wicker ammunition baskets strewed the roadside and brass shell cases glinted in the sunshine. Abandoned equipment was scattered through the wheat-fields as far as he could see. The bodies of soldiers first aid had failed to save surrounded the blood-drenched ground of the dressing stations. More of the slain, like fallen scarecrows tumbled among the grain they once had protected, struck the observer with the terrible meaning of the word "missing." Everywhere the tragic waste of war confronted him: carcasses of horses, some artillery mounts, most of them farm horses slaughtered in their stable yards; smashed motor-trucks, automobiles, airplanes; trampled harvests; villages, with every home and shop gutted and wrecked.

Thirty kilometres farther on, devastation gave way to the play of the forces which had created it—which still were wreaking it. The correspondents were witnesses of a spirited artillery duel which ended with the recapture of Soissons by the Allies.

Late in the afternoon, the three Americans returned to Paris with the story which red seals and their determination to report the news had won them. Next day they were ready to try their luck once more. Fortescue and Morgan, joined by Ellis Ashmead-Bartlett, voted for Soissons again. Davis insisted on Rheims. There was some sort of a cathedral there, he said. Neither he nor his companions knew that it was one of the most celebrated in Europe. Ordinarily he was not much interested in cathedrals, Davis confessed, but something told him there would be copy in this one.

So, playing the lone hand he preferred, his remarkable news instinct led him to another great story of the war. As his car approached along the Paris road, the majestic proportions of the great church dominating the countryside loomed before him. He drove into a city ringed in smoke. Outside the town, French batteries were in action. But the German fire in reply was falling in the heart of the city. Not accident but intent, Davis stoutly maintained. Two days on the scene confirmed his belief that both the German excuses for the destruction of the cathedral were false. A ranging fire to bracket the French artillery positions might explain some of the shells which struck the Cathedral and houses throughout the city, but not the hail of high explosive which rained down for four days. As for the claim that the shelling was justified because the Cathedral towers were being used as observation posts, Davis believed the word of the priests that the charge was a lie.

Past pools of blood at the portals of the Cathedral, marking the trail of wounded Germans carried into the nave after the retreat of their army, Davis followed a curé with a face strong as those of the saints carved in stone. The curé paused to guide a blinded German officer searching for the water pail; then led the correspondent through the ruin shells had wrought. Shattered carvings, crumbled statues, and everywhere fragments of the precious, irreplaceable blue glass of the famed windows. It was a sight that wrenched the heart of the beholder, this wanton destruction so newly done. Even its description would prove a painful task.

All that day while the bombardment raged about him, Davis "covered" Rheims, staying there for a night during which the guns were silent, and again under fire returning to Paris next morning to write his story. Two days later he was back with his three comrades to report a havoc more frightful than ever.

R. H. D. (LEFT) AT PLATTSBURG, 1915

R. H. D. TAKES HIS EASE AFTER DINNER

From a sketch made at Marion, Mass., by Ellen Emmet, in 1903.

A shell had set fire to the roof of the Cathedral and the priests and people had fought the flames desperately, with rescue parties carrying out the German wounded under streams of molten lead and falling timbers. Ready for his relation, too, was an account of the dramatic moment when the Archbishop of Rheims and his clergy, their Cathedral blazing behind them, had protected the German prisoners against infuriated citizens seeking revenge for their own 400 dead, killed by the bombardment.

To Davis now, the mangled edifice looked like the face of a beautiful saint, scarred with vitriol. The spirit of the place seemed to have fled from its abode so pitilessly destroyed. What he had written on his first trip would pale beside the story of outrage he was ready to cable this time when he reached Paris.

II

When he reached Paris . . . that was easier planned than accomplished. Makeshift passes were about to collapse under the strain, and the French military authorities were tired of being flouted by elusive reporters.

Troops gathered in Davis, Ashmead-Bartlett, Fortesque, and Morgan and marched them before the general in command of the area. The others stepped aside to let Davis arrange their release, for they knew that he could assume an air of grandeur which aroused awe even in generals. However, this general refused either to be awed or to accept Davis's offer of five francs to the French Red Cross for every word in his Rheims story that was censorable. He recognized their passes as worthless and ordered them confined under guard for eight days.

Eight days incommunicado with the front-page story they had to file deteriorating into stale news! Ashmead-Bartlett pleaded vainly with a French officer who knew him. Fortescue swore like the trooper he had been. As the correspondents were herded off to be corralled in a barnyard, Davis, almost choking with rage and humiliation, erupted with a regular oration.

"I am Richard Harding Davis," he announced.[1] "I am an American citizen and no one has a right to lock me in a farmyard. I am a free-born American citizen. I refuse to be treated in this manner. I demand my immediate release, or that I be allowed to communicate with Mr. Herrick, my Ambassador in Paris. I have come all the way from America to help France. I have done my best and now you wish to lock me in a dirty pigsty. I will never enter it!"

But he was forced to, along with the rest, and they remained there until night when, guarded by gendarmes, they were put in motor cars, driven to Paris, and shut up in the Cherche-Midi Prison. There Davis and Fortescue staged another rampage with no more effect than their first. Finally they calmed down sufficiently to send out for dinner which, brightened by champagne presented them in the *caves* at Rheims, developed into a merry meal. It was then that Ashmead-Bartlett, who admired Davis highly for his abilities and generosity but had discovered that his knowledge of history was shaky, was inspired to a jest.

Did Davis realize, he asked, that this was the very prison graced by Marie Antoinette and from which she had ridden in a tumbril to her death under the guillotine?

"Is that true?" Davis demanded eagerly. If his history course at Lehigh had mentioned the fact that the prison in question was the Conciergerie, his mind at that moment may have been dwelling on the next football game.

[1] From Ellis Ashmead-Bartlett's *Some of My Experiences in the Great War*. London, 1918.

"Yes," the other assured him. "Think of a night spent in her cell and what you could write."

Davis, shown the "historic" cell, was entirely reconciled to imprisonment. So much so that when French officers arrived to escort the Americans to more comfortable quarters at the Invalides, he rose and in his sketchy French delivered an enthusiastic refusal to stir a step out of the Cherche-Midi.

"No! Je refuse absolument de partir ici. Je desire dormir avec Marie Antoinette."

The others howled with laughter. Davis was immensely annoyed but forgave the joker later.

They were released the next morning and Davis rushed his Rheims story to the censor who at once appreciated its value to France. "But I insist this go at once," the official decreed. "It should have been sent twenty-four hours ago."

III

In this war, declared Davis, war correspondents were fighting for their professional existence, for their ancient right to stand on the firing-line to try to describe the indescribable. No longer welcome, persecuted, harassed, they were being counted out as spies. Davis's answer was that he was on the level; that he had no wish to pry: that his heart was in the cause of the Allies; that a trustworthy correspondent could be accredited and depended upon not to divulge military secrets.

"This is a world war," he wrote, "and my contention is that the world has a right to know, not what is going to happen next, but at least what has happened. If men have died nobly, if women and children have cruelly and needlessly suffered, if for no military necessity and without reason cities have been wrecked, the world should know that."

But the strategist, the propagandist, and the morale maintenance man decreed otherwise, and now that the chaotic confusion of the first months of the conflict were passing, they were making their dictate good, trapping correspondents right and left and cooping them up in Tours or banishing them. Davis, who like so many of his colleagues had worked every trick of the trade to baffle blustering generals and outwit indignant staffs, realized that the game was up, at any rate for the time being. He wrote his wife he was fed up on being arrested, his contract was up October 1, and he was coming home.

Louvain and Rheims had left deep scars on the consciousness of the veteran correspondent sailing home from his sixth war. War had brought him fame and fortune. Saluting the great adventure, he had chronicled its valor and heroic sacrifice, and his battle stories had stirred the pulses of many thousands. He had not shut his eyes to the horrors and tragedies of war. The smoke of crashing volleys and bursting shells had half veiled them from him, and the vision of gallant charges dimmed the memory of stricken fields.

Only once before and briefly—at the concentration camps during the Cuban Insurrection—had he contemplated the obverse of the medal now inexorably thrust before his eyes by the holocaust at Louvain, the slaughter along the Paris highway, and the impact of the mailed fist on the great Cathedral. Like his mother half a century ago, he was constrained to cry out against war which "strikes blindly, brutally, which tramples on the innocent and the beautiful."

Davis nevertheless had not become nor would he ever be an advocate of peace at any price. Whatever the cost, he would not shrink from war in self-defense. And such a conflict, he believed with burning conviction, was being waged by the Allies against a nation driven war-mad by its military aristocracy.

The preface to *With the Allies* was a call to arms.[2] "If President Wilson had seen what I have seen," the author proclaimed, "he never would ask that the people of the United States preserve the mental attitude of neutrals." The policies of Woodrow Wilson, the idealist, the intellectual, were incomprehensible to the direct and impulsive Davis. To him the course was clear in September, 1914. When one opponent was fighting honestly and his adversary was hitting below the belt—when a mad dog was loose in the world—then neutrality was unworthy and cowardly.[3]

Davis had sailed to Europe to report a war. He returned to his own country to preach a crusade.

IV

Even the cause to which Davis had given himself with that whole-souled fervor of his must be temporarily eclipsed by the joy of his safe homecoming after perilous months and by the birth of a daughter January 4, 1915. He who always had loved children was infinitely happy in the possession of a child of his own. Although only fifteen months of life remained to him, he would live to see the little girl begin to fulfil promise of in-

[2] Its author received the following letter from Roosevelt, written on a piece of White House stationery which was frugally being used up at Sagamore Hill:

Dear Davis:

That's a capital book of yours! I particularly like your preface and your chapter on the burning of Louvain and the way you touch up the Americans who are absorbed only in their own preposterous affairs on the other side in the midst of this terrible disaster.

With hearty regards to Mrs. Davis.

Faithfully yours,
THEODORE ROOSEVELT.

[3] When Wheeler cabled that the papers of the Syndicate desired "neutral" despatches, Davis replied that dictation was "unexpected"; that the papers "could go to name-of-place censored." He added an offer to surrender his contract. It was not accepted.

heriting her mother's good looks and charm and his. He named her Hope Harding after the heroine of *Soldiers of Fortune* and his mother's family name and commenced to lay elaborate plans for her future. In spite of a heavy snowfall, the far-from-diffident father wished to move the baby out to Crossroads at once to initiate her into a healthy existence. "Oughtn't we begin to harden her?" he protested the doctor's veto.

With the Allies was out and off to a sale of 40,000 copies. The author was busy with short stories and articles, but appeals in behalf of the soldiers of the Allied armies invariably had first call on his pen. With all the eloquence he could command, he urged contributions to the Belgian Soldiers' Tobacco Fund and to the Lafayette Fund for France. He spared neither his literary skill, the prestige of his name, his time, nor his own money which he poured out in gifts greater than he could afford.

For Preparedness he toiled unceasingly, believing with absolute assurance that sooner or later his own country must enter the conflict. How miserably unready she was! The lessons of the Spanish War had been forgotten in the roseate haze of its fortunate outcome. Davis had dared then to point out military weaknesses in the face of bitter criticism and he dared now. He would, he declared, support an adequate standing army for the same reason that he insured his house. "Americans don't want a competent army," he remarked in a talk with Thomas Beer, "because they prefer the amateur to the expert. The bad thing about the United States is that it only likes professionalism in sports."

Events began to play into the hands of Davis and the far-sighted minority crusading for Preparedness. When the waves closed over the torpedoed *Lusitania,* carrying down 114 Americans, among them Charles Frohman and others of his friends,

MISS HOPE HARDING DAVIS AT MT. KISCO

BESSIE McCOY DAVIS AND HER DAUGHTER HOPE
AT MT. KISCO

he saw the hastening of the inevitable and redoubled his efforts. Yet Wilson's unfortunate phrase, "Too proud to fight"
(it irked Davis intensely), was current, and War Department
orders blocked General Wood's activity for student training
camps in the summer of 1915, until Bernard Baruch and others
financed them.

A business men's camp was scheduled to follow in August.
Since recruiting was slow at first, supporters ready to back
their sentiments with action came forward to enlist. Soon the
rolls listed noted names: Mayor John Purroy Mitchel of New
York, Robert Bacon, former Secretary of State and Ambassador to France; Arthur Woods, New York Police Commissioner; George Wharton Pepper, Willard Straight, Richard
Harding Davis. Others rallied—bankers, professors, farmers,
artists, lawyers, doctors, journalists, politicians, diplomats, man-
ufacturers, sportsmen. Not since the Rough Riders had such
an outfit worn Uncle Sam's uniform as these battalions mustering a strength of 1200 at Plattsburg, N. Y.

Davis, erect and soldierly in his khaki, plunged with zest
into military life he had reported for so many years. Reveille,
drills, riding (he could sit an army saddle better than the
huntsmen and polo players unused to them), tent pitching,
policing—he shirked none of it. But he was fifty-one years old
and the long hikes with full pack under the August sun told
on him. Young John McCloy, nephew of his one-time *Sun*
city editor, watched Davis's face grow livid and stern as the
column swung along through the dust. The fine body which,
except when sciatica struck, always had served him so well,
was beginning to fail. His pride and his patriotism carried
him on. He would rather have died than fall out of ranks.
Sticking to it for mile after mile, he finished the gruelling
marches in line with men half his age. At night by a fire at

the end of the company street he admitted to Pirie MacDonald, the photographer: "I'm a little bit afraid I've overdone." Few others learned how stoically he was enduring the alarming pains around his heart. Theodore Roosevelt visited camp and found his old comrade of the Spanish War doing full duty. Frank O'Malley, covering Plattsburg for *The Sun,* continued to file stories which featured the splendid example his idol was setting.

Writing his tender, homesick letters to his wife, Davis begged her to put on his wrist watch and his horn spectacles and hold Hope the wrong way so she would be reminded of her dad. The end of the encampment released him to return to his family but only for a few happy weeks. Then he was irresistibly drawn back to the war by the message that the entire French front from Flanders to the Vosges was open to him. No more arrests and imprisonments for a friend of France. She finally had realized that every ringing word Richard Harding Davis addressed to his countrymen was worth a dozen vaguely optimistic communiques.

CHAPTER NINETEEN

TALE OF A DESERTER

I

ONE hesitates to read love letters written without reticence or reserve unless one chances upon them years later, yellowed with age, bound with lavender ribbon and breathing the fragrance of a half-forgotten romance. Yet in telling the story of a man's life, nothing affords a clearer glimpse into the innermost recesses of his heart. The letters which Bessie McCoy Davis, proud of the devotion of her Richard, permitted to be published shortly after his death under entirely understandable circumstances,[1] afford this precious insight.

He wrote her one of his most adoring missives when he was crossing the Atlantic to the war for the last time.

Dearest One: On Way to France, Oct. 18, 1915.

You are much more brave than I am. Anyway, you are much better behaved. For all the time you were talking I was crying, not with my eyes only, but with *all* of me. I am so sad. I love you so, and I will miss you so. I want you to keep say-

---

[1] Davis's sudden death left his family provided for by such property as Crossroads Farm and his copyrights but almost destitute so far as ready money went. Gouverneur Morris wrote his fine appreciation of R. H. D. to supply some; then joined with other friends to arrange for the publication of Davis's letters which Charles Belmont Davis was commissioned to edit. H. J. Whigham, editor of *The Metropolitan Magazine,* published them in that periodical, and Arthur Scribner, of Charles Scribner's Sons, brought them out in book form. When these two friends found that the proceeds would go into the estate and not become available until it was settled, they doubled the price agreed upon, thus putting the second half of the sum at the disposal of the widow and child. Bessie McCoy Davis, knowing that the latter part of her husband's career and his happy life with her must go untold in the series and the book unless through his letters to her, willingly furnished them.

ing to yourself all the time, "This is the most serious effort he ever made, because the chances of seeing anything are so *small,* and because never had he such a chance to *help.* But, all the time, every minute he thinks of me. He wants me. He misses my voice, my eyes, my presence at his side when he walks or sleeps. He never loved me so greatly, or at leaving me was so unhappy as he is now."

Goodby, dear heart. My God-given one! Would it not be wonderful, if tonight when I am up among the boats on the top deck that girl in the Pierrot suit, and in her arms, Hope, came, and I took them and held them both? You will walk with her at five, and I will walk and think of you and love you and long for you.

God keep you, dearest of wives, and mothers.

RICHARD.

"Because never had he such a chance to help." From the moment he reached Paris he took full advantage of that chance. At the Beaux Arts where Americans were running a relief league for families of French fellow-students called to the colors, they cheered his promise to write a story about their work. Whitney Warren, the league's head, explained that what Davis previously had written in behalf of Mrs. Warren's fund for war orphans had brought in $5000. President Poincaré was glad to receive the correspondent, who brought a letter of introduction from ex-President Roosevelt,[2] and to transmit through him a message of thanks for American aid of the French Red Cross.

Passes were given him as freely as they had been sternly de-

[2] This was the second such letter T. R. had given, the first having been destroyed as incriminating by Davis when taken prisoner by the Germans in Belgium. Informed of this, Poincaré fingered the thin paper of the second letter and remarked that it could have been eaten and readily digested had an emergency risen again.

nied before. Half doubting his luck, Davis found himself escorted with courtesy through ten out of the twelve French sectors of the Western Front. Back to the Wheeler Syndicate newspapers flowed graphic descriptions of the new trench warfare. Of the mud trenches of Artois and shell-torn Arras. Of Rheims again and the zigzag entrenchments of Champagne where he explored the front line by moonlight while projectiles whined over his head and rats scurried around his feet. Of the deep dugouts and fortresses of concrete sunken in the chalky soil of Verdun,[3] and of the St. Mihiel salient which reminded him of an ill-mannered boy sticking out his tongue. Of the quiet sector of the Vosges Mountains where shell-proof shelters had the look of hunting lodges and soldiers that of hunters cautiously stalking big game.

Through all this tour of the trenches, Davis played fair, attempting to slip nothing past the censor. So strictly did he conform to the ethics of war correspondence that he was moved to an angry public denunciation of another American correspondent who while visiting the front line had seized a rifle and taken a shot at the Germans. If the indignant but inconsistent critic remembered that day long ago at Las Guasimas when he had charged the Spaniards blazing away with a carbine, he may have soothed his conscience with the reflection that his lapse had occurred while his own country was at war.

France fighting on her own soil and the gallant efforts with which the whole nation backed her armies in the field—these were the vital interests which inspired Davis to file scores of despatches appealing for American admiration and sympathy. But trench warfare had become static. The newspapers of the Wheeler Syndicate demanded that their correspondent pro-

[3] Davis visited Verdun and the Vosges after his return from Salonika.

ceed to the Balkan front where the troops of the Central Powers were driving the forces of the Entente through the snowy mountain passes of Serbia down upon technically neutral Greece and the sea. Davis dissented from their judgment but obeyed. He left November 13, 1915, with all the reluctance of a reporter detached from an interesting assignment and sent on one which he firmly believes will not pan out.

II

The pattern of his life seemed to be repeating itself. Again he sailed the Mediterranean. Again with John Bass, comrade of the Græco-Turkish War, he found Athens in armed turmoil. Regiments marching all day through the streets and crowds cheering orators reproduced a scene from *The Galloper*. "In Athens," Davis remarked, "the local color was superior to ours, but George Marion stage-managed the mob better than did the Athens police." After a brief stay, the correspondent sailed for Salonika via Volo. As he landed, the coldest winter in years closed about him, causing him intense suffering and sapping his vitality.

Salonika, port and base for the Allies by invitation of Premier Venezelos, King Constantine regardless, was packed and jammed. In his long experience with cities swamped by conventions, inaugurations, and coronations, Davis never had seen one so deeply submerged. Tens of thousands of troops landed to cover the retreat, thousands of refugees from Serbia, and swarms of spies, who lined the quay in solid formation and kept tally of everything, quadrupled the population.

Davis's ears rang with a piercing, continuous, monotonous cry, the peculiar "clamor of Salonika." Imagine it, he urged in a masterly bit of description, "increased by the rumble and roar over the huge paving-stones of thousands of giant motor-trucks; by the beat of the iron-shod hoofs of the cavalry, the iron-shod boots of men marching in squads, companies, regiments, the shrieks of peasants herding flocks of sheep, goats, turkeys, cattle; the shouts of bootblacks, boatmen, sweetmeat venders; newsboys crying the names of Greek papers that sound like 'Hi hippi hippi hi,' 'Teyang Teyang Teyah'; by the tin horns of the trolley-cars, the sirens of automobiles, the warning whistles of steamers, of steam-launches, of donkey-engines; the creaking of cordage and chains on cargo-hoists, and by the voices of 300,000 men speaking different languages, and each, that he may be heard above it, adding to the tumult."

There was not a hotel room to be had in the seething city, but John T. McCutcheon, James H. Hare, and William G. Shepherd gladly shared with Davis their quarters in the Olympus Palace Hotel. The new arrival failed to wear out his welcome even when he woke his hosts every morning gasping and splashing in his portable tub. Neither zero weather nor icy water could halt that daily rite, for physical immaculacy was as strongly an inbred characteristic of his as were mental and moral cleanliness. The average man under such conditions might be satisfied with "casual ablutions." Not Dick Davis; he said he always had begun the day with a cold bath and did not dare stop. The shock to a heart out of kilter was grave. His body did not react, seemed never to grow thoroughly warm. But, teeth chattering, he kept it up.

The roommates filtered the wild rumors of Salonika for news and pictures, each following his own method. Shepherd, who was covering the war for the United Press in the quiet, thorough way he reported any story, was the recipient of advice from the man he had watched dining at Vera Cruz arrayed in the full glory of evening clothes.

"Bill, you're no window-dresser," Davis informed him. "You don't dress your stuff up and you take yourself too casually. I find out that no matter how good your stuff is, you've got to take it to the window, tie a blue ribbon around it and tell everybody how good it is."

III

As the retreating columns of the Allies drew back through Serbia toward the Greek border, General Sarrail gave permission to the corps of correspondents in Salonika to visit the front. Davis, again in his element of action, forgot the bitter cold and the snow. The courage of a lone British battery, commanded by two officers who were mere youngsters, pounding away at the advancing Bulgarians, warmed him. Mc-Cutcheon complained that the return shelling was coming too close; Davis answered that he rather liked the thrill of it. But as a shell burst even nearer, he ducked and his companion called over sarcastically: "I thought you weren't afraid." "Yes," Davis answered, "but I don't want to go home in the fifth inning."

When the French staff dined the correspondents in a concrete shelter, Davis enlivened the occasion with his brilliant talk. McCutcheon also entertained by decorating its walls with inimitable caricatures. Jimmy Hare, who had been out scouting with his camera, was a tardy guest.

"Very bad manners of you, Jimmy," Davis, the stickler for etiquette, scolded him.

"I apologize to you, Mr. Dyvis," the Cockney voice piped back impudently.

"You shouldn't apologize to me." This with a meaning glance toward the French general.

R. H. D. AND CAPT. PUAUX OF THE GENERAL HEADQUARTERS
STAFF IN THE RUINS AT GERBEVILLER

"RICHARD" (Richard Harding Davis)

From Town and Country, March, 1916.

CARICATURE OF A WAR CORRESPONDENT BY VIM

"I don't notice the general syin' anything," came the retort.

"I'll take it up with you outside," promised the mentor sternly.

Outside Hare belligerently took it up himself.

"I don't know as my lyteness was any business of yours, Mr. Dyvis," he challenged.

A grin broke over Davis's face as he looked down at the cocky little photographer.

"I don't know as it was either, Jimmy," he finished.

There was no further opportunity for entertainment or etiquette. The fierce onslaught of the German-Bulgar legions soon brought orders that the press stand not on the order of its going. Crowded into a filthy, frigid freight car, the French, British, Italian, and American correspondents sat against the walls while the car was coupled into a train full of refugees. None in the silent, depressed group would have believed that night that the Allies would be able to cling to Salonika; that ultimately they would sweep back through Serbia in triumph.

A brakeman's lantern gleamed at the door and Davis, who had commandeered it, climbed in. His compatriots gathered around him on the floor in the centre of the car. Cards, chips, and a bottle of Irish whisky appeared, and for hours of the run back to the coast a poker game was waged that lived up to all the merriest and most picturesque traditions of the great American indoor sport. The foreigners, watching the wild Yankees at their pastime, forgot their dejection. Next day one of the British correspondents approached his American confrères to compliment them.

"I was proud to be an Anglo-Saxon," he declared. "The way you chaps kept your peckers up in that cold, dirty car was splendid."

The others glanced at Davis. They had not realized how well he had staged the scene.

"That was a game for the Stars and Stripes last night," said Davis.

IV

Since the enemy's pursuit halted at the Greek border, the Allies need not now make a desperate stand with the sea at their backs. The war would shift to other theatres, and Davis prepared to leave for home. Yet the papers of the Wheeler Syndicate could not have regretted sending their correspondent to Greece nor could he his going. His despatches, informative and colorful, supplied the most interesting material for his second book on the war, *With the French in France and Salonika*. Best of all, Salonika gave him what many regard as the finest story he ever wrote, *The Deserter*.[4]

To few of the millions of fictioneers who have racked their brains for an idea is it vouchsafed that a plot walk right into their workroom. *The Deserter* was just such a gift of the gods to Davis.

The vast apartment in the Olympus Palace Hotel was the setting, he himself became the narrator and his roommates the supplementary characters. With brief, sure strokes he drew them to the life. *Uncle Jim* (Hare), the veteran of many wars, and of all the correspondents, in experience the oldest and in spirit the youngest. *The Kid* (Shepherd), the only Boy Reporter who jumped from a City Hall assignment to cover a

---

4 This timely and highly popular story was first published in *The Metropolitan*, September, 1916, under the title, *The Man Who Had Everything;* then in a collection of Davis's stories, *The Lost Road;* then separately as a small volume. It is also included in Roger Burlingame's excellently chosen anthology of short stories by Davis, *From Gallegher to The Deserter*. *Gallegher, The Bar Sinister, The Consul, The Deserter*—these four at least are worthy to survive as monuments to the man who possessed in a high degree the precious gift of the story-teller and used it with honest, unaffected craftsmanship.

European War. "I don't know strategy," he would boast; "neither does the Man at Home. He wants "human interest stuff, and I give him what he wants. I write exclusively for the subway guard and the farmers in the wheat belt." And there was *John, the Artist* (McCutcheon), who could write a news story but whose front-page cartoons made up people's minds for them; whose thoughts were as brave and clean as they were clever.

Into this group strode *Hamlin,* the fictitiously named, would-be deserter,[5] a young American serving as a sergeant with the British R. A. M. C.—the Medical Corps. Sick from half-healed wounds, his nerves worn to the quick by hideous experiences and hardships endured through months of war, he was through with it all, he was clearing out. " 'It isn't the danger,' he protested. 'It isn't *that* I'm getting away from. To hell with the danger! It's just the plain discomfort of it! It's never being your own master, never being clean, never being warm.' " So he had come to the *Artist,* an older graduate and fraternity brother of his college, to obtain the civilian clothes and passage home that would make his desertion possible. Gravely and reluctantly, *John* had made the arrangements.

How the four correspondents, who saw the boy was too sick to realize what he was doing, dissuaded *Hamlin* in the hours before the steamship sailed; how, again in his muddy, blood-stained uniform, he returned to duty, cursing them—these make up a yarn spun with such skill and artistry that it should not be spoiled by further synopsis.

No sooner had the door slammed behind the young soldier than Davis exclaimed:

"I yelled first. This is my story. The best war story I ever knew!"

[5] The four correspondents took and kept a pledge never to reveal his real name.

The others made no counter-claims. For this was no news story but a human document in the highest sense, the tale of a struggle in a man's soul. Davis's friends knew how well he could write it and he justified their confidence, telling it beautifully, simply, with infinite understanding. McCutcheon, reading it, recognized that the theme unconsciously mirrored the author's own ideals of honor and duty. *The Deserter,* he declared, "belongs in patriotic literature by the side of Edward Everett Hale's *The Man Without a Country.* The motif is the same—that of obligation and service and loyalty to a pledge."

Davis never heard the sequel to the story. Soon after its enaction, he was given a glorious farewell dinner by Mr. and Mrs. John Bass and sailed for France and home. Three weeks later a message summoned his former roommates to a Salonika pier where a Red Cross lighter was transshipping scores of sick and wounded to hospital ships bound for Alexandria. *Hamlin,* lying thin and pale on a stretcher, showed no trace of his former bitter resentment against the men whose appeals had changed the course of his life. Smiling up at them, he answered their eager questions as to how he had fared when he returned to camp that night after overstaying his leave.

"Oh, they gave it to me good," he said.[6] "But they still think I got drunk. They took away my stripes and made me a private. But I was sick the night I got back to camp and I've been laid up ever since. They say there is something the matter with my intestines and they're going to cut me open again. Gee, but the captain was surprised! He said he had always counted on me as a teetotaler, and that he was grieved and dis-

---

[6] From McCutcheon's introduction to *The Deserter.* New York, 1920. Davis does not relate in the story that *Hamlin* had shaved off his mustache, which he was required to wear as a British non-commissioned officer. This was damaging evidence of intent to desert. His advisers told him to report that he had been with a girl who objected to mustaches and persuaded him to cut it off; and that story was accepted by his commander.

appointed in me. And just think, I've never taken a drink in my life!"

They said good-by and this time it was a friendly one. It fell to Shepherd to add a dramatic postscript to *The Deserter*.[7] Three months later in London he felt an arm flung around his shoulder and turned to look into the healthy, cheerful face of *Hamlin*. At luncheon the grateful soldier brought his story up to date. Recovered from his operation, he had been sent to England to convalesce. After his discharge from the hospital, he had been paraded to receive the Distinguished Conduct Medal for bravery in Flanders ten months before, when he went out into No Man's Land under fire to carry a wounded comrade back to safety. Now, a sergeant again, he was about to return to France with his regiment.

One note saddened their reunion. Shepherd told of Davis's recent death of which *Hamlin* had not heard. The boy was deeply touched that one of the four who had done so much for him was gone. He groaned that Davis had died thinking him yellow.

"If he thinks at all," Shepherd answered gently, "he knows now you're all right."

[7] *The Scar that Tripled,* by William Gunn Shepherd. New York, 1918. As for the final sequel of *Hamlin's* story, he survived the war. A letter from his mother informed McCutcheon of her son's recent death from tuberculosis.

CHAPTER TWENTY

OBIT

I

RICHARD HARDING DAVIS sacrificed his life for his country and for principles he held highest and dearest, as surely as if he had fallen in battle. Wearing her uniform in the long, hot marches at Plattsburgh, striving for her future allies in France and freezing Salonika, he had sustained fatal injuries to his heart. Like a soldier wounded in action but refusing to be sent to the rear, he would not retire and rest when he came home in February, 1916. His simple and intense patriotism, his inflexible sense of duty spurred him on.

There was his book, *With the French,* to be finished, with its danger signal that the day was nigh when America must send men, not only munitions, overseas; with its plea for Preparedness to reduce the terrible toll of approaching war; with its appeals for war-blinded soldiers for whom he, who could see so much and so well, felt such deep compassion.

Warned by fainting spells, he could not but realize the risk he ran by his strenuous and unremitting endeavors. He disregarded it with quiet courage and flung himself into the heated controversies of that pre-war year. In an article he charged that American shoes with paper soles had been sold to the French Army and he had brought back several pairs to prove it. A suit for libel (dropped after his death) was threatened by the American manufacturer. Davis's answer was to instruct his attorney, Roland S. Morris, to fight it through court, cost what it might.

His fighting blood boiled again when he read newspaper reports that James H. Maurer, President of the Pennsylvania State Federation of Labor, speaking in a New York City high school, had shouted, "To hell with the Flag!" The labor leader subsequently issued a complete denial. He stated, and was corroborated by twenty-five auditors, that he had been quoting a captain of Pennsylvania State Constabulary dispersing a miner's funeral procession; that when the miners had objected that their assembly was a peaceable one with the American flag at its head, the officer had yelled the insult. But Davis, wrathfully reading the first stories and assuming they were correct, never learned the explanation.

On the evening of April 11 at Crossroads Farm, he had sent a telegram of strong protest against the alleged Maurer utterance to Mayor Mitchel. An article on Preparedness, the preface to *With the French,* lay on his desk. His firm, clear pencilling was fresh on its final paragraph——

. . . "That France and her Allies succeed should be the hope and prayer of every American. The fight they are waging is for the things the real, unhyphenated American is supposed to hold most high and most dear. Incidentally, they are fighting his fight, for their success will later save him, unprepared as he is to defend himself, from a humiliating and terrible thrashing. And every word and act of his now that helps the Allies is a blow against frightfulness, against despotism, and in behalf of a broader civilization, a nobler freedom, and a much more pleasant world in which to live."

It was his last message, the fiery cross he must drop for other hands to catch up and carry on. He left his desk to make a telephone call to Martin Egan in New York City. The conversation ended abruptly but Egan suspected nothing wrong. Mrs. Davis, who had retired early, called from upstairs to her husband about midnight. Receiving no answer, she hurried down to find him dead beside the telephone. He had gone swiftly, as he wished to when his time came, still in harness, never knowing the feebleness and enforced inactivity of old age. "The gods loved him," said Gouverneur Morris, "and so he had to die young."

II

Word that Richard Harding Davis was dead did not reach New York City until the following morning. Evening papers at once swung into action. City editors switched the call to rewrite men to note the details. Copy boys brought clippings and typed manuscripts in fat envelopes labeled "Davis, Richard Harding," from the "morgues." Those invaluable libraries for years had clipped from their own issues and those of other newspapers all stories containing references to him, as is the practice in the case of any person appearing more or less frequently in the news. To save time, Davis's obituary, like those of other noted men or women, had been prepared in advance of his death.

Typewriters clicked as the rewrite men pounded out their leads to the "obit." Copy desks wrote their headlines. Pneumatic tubes shot the copy to the linotypes. Forms were locked, matrices made, plates cast, and the presses whirred, printing the edition. Again the rewrite men bent over their machines and clippings to turn out the more finished stories which would follow in later editions. These the "day side" of the morning papers used for reference in compiling accounts from their own material.

Surely any newspaperman, when the symbolic "30" which means the end of the piece is written beneath the story of his

From a photograph © Pirie McDonald.

RICHARD HARDING DAVIS

R. H. D. ON THE WESTERN FRONT, 1915

life, would have one overwhelming desire, were he permitted to wander back on this earth as a wraith—to rustle through the familiar sheets of newsprint once more and read his "obit." Not even the old fellows, who have toiled through a lifetime of obscurity and anonymity at newspaper wages, never rising out of the rut, would be doomed to disappointment, for as a final *amende honorable* they are awarded headlines and a story far beyond their news deserts. Richard Harding Davis, for so many years a celebrity in his own right, required no favors. His shade could have glowingly read his "obit." on many a front page.

The great press associations flashed the story of his death to their subscribers throughout the country. Correspondents of foreign newspapers cabled it abroad. *The New York Evening Telegram* brought out an extra. All the New York newspapers and papers throughout the United States gave him columns, some featuring his work as an author, some as a playwright or a war correspondent, some his tireless efforts in the cause of Preparedness. Space was lavished on a man whose name and fame were a watchword to millions of devoted readers. Even so it was difficult to compress the relation of his crowded career within the necessary limits. Editorials added their eulogies of a life lived so fully and so glamorously.

The tribute Davis perhaps would have liked best of all was printed by *The New York Journal,* the paper he had served so efficiently at Moscow and in Cuba and which he had refused ever to serve again after its misinterpretation of his *Olivette* despatch. Admirable for their restraint, simplicity, and pith, *The Journal's* three sentences might well stand as his epitaph:

"He gave pleasure to many.

"He worked hard for his success and deserved it.

"He was a courageous man."

III

He lived as did his heroes, said *The New York Sun,* and fell short of them only in never knowing poverty. Yet for a while after Davis's death, his family was reduced to absolute want.

Generous and extravagant though he was, he cannot be accused of utter improvidence. One of the most successful authors of his day, he earned $100,000 each of the last five years of his life and is believed to have been worth nearly a million dollars at one time. While he spent his money freely and enjoyed the spending vastly, he was by no means an arrant spendthrift. He owned Crossroads Farm and copyrights which were a valuable provision for the future. Ill as he was, he had no thought of surrender and he was toiling away with his old-time confidence. It was rather the writing-man's vagueness about business matters and the artistic temperament, which Mrs. Davis shared, that left his family in a dilemma at his sudden demise, with only a pitifully small amount of cash on hand and the assets of his estate tied up pending its settlement.

Bessie McCoy bravely returned to the stage. Friends of Davis —no man ever had more loyal ones, as the volume, *R. H. D.: Appreciations,* proves—rallied to her aid as soon as they learned of the situation, and the sale of the magazine and book rights of Davis's letters met the emergency. Income from an estate of $50,000, gradually tripled by book and play royalties and film rights, was made available for Mrs. Davis's support and upon her death in 1931 became their daughter's inheritance.

IV

The name of Richard Harding Davis is not enrolled among the illustrious of literature, nor was he under the illusion that it was or would be. For him it was enough that men and women, boys and girls, eagerly awaited the appearance of his novels. That they who were too poor to buy magazines haunted public libraries for issues with stories of his. That people laughed at his farces or were thrilled by his plays and forgot their troubles. That so many youngsters found inspiration for their writing careers in his success. "Romance was never dead while Davis was alive."

It is as a great reporter, the greatest of his day, that his fame is lasting. For thirty years, he watched and vividly recorded the march of events, following the wise counsel his mother left.

"It has always seemed to me," wrote Rebecca Harding Davis, "that each human being before going out into silence, should leave behind him, not the story of his own life, but of the time in which he lived,—as he saw it,—its creeds, its purpose, its queer habits, and the work which he did or left undone in it."

As she bade, her son made history live and breathe—in his despatches, his articles, and his letters. Through their pages, through the memoirs of his contemporaries, and the annals of his period, strides the gallant and lovable figure of Richard Harding Davis, ever knightly and adventurous, ever romantic, forever young.

ACKNOWLEDGMENTS

"Dick would have loved it that a book was being written about him," Colonel Frederick Palmer remarked when he was giving me his recollections of the subject of this biography. He would have been pleased, too, I think, that most of whatever may be of value and interest in this volume derives from the memories of his friends; and that those memories, warmly affectionate though most of them are, were imparted with an open honesty and freedom from bias which recognized that a balanced, credible portrait was desirable.

Seldom is it the lot of a biographer, so often doomed to musty tomes, barely decipherable letters, and tattered manuscripts, to accomplish the bulk of his research from living sources, among such charming, kind, and distinguished people as are these friends of Richard Harding Davis. The frequent appearance of their names in the text testifies how deeply I am indebted to their courtesy and helpfulness.

I must express my gratitude in particular to the following:

To Mr. and Mrs. Charles Dana Gibson to whom this book is dedicated. I had their aid and encouragement from the beginning. It seems particularly fitting that Mr. Gibson's drawings, reproduced here by his permission, should illustrate a book about Dick Davis, as they did those by him.

To Miss Hope Harding Davis, who generously made available to me many of her father's papers, photographs, and mementos.

To Mr. M. A. DeWolfe Howe and Mr. Martin Egan for splendid material and invaluable assistance in revision. Also to Messrs. Franklin Clarkin, H. J. Whigham, William G. Mc-

Cloy, William G. Shepherd, and Arthur H. Folwell. And to Mr. Howe and Mr. Vincent Starrett for the loan of photographs.

To Mr. Maxwell E. Perkins, editor of *Scribner's,* whose suggestion of this biography came at a time when it meant much to me, and whose advice was of great service. Also to Mr. Joseph H. Chapin, art director of *Scribner's.*

To my wife, for her devoted and indispensable help throughout the writing of this book.

I appreciate also the testimony of those who frankly disliked Mr. Davis and whose candor presented the other side of the picture.

My literary sources: Mr. Davis's own books, his letters, memoirs mentioning him, newspaper files, and so on, are acknowledged in my text and footnotes. Chief among them were *Adventures and Letters of Richard Harding Davis* (New York, 1917), edited by his brother, Charles Belmont Davis; and *Richard Harding Davis, a Bibliography* (New York, 1924), compiled by Henry Cole Quinby. That excellent work obviates the necessity of any Davis bibliography here.

The unique Talcott Williams collection of newspaper clippings in the "morgue" of the School of Journalism, Columbia University, was of immense service to me. I am also grateful to other libraries whose facilities were courteously extended: to the Library of Congress, the New York Public Library, the New York Society Library and its assistant librarians, Mrs. F. G. King and Miss Helen Ruskin; the Richards Free Library, Newport, N. H., and the library of the Yale Club of New York City.

FAIRFAX DOWNEY,
New York City, 1933.

REBECCA HARDING DAVIS[1]

PORTRAIT OF A PIONEER

Reprinted by permission of *The Colophon*.

THE black man, the red man, and the white laboring man—each was championed by an American woman author who couched quill, settled herself in a side-saddle on Pegasus, and did battle and book against the oppressor. A few years after Harriet Beecher Stowe dealt her lusty buffet for *Uncle Tom* she had half a nation at her back and victory was hers. Helen Hunt Jackson's fight in behalf of the Indian in *Ramona* and earlier works was none the less gallant for being late and losing. It was the lot of Rebecca Harding Davis, paladin for mill workers and slum dwellers, to see decades pass before her onslaught gained ground. Then, ironically, the memory of her own early challenge had faded.

The Civil War in prospect or in progress failed to divert the attention of the country from the short story and the serial in which Rebecca Harding first espoused her cause. They won her a triumphal trip to Boston, there to be welcomed into the exclusive fold of literature by Emerson, Holmes, and Hawthorne. Her pen achieved for her a long, prominent, and profitable career. Today she is remembered by those on whom her character and wisdom made their impress—she died only in 1910—or identified by her last two names as the mother of Richard Harding Davis. The blows she struck for labor re-

---

[1] "Dick Davis's mother," Martin Egan wrote the author, "was the controlling influence of his life and no one could fully understand him without knowing about her. The bond between them was an amazingly strong one and never in my life have I known a man who had greater devotion for his mother than Dick had."

sounded but they were premature for the assurance of her own fame; they sank unseen foundations on which later reformers built.

A true sister of the American pioneer women of the mid-nineteenth century, Rebecca Harding resolved in her teens to do her pioneering at home; to grasp the pen instead of the rifle, to cling to the crinoline rather than the covered wagon, and to warm herself at a Franklin stove, not a campfire. One might press forward no less indomitably toward the winning of a literary West. The perils were social and not physical but they were no less real. All around her in the man-monopo-lized wilderness of the craft she was choosing lurked savages shooting arrows of vituperation at females who dared write for publication. Such creatures, whooped the braves, were inele-gant, ungenteel, and hardly a step above the oldest profession, which, at that, was infinitely more feminine.

Undaunted, Rebecca Harding chose—chose on the inspira-tion of the trail which had been blazed. Bold women had written and succeeded magnificently. There was Mrs. Stowe for one; her reputation was well established before *Uncle Tom's Cabin* appeared. There were Susan and Anna B. War-ner, daughters of a New York lawyer. Susan's *The Wide, Wide World,* a two-volume novel of American domestic life, was selling by the hundreds of thousands in 1849, flooding the country as copiously as tears saturated its pages. Anna had struck a typical American note with *Dollars and Cents,* and the sisters were carrying on separately and as collaborators. Maria E. Cummings had a best seller, too, in the didactic *The Lamplighter.* And there were others penning romances which people bought even if a female's name was on the title page, although many a cautious authoress remained anonymous.

So Miss Harding decided to write, and the strength was not

in her at first to resist scribbling reams on dark conspiracies in Italian palazzios and stately romances in English castles, *à la mode*. Then one of those cruelly frank friends, whom every author should own, damned her effusions one day by remarking: "Try and tell us about the butcher next door, my dear." The author awoke to the fact that her foreign travel was nil and her education more homely than classical. Yet she had seen an unusual share of her native land and her own people. Born in 1831 in Washington, Pennsylvania, she had spent her childhood in Alabama and her young womanhood in the industrial town of Wheeling, (then) Virginia. Why should she not write of life as she saw it? Must the familiar lack value? There must be individuals she knew capable of a love terrible in its strength—tragic drama even in mill towns and villages. "You want something to lift you out of this crowded, tobacco-stained commonplace, to kindle and chafe a glow in you," she mused in one of her prefaces. "I want you to dig into this commonplace, vulgar life, and see what is in it. Sometimes I think it has a new and awful significance that we do not see."

The spark for her tinder glowed in her home town of Wheeling. Pity had enlisted her in what would later be called settlement work among the Welshmen and other immigrants. They toiled harshly and squalidly, the men in the iron mills, the women as cotton spinners. She grasped her pen and unsparingly pictured the sullen smoke settling everywhere, the foul smells, the stagnant and slimy life of the workers in the mills and their miserable hovels, the furnaces glowing by night like a street in Hell, the nightmare fog of an existence from which drunkenness was the only escape. "If I had the making of men," she wrote bitterly, "these men who do the lowest part of the world's work should be machines,—nothing more— hands. It would be kindness." Through her inferno scenes she wove the tale of a young Welsh puddler with a genius for sculpture and of the deformed girl who adored and stole for him; a stark, powerful story ending with suicide in a jail cell. She did not sign it. People were sure a man must have written it, probably some Russian revolutionary. It was incredible as the work of a young American woman in the year 1860.

The author sent this long short story to the *Atlantic Monthly*. Back came a letter which she carried around half a day not daring to open. It contained an acceptance, seal of the splendid approval of Mr. Ticknor and Mr. Lowell, and a check for fifty dollars.

II

This one short story, *Life in the Iron-Mills,* made Rebecca Harding famous. Thirty years later, in still spacious days, *Gallegher* would do the same for her son. Her success and an acquaintance with Hawthorne through correspondence induced her to journey to Boston. There she strolled with him through a cool, green cemetery and noted his mocking comment: "We New Englanders begin to enjoy life—when we are dead." There she contemplated with awe Emerson, Yankee of the Yankees, and felt the philosopher was most certainly studying her soul. There she was drawn by the magnetism of Oliver Wendell Holmes, the Autocrat, "finest fruit of the Brahmin order of New England he had first classified and christened." She received Louisa Alcott, who had been to Concord to get a dress worthy to appear in before her, and was confided in by the author-to-be of *Little Women* that she once had taken a place as a second girl.

All of the mighty *Atlantic* coterie sat at the feet of this young woman to listen eagerly to her first-hand account of the war, for she was fresh from the border where West Virginia and the

Old Dominion were sundered. Bronson Alcott's windy pane-gyric to the effect that war was an armed angel waking the nation to a lofty life had short shrift from the visitor, who had looked on the conflict's ugly face. "War," she ventured to declare, "may be an armed angel on a mission, but she has the personal habits of the slums." Whereat twinkling little Doctor Holmes laughed and conceded, "Et in Arcadia, ego."

Rebecca Harding's *Margret Howth,* run serially in the *Atlantic* and later published as a book, also was attracting Bostonian and national approbation. Here, as in her previous story, she had broken away from the ultra-romantic, sickly sentimental trend of the period to do pioneer work, and she realized it. "A Story of Today," she called it, but not the today of 1862. "I write from the border and the battlefield," she began it, "and I find in it no theme for shallow arguments and flimsy rhymes. The shadow of death has fallen on us; it chills the very heaven. No child laughs in my face as I pass down the street. Men have forgotten to hope, forgotten to pray." Her book, she promised, would not echo the hackneyed cant of men and bloodthirstiness of women in the fervors of war feeling; it would tell a plebeian story of every-day drudgery, a great warfare as old as the world, and readers might like it or not.

Amazingly, they liked it, this novel whose heroine was a homely woman bookkeeper and whose men included the hero who abandoned his career as a merchant prince for her and a reformer who strove in the foul stratum of the under-life of the American slums. Her thesis was that the great idea of American sociology is to *grow.* Why, she demanded, should an employer's responsibility halt at the narrow limits of the payroll? Throughout she reiterated the dumb question asked by the sordid, massed lives and deaths of workers. "This terrible dumb question is its own reply. . . . From the very extremity of its darkness it is the most solemn prophecy which the world has known of the hope to come."

Anything but a romance of moonlight and honeysuckle was *Margret Howth*. Although it was published anonymously, L. Clarke Davis, a young journalist, took the trouble to ascertain its authorship. His admiration for the character of a woman who could do such work led to a meeting. Miss Harding was not beautiful and she was larger than he, but the charm of her personality and her ability were all he had hoped. They were engaged when she went to Boston.

Rebecca Harding left the pleasant but not entirely satisfying company of philosophers without great effort. After all, she opined, they were not guiding the world; they were in it but not of it. Celibate discipleship did not appeal to her. In token thereof she shocked the modern Athens by her radical utterance of the axiom that women desire men, gathered her hoop skirts and her portmanteaux, and went home to be married.

III

The young couple began life together in Wheeling, but slaughter, rapine, and profiteering were too close to be endured. Julia Ward Howe might see the glory of the coming of the Lord; the gaze of Rebecca Harding Davis was repelled by the filthy garments of the deity of war. She was incapable of an exaltation which would blind her to the effect on the individual of daily blood, to the spectacle of right, wrong, and the Ten Commandments shaken to the base, to brother shooting down brother, to girls thrown in jail for playing "Dixie" on their pianofortes. A sincere pacifist, she could not condone fire and sword as the settlement of a quarrel, however just.

These sentiments and considerations of livelihood drove the

Davises across the mountains to Philadelphia, which they made
their home for life. Clarke Davis began the rise in journalism
which brought him to the managing editorship of *The Inquirer* and *The Ledger*. The family income was always supplemented by the marked and continued success of his wife's
authorship. Her steady production of novels and short stories
alternated with articles and editorials for *The New York Tribune,* to the staff of which she was invited in 1869, and for other
publications.

She bore two sons and a daughter and performed the considerable feat of combining upbringing, housekeeping, and writing, retaining the best features of each. Calm and benign but
determined, she was a splendid mother. For each child she
wrote a Book of Days. Many of the finer facets of the character of her celebrated son Richard, as well as much of his ability,
were due to her rearing. She was also a neighborhood oracle.

The Davises were a devoted, mutually admiring family. To
their Philadelphia house, which they called "The Center of the
Universe," came many notables, particularly of the stage, for
Clarke Davis was a deep student of the drama and its literature. Their list of guests forms a roster of almost all the theatrical celebrities of the latter half of the nineteenth century.
The Drews and Barrymores were intimates. So was Joseph
Jefferson. Mrs. Davis heard Edwin Forrest's most sonorous
rendition of the Curse of Rome when young Richard stumbled
over that actor's gouty foot. Dion Boucicault, Henry Irving,
and Ellen Terry attended the Davis pre-matinée breakfasts, as
did Augustin Daly, with Ada Rehan, Mrs. Gilbert, and John
Drew in his train.

Ranking high among the women leaders of her time, Rebecca Harding Davis commanded wide attention and respect
for the sentiments she expressed so emphatically. Her inde-

pendent bearing in person and print belied her own dictum that "women go through life as babies learn to walk,—a mouthful of pap to every step, only they take it in praise and love." Women's rights she advocated but only in diluted doses. Flaming feminists found entirely too many old-fashioned notions in her precepts; men, alarmed by increasing revolt against their omnipotence, were sustained and soothed by Mrs. Davis's pronouncements in her *Pro Aris et Focis*.

Don't put out the fire on the hearths of your homes, she pleaded with her sex in that unique volume, warning of emancipation's trend toward irreligion. If women required more extended rights in marriage, let them do away with the fiction of love. Where you are reluctant to obey, don't marry, she advised, since obedience is rendered a husband in accordance with the laws of the kingdom of Christ. But—and here was sagacity—let a spouse or a father be assured that obedience is yielded more willingly to him who says not "You must" but "I think we should."

Votes for women? Comparatively few, she hazarded, would care to cast the ballot if they had it, being too lively in feeling not to be hasty. And deep thinking, the author made bold to state, in a moment of Homeric nodding, was fatiguing to the mental constitutions of most women and apt to prostrate them. Still she would admit women to be man's inferior in one respect only. O my sister, she begged, wipe off the foul, fatal spot of fibbing from thy escutcheon.

As for careers for women, Mrs. Davis was too absorbed in her own to offer much by way of vocational freedom. "In literature," she wrote, "woman has enjoyed legitimate triumph sufficiently near the success of men to satisfy her ambition." Otherwise she saw no opening save in overcrowding teaching, governessing ("the only real resource of an educated lady"), and benefaction of the poor. Love and motherhood, finished this fundamentalist, were the aim and the end.

No pussyfooting on sex for Rebecca Harding Davis. Her forthright candor on that subject was a matter for marvelling in the nineteenth century, and no man dared match her. In the 'Nineties, from her summer home in Marion, Massachusetts, she took note of the plethora of Down East spinsters and, seized with pity, composed an essay, "In the Grey Cabins of New England," which the *Century* valiantly printed in February, 1895. Go West, young (or middle-aged) virgin, go West, was the burden of the Davis counsel. There might be found natural destiny and happiness. The West, in the phrase of Beer, was full of cowboys and such things ready to assist in the production of babies. Frances Willard, in comment, asked Mrs. Davis if she did not think that membership in the greatest spiritual movement since the Saviour's time was enough for the maiden ladies of New England. Rebecca, stout Christian though she was, smiled in silence.

IV

Critics agree that the later writings of Rebecca Harding Davis failed to fulfil her early promise. Her novels fell into the conventional grooves of the period. Love vs. money is often their conflict. Their homely scenes wear the color of authenticity, they reveal the beauty and sincerity of her own life, and through them runs an under-current of deep religious faith. Her theme in *Dallas Galbraith* declared that "in the story of the humblest man there is no such thing as luck or chance—that God is under the hardest circumstances, and that God is good." These books are outmoded for the taste of the cynic who believes in the "breaks," for the modern reader impatient of moralizing and insistent on pace.

Yet the arresting quality of her articles on social subjects survives, as does the charm of her reminiscences, especially in *Bits of Gossip.* "It has always seemed to me," she prefaced that volume, "that each human being before going out into the silence, should leave behind him, not the story of his own life, but of the time in which he lived,—as he saw it,—its creed, its purpose, its queer habits, and the work which he did or left undone in it. Taken singly, these accounts might be weak and trivial, but together, they would make history live and breathe."

These fragments of her remembrances, together with those previously given, will, I think, confirm her theory. Her Virginia childhood in the 'Thirties when British-hate was part of religion, where conversation was interlarded with scraps of Greek and Latin, and poets referred to their endeavors as courting the Nine . . . Boston and the Brahmins in the 'Sixties . . . the Civil War with its mobs of men who volunteered not through patriotism but unemployment, and the '64 bear market in enlistment bounties due to increased immigration . . . Horace Greeley gripping his audiences in spite of his squeaky voice and the yellow bandana he sawed across his knees . . . Wendell Phillips orating at a group of gray-clad Quaker women with the effect of an archer shooting barbed arrows into down cushions . . . a ranting Congressman making a speech that sounded like a performance on a leaky, discordant accordion.

Richard Harding Davis, a great reporter and a crusader on occasion, though never with the stern strength his mother displayed in her early days, wrote her a letter for her seventieth birthday in 1901. There was never a more loyal and loving son, but his tribute need be little discounted. "From the day you struck the first blow for labor in *The Iron-Mills* on to the editorials in *The Tribune, The Youth's Companion,* and *The Independent,*" he wrote in part, "with all the good the novels, the stories brought to people, you were always year after year making the ways straighter, lifting up people, making them happier and better. No woman ever did better for her time than you and no shrieking suffragette will ever understand the influence you wielded, greater than hundreds of thousands of women's votes."

Toward the end of her life of seventy-nine years, Rebecca Harding Davis looked back, found the fogs and prejudices of youth melted away, and inscribed her own epilogue:

"Now I only see men and women slaving for their children; husbands and wives sacrificing their lives to each other; lovable boys, girls with their queer new chivalric notions. I see the fun, the humor, the tragedy in it all; the desperate struggle of each one, day by day, to be clean and decent and true."

A CHECK LIST OF THE WORKS OF REBECCA HARDING DAVIS

Margret Howth. Boston, 1862.
Life in the Iron-Mills. (In Atlantic Tales, a Collection of Stories from *The Atlantic Monthly.*) Boston, 1866.
Dallas Galbraith. Philadelphia, 1868.
Waiting for the Verdict. New York, 1868.
Pro Aris et Focis. New York, 1870.
John Andross. New York, 1874.
Kitty's Choice. Philadelphia, 1874.
A Law Unto Herself. Philadelphia, 1878.
Balacchi Brothers. (In Stories by American Authors, Vol. I.) New York, 1884.
Natasqua. Philadelphia, 1886.
Silhouettes of American Life. New York, 1892.
Dr. Warrick's Daughters. New York, 1896.
Frances Waldeaux. New York, 1897.
Bits of Gossip. Boston, 1904.

INDEX

INDEX

Abbey, Edwin Austin, 77
About Paris, 105
Adams, Evangeline S., 204 n.
Adams, Maude, 84, 115, 130
Adams, Samuel Hopkins, 229
Adventures and Letters of Richard Harding Davis, 54 n., 201 n., 300
Adventures of My Freshman, 25
Albert, King of Belgium, 251
Alcott, Bronson, 5, 305
Alcott, Louisa M., 5, 13, 304
Aldrich, Thomas Bailey, 205
Alexander III of Russia, 118, 123
Alfonso XIII of Spain, 220
Alix of Hesse-Darmstadt, Princess (Czarina of Russia), 118, 123, 125
Alvarez, Madame, 128, 234
Alvarez, President, 128, 234
Arcadia Club, 23 f.
Arch Street Theatre, Philadelphia, 13
Ashmead-Bartlett, Ellis, 271, 273 f., 274 n.
Asquith, Premier and Mrs. Herbert H., 140, 270
Associated Press, 45, 207 f.
Astor, John Jacob, 200
Astor, Mrs. William, 72
Athens, Greece, 104, 139, 284
Atherton, Gertrude, 87
Atlantic Monthly, 4, 5, 304 f.

Bacon, Robert, 279
Balliol College, Oxford, 98 ff.
Baltimore, 30
Bar Sinister, The, 177, 288 n.
Barrie, Mrs. James M., 140
Barrie, Sir James M., 140
Barrymore, Ethel, 12, 13, 130, 140, 175, 196, 221, 307
Barrymore, John, 13, 202, 307
Barrymore, Lionel, 13, 307
Barrymore, Maurice, 13, 307
Baruch, Bernard, 279
Bass, John, 137 f., 208 f., 284, 290
Beauregard, General P. G. T., 113
Bedford, General Forrest, 3
Beer, Thomas, 4 n., 18 n., 78 n., 80 n., 111, 112 n., 171, 278, 309
Belmont, Mrs. August. *See* Eleanor Robson

Benedict, Commodore E. C., 84
Benedict, Helen (Mrs. Thomas Hastings), 84
Bennett, James Gordon, the Younger, 143, 179
Bennett, James O. D., 257 n.
Bernhardt, Sarah, 37, 112
Bethlehem, Pa., 16, 17, 28, 28 n.
Birch, Reginald, 13
Bishop, The, 169
Blackwood, Algernon, 56, 57
Boer War, 178 ff., 209, 231, 258, 262
Bonsal, Stephen, 146, 153
Booth, Edwin, 14, 205 f.
Booth, John Wilkes, 205
Boston, 6, 18, 224, 301 f.
Boucicault, Dion, 14, 307
Bourget, Paul, 122
Bowery, The, 39, 192 f.
Breckinridge, U. S. Minister, Clifton R., 121
Brewster, Francis E., 48
Bridges, Robert, 75, 75 n.
Brill, William, 214
Brisbane, Arthur, 52, 54, 56, 57, 59, 64, 67, 69 f., 72, 77, 85, 87, 229
Broadway, 64, 65
Brodie, Steve, 192, 192 n., 193
Brown, E. W., Jr., 48
Brown, Henry J., 48
Brown, R. D., 48
Brussels, 2, 248 ff., 265
Bryan, Secretary of State William Jennings, 245, 248
Budapest, 126
Buller, Lieutenant-General Sir Redvers H., 178 f.
Bunner, H. C., 76, 97
Burnett, Frances Hodgson, 13, 219
Burnside, Major-General Ambrose E., 8
Byrnes, Inspector Thomas, 60

Cabot, Helen, 164
Cairo, Egypt, 104 f.
Camp, Walter, 170
Cape Town, South Africa, 178, 182
Capron, Captain Allyn K., 154 f.
Captain Kidd, 203 n.
Captain Macklin, 11, 94, 114, 201, 201 n., 202, 202 n.

315